Monique W. Morris is co-founder of the National Black Women's Justice Institute and formerly served as Vice President for Economic Programs, Advocacy, and Research for the NAACP. The author of the novel *Too Beautiful for Words*, she lives in the Bay Area with her husband and two daughters.

Khalil Gibran Muhammad is the director of the Schomburg Center for Research in Black Culture at the New York Public Library and the author of *The Condemnation of Blackness: Race, Crime, and the Making of Modern Urban America*.

Also by Monique W. Morris

Too Beautiful for Words: A Novel

BLACK STATS

African Americans by the Numbers
in the Twenty-First Century

MONIQUE W. MORRIS

THE NEW PRESS

NEW YORK
LONDON

Requests for permission to reproduce selections from this book should be made
through our website: https://thenewpress.com/contact.

Published in the United States by The New Press, New York, 2014
Distributed by Two Rivers Distribution

LIBRARY OF CONGRESS CATALOGING-IN-PUBLICATION DATA

Morris, Monique W., 1972-
    Black stats : African Americans by the numbers in the twenty-first century /
Monique W. Morris.
        pages cm
    Includes bibliographical references and index.
    ISBN 978-1-59558-919-4 (pbk.) -- ISBN 978-1-59558-926-2 (e-book) 1. African
Americans--Social life and customs--21st century--Statistics. 2. African Americans
--Social life and customs--21st century--Statistics. 3. African Americans--
Statistics. 4. African Americans--Statistics.   I. Title.
E185.86.M637 2014
305.896′0730905--dc23

                                            2013035282

The New Press publishes books that promote and enrich public discussion and
understanding of the issues vital to our democracy and to a more equitable world.
These books are made possible by the enthusiasm of our readers; the support
of a committed group of donors, large and small; the collaboration of our many
partners in the independent media and the not-for-profit sector; booksellers, who
often hand-sell New Press books; librarians; and above all by our authors.

www.thenewpress.com

Book design and composition by Bookbright Media
This book was set in Avenir LT and Jockey

Printed in the United States of America

10 9 8 7 6

In memory of Dr. William Manning Marable
(1950–2011)

CONTENTS

Preface   ix

Acknowledgments   xi

Introduction   xiii

The Basics   1

Education   3

Environment   22

Entertainment and Sports   32

Health   43

Justice   58

Lifestyle and Identity   83

Military Service   93

Money and Jobs   99

Politics, Voting, and Civic Engagement   115

Science and Technology   123

Coda: African Americans by Gender

Black Females   137

Black Males   150

Afterword   160

Resources for Additional Information   162

Notes   164

Index   208

The United States is home to more than 40 million people of African descent—a diverse community whose primary ancestry derives from the Black racial and ethnic groups of Africa. They came to the United States not only from the "mother continent" but also from Caribbean islands, Europe, Asia, and South America. Scholars often interpret race as a socially constructed phenomenon, its divisions shaped by common social norms, understandings, and perceptions. As legal scholar Ian Haney López wrote, "Human fate still rides upon ancestry and appearance. The characteristics of our hair, complexion and facial features still influence whether we are free or enslaved. . . . Human interaction rather than natural differentiation must be seen as the source and continued basis for racial categorization."[1] Race, as a social construct, continues to play an important role in shaping the life outcomes of individuals in the United States. The complexity, versatility, and diversity of life among Black Americans have been documented and widely discussed for more than four centuries.

This book is designed to provide a statistical snapshot of the lives of Black Americans, juxtaposing where possible their conditions with those of other racial and ethnic groups. The use of data is a powerful tool for understanding how these conditions may have changed or where they have remained the same. Data track specific points along the "color line" that W.E.B. Du Bois famously declared would dominate the modern public discourse—and consciousness—about human relations in the United States.[2] Because data are able to highlight both equality and disparity, they remain an essential component in evaluating progress on racial equity, building a more inclusive democracy, illustrating our narratives, and deciding where to intensify our advocacy for racial justice.

The data in this book were collected from a variety of secondary sources, including, but not limited to, federal agencies, foundations, journals, nonprofit organizations, and corporate surveys. Where appropriate, figures presented here have been rounded to the nearest whole number or nearest tenth. Where political or research concepts are introduced, I have offered additional information on the context or framework that informs the statistics included in that section.

"Black" and "African American" are used interchangeably in this book to refer to people of African descent. "African American" always refers to people of African descent who are nationally identified with the United States. "Black" is a larger umbrella term that describes individuals throughout the African diaspora, including Caribbean and Latino Americans.

Every day Black Americans are the subject of memes that do little more than caricature their life experiences for public consumption. While the election of President Barack Obama delivered an image more powerful than many could have imagined, we must not lose sight of the more general narrative, and that can be constructed through data.

Throughout his work, social scientist Manning Marable reminded us that history is not only about the times long past: understanding contemporary Black history is crucial to understanding our collective experiences and our interactions with public policies. Each of us has the ability to record a unique story that adds to this rich and inclusive tradition. Examining the information in these pages can inform and develop our thinking about the historic and contemporary conditions and contributions of Black people in America.

Monique W. Morris
August 2013
Oakland, California

A C K N O W L E D G M E N T S

First, I would like to thank the ancestors for their struggle for human dignity and racial justice. Their fight is one that we continue.

No book of statistics on Black Americans would be possible without the rigorous and thoughtful work of the researchers and scholars across the country who collect and analyze data to help bring to the fore the trends that inform our understanding of how African Americans are affected by a host of issues and social policies. I would specifically like to thank the African American and Africana studies scholars, historians, sociologists, economists, educators, environmentalists, social scientists, statisticians, biological scientists, media professionals, criminologists, legal advocates, and other scholar practitioners who collect statistics associated with the topics presented in this book. I would like to thank Steven Pitts and Njema Frazier, who took the time to speak with me regarding some important nuances of their work, which I have presented in this book. I am deeply grateful for my ongoing thought-partnerships with Dereca Blackmon, Stephanie Bush-Baskette, Sarah Bacon, Lesleigh Irish-Underwood, Erika Irish Brown, Lenneal Henderson, Shawn Ginwright, Doug Paxton, and Kimberlé Crenshaw. Our conversations strengthen my work and me. Thank you!

I would also like to honor the libraries, institutes, and other centers that collect data—quantitative and qualitative—toward the goal of informing social policy and improving the conditions of Black people. I would especially like to thank the New York Public Library's Schomburg Center for Research in Black Culture for providing a laboratory for ongoing inquiry about Black life, and its director, Khalil Gibran Muhammad, for writing the introduction to this book.

I am very fortunate to have had the opportunity to work with and learn from Marie Brown. Thank you, Ms. Brown, for all that you bring to the literary world. I am honored to be a part of the community of authors privileged to work with you. I had the extraordinary luck to work with a fantastic editor whose patience and critical feedback expanded and strengthened this project. Tara Grove, thank you!

I am grateful for the support of my family—my husband, Greg, and my daughters, Ebony and Mahogany. What I do is for my children and I pray that their futures will be enhanced by every action that I take. I would like to thank my mother, Katie Couvson; my mother-in-law, Barbara Griffin; and my brothers and sisters for their encouragement along the way (and patience with my busy schedule). I would also like to acknowledge my uncle Benjiman Couvson, for being the first person to show me the beauty of a vast display of books by and about people of African descent. From one book grew a lifelong commitment to African American studies. Thank you!

Lastly, in 1996, as a graduate student at Columbia University, I worked with Manning Marable at the Institute for Research in African American Studies. I supported the research for his book *Black Liberation in Conservative America* by coordinating his column, "Along the Color Line," and maintaining a comprehensive clipping file of major events and issues affecting Black communities across the country. At that time, I fell in love with the stories of Black people—the stories found in the numbers as well as those in narratives. In 2010, only months before he made the transition from mentor to ancestor, Manning sent me a private note in which he mentioned that it was time "to present a new vision for Black freedom." I believe that in order to do that, we must first fully understand the current state of Black freedom in all its iterations—quantitative data being one of them. Thank you, Manning, for this charge. This book is dedicated to you.

Numbers Never Speak for Themselves

Khalil Gibran Muhammad

> There are three kinds of lies . . . white lies,
> black lies, and statistics.
>
> —*M.V. Ball (1894)*

Once upon a time, the world's best social scientist of U.S. race relations set out to debunk all the lies that White people told about African Americans. He had the best training and education money could buy. He had spent three semesters at the University of Berlin, where the eminent German sociologist Max Weber was one of his mentors. And he had a Harvard PhD to boot, the first for his kind. For decades his research was a powerful, if singular, weapon in a slim arsenal aimed at the tyranny of racial ignorance, mythology, and propaganda.

Where his enemies said Blacks were lazy, diseased, criminal, and promiscuous, he shot back with data of hardworking, healthy, and law-abiding Black families. He brooked no racial insult without a statistical rebuttal. Not only did he demonstrate Black success where others had seen only failure, he highlighted evidence of excessive White poverty and immorality, exposing the racial double standards of an earlier post–civil rights, Big Data age.[1] "The world was thinking wrong about race, because it did not know," W.E.B. Du Bois once wrote. "The ultimate evil was stupidity."[2] To this day, his statistical analyses of Black life at the turn of the past century continue to be relevant and essential to twenty-first-century scholarship.[3]

But back then, on the ground, in the real world, far from the academy, Du Bois's Black stats failed to hold the creeping shadow of Jim Crow at bay. Instead the darkness descended upon his generation of those born into freedom in spite of the data showing Black success, White failure, and the manufactured disparities of injustice and inequality. No data-driven counternarrative of Black humanity mattered to the statistical truth of Black inequality in a rapidly modernizing industrial society where social science plus civil rights equaled "separate but equal."[4]

One White supremacist after another cherry picked Du Bois's data on the Black poor and the "submerged tenth" to justify racial oppression. In his groundbreaking work *The Philadelphia Negro* (1899)—a sociological classic of race and urban America, unmatched in statistical detail, analytical scope, and explanatory power even to this day—Du Bois's interpretations and conclusions were roundly dismissed and shamefully ignored. Writing for the nation's most prestigious academic journals, reviewers noted that Du Bois was flat wrong about racism in post-*Plessy* America but praised him for being, as one wrote, "perfectly frank, laying all the necessary stress on the weaknesses of his people, such as their looseness of living, their lack of thrift, their ignorance of the laws of health, the disproportionate number of paupers and criminals among them as compared with the whites."[5] Another reviewer added that "Du Bois's statistics are worthy of careful study," but "they are a little weak in the pages devoted to showing that the negro is not so criminal as he is popularly represented to be."[6] Scholarly assessment counted most in the leading journal of his discipline, the *American Journal of Sociology*, which did not review the book and only mentioned it a decade later in a footnote to an article. One of Du Bois's colleagues in the sociology department at the University of Pennsylvania, the institution that sponsored the study, simply wrote him off as a well-educated and articulate Black man with "chips on his shoulders."[7]

Du Bois grew disheartened and disillusioned. Even as he was personally attacked as an angry Black man and his interpretations disparaged, his data fueled segregationist claims. This was the high price he paid for challenging the racial status quo. He tried to fight fire with fire. He tried to reshape racial knowledge with *better* statistics or more *comprehensive* data. His census data on poverty, education, crime, and unemployment supplemented by 10,000 life histories recorded after nearly a thousand hours of interviews were simply no match for ideology. All the coding and surveying in the world meant little to a White world committed to condemning Blackness.[8]

Du Bois learned a hard lesson that numbers never speak for themselves. Statistics are only an artifact of the power to shape questions we think are worth asking. They are meaningful only in relation to how we interpret them in light of the public policies we seek to enact. In today's Information Age, the power of numbers is unprecedented in its ability to shape our understanding of the world we live in, the people we dwell among, and the scope of the challenges we face collectively. Microprocessors, terabyte servers, and Wi-Fi allow us to collect, quantify, analyze, and distribute data with a speed and scale that even George Lucas could not have imagined a generation ago, let alone Du Bois.

But the basic problem remains the same. Data are not produced in a vacuum. Why, for example, is there no national database of police brutality? How come the Philadelphia police department does not know how many Italian Americans committed armed robbery last year? The former has never been measured, and the latter we stopped collecting in the 1930s. Data are always a reflection of a set of economic, social, political, and, yes, racial choices. The fact of their existence, collection, compilation, and dissemination is a consequence of resource allocation, of choices made by individuals and institutions on what to measure and why.

There is also the problem of second-class data. That is, all statistics are not equal. Even though we know that Whites are the majority of crack users in America compared to Blacks (32 percent), as cited in these pages, it makes no difference. We continue to label crack a Black drug and punish accordingly, where the vast majority of those imprisoned for crack-related drug offenses are African American. This statistical lie is laid bare not by the simple counting of who is in prison (first-class data), but by knowing also who isn't and why. This and other complex social realities, such as biased drug enforcement, are not easily measured. And when such facts come to light, these second-class data have historically had little political or social currency.

Quantitative evidence of racial disparity never proved racism on its own in Du Bois's day any more than it does in our own. Monique W. Morris's *Black Stats* notes that Black youth make up 16 percent of public K–12 students and 9 percent of private school students but make up 35 percent of those who are suspended from school. This would seem an outrage and surely evidence that something is terribly wrong in how Black children are treated by teachers, of whom only 7 percent nationwide are Black. And yet it all depends on what you believe about the hearts and minds of White teachers, the quality of Black parenting, and the role racism plays in shaping social outcomes today. Zero tolerance suspensions and other school-to-confinement pathways among Black girls and boys that often lead to high incarceration rates among African American women and men still mean, in many minds, that too many Black children behave badly in school, charting their own paths to prison. An interpretation of the data as a reflection of racist, punitive policies and practices is an argument, not a fact. That is the lesson of Du Bois's failed social science.

After the better part of two decades, Du Bois renounced his faith in statistics, left the academy, and spent much of the rest of his very long life as a propagandist for the race, telling stories in poetry and prose. He had become a civil and human rights activist first and foremost, using data in the service of racial justice. The stats were simply no longer the story in and of themselves. Du Bois realized that in order to save Black people, their humanity could not be reduced to a chart, table, or graph. And to quote the late jazz critic, essayist, and novelist Albert Murray from forty years ago: now is a "time when an ever increasing number of writers seems to mistake the jargon of social science for insight into the nature and condition of man."

In what follows, Morris carries forward the best of the Du Boisian social science and progressive tradition. Knowledge, she insists, is the predicate of social transformation. I agree.

And from these pages it is clear that mapping the color line today is as essential as it was more than a century ago. The world is a complex place. Most of us rely on our beliefs and the fragments of life we catch in the morning paper, our favorite blog, or cable news to understand it. The best work of social scientists offers us a fuller picture to be sure. Their data can test our beliefs and our perceptions. When researchers cast as wide a net as possible, as Morris does here, we all learn something new. As a music lover, I learned that R&B, that old soul music linking Ray Charles to Aretha Franklin to Alicia Keys, outsells hip-hop albums two to one (49.7 million to 24.2 million units in 2012). Rhythm and blues is number three in overall record sales behind rock and alternative. Next time I have my White and Latino neighbors over, I will leave Luther and Mary J. Blige on the playlist. Like me, other readers might find that Americans share much more in common in their private spaces and leisurely pursuits than our indices of residential segregation indicate.

Given that the nation is in the midst of celebrating the fiftieth anniversary of the civil rights movement, *Black Stats* paints a devastating picture of the limits of the movement in terms of economic power and decision making among African Americans. The corridors of power in America are paler than I imagined. Of course, Black poverty is more visible than Black privilege outside of entertainment and sports. But if you had asked me before I read this book what percentage of Black people are executives or senior-level officials or managers in the private sector, I might have guessed 10 percent, based on so much backlash against affirmative action and so many Black elites in corporate America who preach the politics of personal responsibility, using their own success as evidence that only ambition and hard work stand between poverty and prosperity. The number is actually 3 percent.

In the nonprofit sector where I work, the picture of Black influence is even bleaker. Since much of the nonprofit world turns on redistributing private and public funds to help insecure families and individuals, one would think that African Americans would be well represented among the decision makers. Here the opportunity to reverse the legacies of segregation and racism is directly linked to the work itself and presumably by the people who stand to benefit the most. Not true, according to *Black Stats*. African Americans make up 4 percent of foundation presidents, 4 percent of nonprofit executives, and only 7 percent of nonprofit boards of directors. African Americans are much better represented among program officers in foundations. But, as in the corporate boardroom, decisions are still made at the top. Speaking of charity work, Du Bois wrote in *The Philadelphia Negro* that Whites much preferred to give Blacks charity than work. "The same Philadelphian who would not let a Negro work in his store or mill will contribute handsomely to relieve Negroes in poverty and distress." What the data herein on nonprofit employment suggest to me is that those jobs are still hard to come by even when the mission is to relieve "poverty and distress" among Black folks.

And therefore, for many reasons, Du Bois's caution and challenge remain. Statistics will often tell an incomplete story at best or an outright falsehood at worst. They cannot change the world on their own. Beliefs are far more powerful than numbers. Religion and art have endured across the millennia. What we do with the information, what we say about it, the stories we tell from it, and the movements we launch because of it are our way forward. While racial statistics have been foundational to defending White supremacy and maintaining racial inequality, today we must use the benefit of hindsight and a better appreciation for the work required beyond the numbers.

Black Stats is a starting point for unraveling the twenty-first-century color line with all its gerrymandered borders around gender, sexuality, and immigrant status. The struggle for racial democracy has always been a numbers game; knowing the inherent dangers of that game, it is critical that we use this knowledge to paint a fuller picture of Black humanity, disseminating a multidimensional vision of both the present and the road to a just future.

BLACK STATS

The Demographics of Black America

In 1790, the census recorded 757,208 Black people in the United States—including 59,527 free Black people and 697,681 enslaved Black people. By 1860, just five years before the Emancipation Proclamation legally ended the institution of slavery, the recorded number of Black Americans had reached more than 4.4 million, including more than 488,000 who were "free" and more than 3.9 million who were enslaved.[1] From these humble beginnings, the Black population in America has grown to be richly diverse, traveling a dynamic and storied path toward today's fuller embrace of Black American identities.

This collection of statistics reflects that diversity, presented in sets of basic facts, figures, and trends observed in the Black population of the United States.

How many Black people live in the United States?

- Black Americans are the third-largest racial/ethnic group in the United States, behind Whites and Latinos.[2]
- 42 million people in the United States identify as Black or African American, alone or in combination with one or more other races—a record number that constitutes 14 percent of the U.S. population.[3]
- 13 percent of the U.S. population identifies as Black alone. By comparison, 64 percent of the U.S. population reports as White, non-Hispanic.[4]
- 3.1 million people identify as multiracial Black or African American, with 59 percent of this group identifying as Black and White.
- 97 percent of the Black population in the United States is non-Hispanic.
- 38 percent of Hispanics who identify as Black or African American in combination with other races report being Black and White.[5]

How much has the Black population grown in the past decade?

- □ The Black population* grew by 15 percent between 2000 and 2010.
- □ Among Black populations of mixed racial heritage, the number of those who identify as Black and White grew by 134 percent during that same decade.[6]

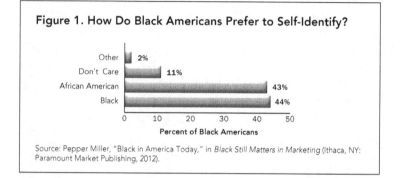

Figure 1. How Do Black Americans Prefer to Self-Identify?

Source: Pepper Miller, "Black in America Today," in *Black Still Matters in Marketing* (Ithaca, NY: Paramount Market Publishing, 2012).

Where were Black people in the United States born?

- □ 91 percent of Black people living in the United States were born here.[7]
- □ 42 percent of foreign-born Black people in the United States—1,496,000 people—entered the country in 2000 or later.[8]

What is the age breakdown of Black Americans?

- □ 8 percent of the Black population is under the age of 5.
- □ 28 percent of the Black population is under the age of 18.
- □ 66 percent of the Black population is age 21 and over.
- □ 9 percent of the Black population is age 65 and over.[9]

---

*"The Black population" refers to the population identifying as Black alone or as Black in combination with other races.

Education is the passport to the future, for tomorrow belongs to those who prepare for it today.

—*Malcolm X*

In 1973, the Supreme Court ruled in *San Antonio Independent School District v. Rodriguez* that the U.S. Constitution does not guarantee education as a fundamental right.[1] As a result, each state has enacted its own laws governing public education, leaving the quality and form of education in the United States as varied as fifty states and the District of Columbia—all responsible for shaping their own educational policies, procedures, and standards—can make them. And within each there is even more variation, due to the differences in practice among all of the school districts and facilities charged with educating America's children.

Nevertheless, education, though plagued by political and pedagogical debates—especially regarding the overemphasis on high-stakes standardized testing—is still widely accepted in this country as the primary road to increased opportunity. Still, many challenges remain with respect to securing a quality education for all children: racial achievement and opportunity gaps, ongoing segregation in our nation's schools, high dropout rates, and a concentration of high-poverty schools in communities of color.

Yet there have also been promising trends showing improved academic achievement among Black students, including increasing access to higher education. The statistics that follow present a profile of these academic achievements and of lingering challenges to full educational equality for Black people in the United States.

DEGREES

How formally educated is Black America?

- 84 percent of Black Americans ages 25 and

older today have earned at least a high school diploma, compared with 88 percent for the nation. This is a dramatic increase from 1970, when just 31 percent of Black Americans had earned at least a high school diploma.

- 20 percent of Black Americans ages 25 and older today have earned a college degree or better, compared with 30 percent for the nation—also a dramatic increase from 1970, when just 4 percent of Black Americans ages 25 and older had earned a college degree or better.[2]
- Black Americans ages 25 and older compose 19 percent of those with one year of college or more but no degree, compared to 15 percent of all Americans.[3]
- Black Americans earn 14 percent of associate's degrees in the United States, while White Americans earn 66 percent of these degrees.
- Black Americans earn 11 percent of bachelor's degrees, while White Americans earn 73 percent of these degrees.[4]
- 0.9 percent of degrees earned by Black Americans are professional degrees, such as law degrees, medical degrees, and business degrees.[5]
- Black Americans earn 13 percent of master's degrees conferred in the United States. White Americans compose 73 percent of Americans with a master's degree.
- Black Americans compose 7 percent of Americans with a doctoral degree (e.g., PhD, EdD, etc.). White Americans compose 74 percent of Americans with a doctoral degree.
- Black Americans compose 7 percent of Americans with a professional degree. White Americans compose 71 percent of Americans with a professional degree.[6]

BLACK EDUCATORS

The teaching profession has a rich history in the African American community. For many Black Americans, particularly women, teaching was one of the first nondomestic occupations that became available during the era of legal segregation. It was noble to teach—teachers held the key to a critical pathway to freedom. To read was to interpret and to be recognized as a legitimate, thinking human being. The teacher, as the purveyor of these skills, was a critical link to racial achievement. The same is true today. Educator Michele Foster has described the Black educator as one who loves his or her students and provides for them a culturally competent learning environment that not only encourages their academic achievement, but also responds to their emotional needs as children growing up in a race-conscious society.[7] Similarly, research led by Jan Hughes has documented the critical role of the teacher-student relationship in the development of a caring school environment conducive to Black student achievement[8]—a relationship that has not been sufficiently developed, just as Black teachers are not sufficiently represented in our contemporary education system.

Between 1890 and 1910, the number of African American teachers rose from 15,100 to 66,236.[9] The growth of the Black teaching profession continued until—as an unintended consequence of desegregation—Black teachers were dislocated by the closure of Black schools. Structural barriers to their participation in schools as credentialed teachers and new occupational opportunities for educated Black Americans also meant that more Americans were selecting non-teaching careers. The decline of Black teachers continues to be of concern to education equity advocates and scholars.

What is the percentage of Black teachers and where do they teach?

- 239,460 teachers—7 percent of the total teaching force in U.S. public schools—are Black.
- 19,800 teachers—4 percent of the total teaching force in U.S. private schools—are Black.
- Only 24 percent of Black teachers are male.[10]

What subjects are Black teachers teaching?

Although data show no particular concentration of Black teachers in a single subject, higher percentages of Black educators are found in special education, technical and vocational courses, and English. Black teachers are least likely to teach a foreign language.

- 8 percent of English teachers are Black.
- 3 percent of foreign language teachers are Black.
- 7 percent of health/physical education teachers are Black.
- 7 percent of math teachers are Black.
- 6 percent of natural science teachers are Black.
- 5 percent of social science teachers are Black.
- 9 percent of the instructors teaching special education, vocational/technical courses, and all other subjects are Black.[11]

Are Black teachers satisfied with their jobs?

- 70 percent of African American teachers are satisfied with the way that their school is run, compared with 78 percent of White teachers.
- Only 37 percent of African American teachers are satisfied with their pay (approximately $49,000 in 2008), compared to 46 percent of Latino teachers (paid approximately $49,300 in 2008) and 52 percent of White teachers (paid approximately $49,570 in 2008).[12]

How many Black senior administrators are there?

- 11 percent of all K–12 school principals are Black.
- 21 percent of urban (metropolitan) school principals are Black.[13]

What percentage of college faculty are Black?

- Nationwide, Black Americans compose approximately 6 percent of faculty on college campuses.[14]
- African Americans hold 5 percent of chief academic officer/provost positions nationwide.[15]
- At the University of Phoenix (a for-profit college), 19 percent of the total faculty is African American, three times the national level of Black faculty appointments.[16]

How many senior Black administrators are leading institutions of higher learning?

- 14 percent of all college presidents are people of color.
- 6 percent of college presidents are Black.
- Black people hold 6 percent of chief of staff positions and 12 percent of executive vice president positions at colleges or universities.[17]
- 11 percent of deans and 9 percent of associate or vice deans of law schools are Black males; 14 percent of deans and 16 percent of associate or vice deans of law schools are Black females.[18]

27 percent of all African American teachers came into the classroom through alternative certification routes.[19]

BLACK STUDENTS

Black educators have occupied a unique and storied role in the development of Black achievement, but Black students have been subjected to a different kind of narrative. Plagued by segregated learning environments that often represented unequal access to quality education, Black children have remained disproportionately vulnerable to the legacy of racial bias and poverty that socially reproduce underachievement. However, although in smaller numbers than their racial and ethnic counterparts, Black students are represented in advanced courses and competitive institutions. Overall, while Black American students have struggled to define their collective identity as a high-achieving learning community, they continue to construct new narratives about what it means to be a Black student.

How many Black children are in preschool or receiving early education?

- 14 percent of Black four-year-olds are in home-based care provided by a relative.[20]
- 4 percent of Black four-year-olds are in home-based care provided by a nonrelative.[21]

- 53 percent of Black four-year olds are in preschool or kindergarten programs.[22]
- 62 percent of Black four-year olds are in center-based child care.
- 25 percent of Black four-year-olds attend a Head Start program.[23]

How many Black students attend private schools and which ones?

- 9 percent of all private schools are Black and 6 percent of all students enrolled in National Association of Independent School (NAIS) private day schools are Black.[24]
- Black youth make up 7 percent of children in private Catholic schools and 11 percent of other conservative Christian schools.
- Black youth make up 10 percent of all students in nonsectarian private schools and 21 percent in nonsectarian special education schools.[25]
- 7 percent of NAIS boarding-school students are Black.[26]

How many Black students are educated in public schools?

- 16 percent of students enrolled in American public schools are Black, a proportion that is expected to last through 2022.
- Larger percentages of Black children are educated in public schools in the South:
  - In the Northeast, Black children compose 16 percent of public school pre-K–12 students.
  - In the Midwest, Black children compose 16 percent of public school pre-K–12 students.
  - In the West, Black children compose 6 percent of public school pre-K–12 students.
  - In the South, Black children compose 24 percent of public school pre-K–12 students.[27]
- More Black students (36 percent) attend a "chosen public school" (i.e., a public school other than their assigned public school) than do their White (20 percent) and Latino (26 percent) peers.[28]
- Black students make up 69 percent of students in the District of Columbia public schools.[29]

How segregated are the schools Black children attend?

School segregation and racial isolation may be found at the district level, school level, and classroom level. The measurements below capture trends associated with the racial isolation of and in schools.

- □ 46 percent of Black students in the United States attend a predominantly Black school.[30]
- □ 29 percent of Black students attend predominantly White schools.* This represents a decline in Black students' exposure to White students (and vice versa). In 1988, the year considered to be the peak of desegregation for Black students, the average Black student attended a school that was one-third White.
- □ 39 percent of Black students are educated in "intensely segregated" schools (90–100 percent students of color), a slight increase since 1988, when one-third of Black students had an intensely segregated educational experience.[31]

How many Black students are in special education classes?

The placement of African American children into special education courses is extremely controversial. Education scholar Beth Harry and others have documented the problematic and arbitrary classifications that route Black children into special education classes.[32] Researchers have also found that Black children may be tracked into special education for behavioral issues, rather than for cognitive or developmental problems.

- □ Black students compose 22 percent of all students receiving special education.[33]
- □ 16 percent of Black males in the ninth grade receive special education services, compared with 12 percent of Latino males and 13 percent of White males in the ninth grade.
- □ 7 percent of Black females in the ninth grade receive special education services, compared with 8 percent

---

*"White" schools are those in which 50–75 percent of the students are White.

of White females and 6 percent of Latinas in the ninth grade.[34]

How many Black students are educated in low-performing schools?

- 46 percent of Black students are educated in schools that fail to meet the Adequate Yearly Progress requirements (academic standards established by the No Child Left Behind Act of 2001).[35]
- Approximately 58 percent of Black students and 50 percent of Latino students who drop out of high school were attending one of the nation's lowest-performing high schools.[36]

How many Black students are educated in public charter schools?

- 30 percent of the students in public charter schools identify as Black or African American.[37]
- New Orleans is home to the greatest proportion of Black students attending charter schools (86 percent of the student population) in an area where the share of charter schools is over 50 percent.
- In other areas where the share of charter schools is above one-third, Black students compose a significant proportion of the charter student population: the District of Columbia (82 percent), Detroit (86 percent), and Kansas City (73 percent).
- Nationwide, Black youth compose 27 percent of low-income charter schools students.[38]

How many Black students are homeschooled?

- Less than 1 percent of Black children ages 5 to 17 are homeschooled, compared to 3 percent of students overall.
- The percent of Black children being homeschooled declined by 27 percent between 1999 and 2007, falling from 84,000 to 61,000 students.
- Fewer Black children are homeschooled than White and Latino children (1,159,000 and 147,000, respectively).[39]

How many Black students are educated in high poverty schools?

Nationwide, Black students are disproportionately educated in schools defined as high poverty, meaning that 76 percent to 100 percent of attending students qualify for free and reduced-price lunches through the National School Lunch Program. These schools tend to lack the resource infrastructure present in low-poverty schools, and various factors associated with limited funding can produce a challenging learning environment for students. As the data below show, Black children are more likely to be concentrated in high-poverty elementary schools than in high-poverty secondary schools.

- ▢ 42 percent of Black children are educated in all high-poverty schools (both elementary and secondary). By comparison:
  - ▪ 38 percent of Latino children are educated in high-poverty schools,
  - ▪ 31 percent of Native American children are educated in high-poverty schools,
  - ▪ 15 percent of Pacific Islander and Asian children are educated in high-poverty schools, and
  - ▪ 6 percent of White children are educated in high-poverty schools.[40]
- ▢ 46 percent of Black children are educated in high-poverty elementary schools. By comparison:
  - ▪ 45 percent of Latino children are educated in high-poverty elementary schools,
  - ▪ 35 percent of Native American children are educated in high-poverty elementary schools,
  - ▪ 14 percent of Pacific Islander and Asian children are educated in high-poverty elementary schools, and
  - ▪ 7 percent of White children are educated in high-poverty elementary schools.
- ▢ 21 percent of Black children are educated in high-poverty secondary schools. By comparison:
  - ▪ 21 percent of Latino children are educated in high-poverty secondary schools,
  - ▪ 17 percent of Native American children are educated in high-poverty secondary schools,

- 7 percent of Pacific Islander and Asian children are educated in high-poverty secondary schools, and
- 2 percent of White children are educated in high-poverty secondary schools.
- Only 7 percent of Black children are educated in low-poverty elementary schools.
- Only 12 percent of Black children are educated in low-poverty secondary schools.[41]

Are Black parents involved in their children's education?

Black students are slightly more likely than their non-Black counterparts to have their homework checked for completion by an adult.

- High school: A greater percentage of Black students (83 percent) have had their homework checked by an adult than White (57 percent) or Asian (59 percent) students.[42]
- Black parents are less likely to attend school-based events or volunteer for school fund-raising events than their White counterparts:
  - K–12th grade: 62 percent of Black male students and 68 percent of Black female students report that at least one parent attended a school or class event, compared with 80 percent of White students, 72 percent of Asian students, and 65 percent of Latino students.
  - K–12th Grade: 32 percent of Black male students and 39 percent of Black female students report that their parents had volunteered in school or served on a school committee, compared with 54 percent of White students and about 32 percent of Latino students.[43]

SCHOOL DISCIPLINE AND PUSH-OUT

School-to-confinement pathways include policies, practices, and conditions that facilitate the criminalization of students in educational environments and school processes that result in the confinement or incarceration of youth and young adults. High-stakes testing, poor student-teacher and student-administrator relationships, racially biased implementation of dress codes, and the absence of alternatives to exclusionary discipline fuel the punitive practices that in various ways push many Black youth out of classrooms and schools.

How are Black youth affected by school discipline?

- ❑ Black youth make up 16 percent of public school students and 9 percent of private school students in grades K–12 nationwide[44] but account for:
    - 35 percent of in-school suspensions,
    - 35 percent of those who experience one out-of-school suspension,
    - 46 percent of those who experience multiple out-of-school suspensions, and
    - 39 percent of those who are expelled.
- ❑ 20 percent of Black boys and more than 10 percent of Black girls have experienced an out-of-school suspension.[45]
- ❑ One out of every seventeen Black schoolchildren has been suspended at least once.
- ❑ One out of every four Black children with disabilities in grades K–12 has been suspended at least once.[46]
- ❑ Five of the nation's largest school districts produce a rate of Black youth suspensions greater than 70 percent:
    - Prince George's County, Maryland: Black students make up 71 percent of student enrollment but account for 87 percent of school suspensions.
    - Philadelphia: Black students make up 62 percent of student enrollment but account for 78 percent of school suspensions.
    - Chicago: Black students make up 45 percent of student enrollment but account for 78 percent of school suspensions.
    - City of Charlotte/Mecklenburg County, North Carolina: Black students make up 44 percent of student enrollment but account for 75 percent of school suspensions.

- Duval County, Florida: Black students make up 46 percent of student enrollment but account for 72 percent of school suspensions.[47]

How are Black students affected by seclusion and restraint in school?

- 16 percent of students without disabilities who are subjected to seclusion in school are Black.
- Black youth make up 21 percent of youth with disabilities and 44 percent of students who are subjected to mechanical restraint (this includes any device or equipment used to restrict a student's freedom of movement).[48]

How many Black students are dropping out of school?

Measures for the tracking of dropout rates vary according to how the issue is defined and how specific student populations are classified. However, most studies define "dropout" as a failure to complete school according to compulsory state education law. Although Black students have historically had higher dropout rates than the nation as a whole and than their counterparts from certain racial and ethnic groups (with the exception of Latino and Native American youth), more Black students are now completing their secondary education.

- The current national dropout rate is 8 percent for Black youth ages 16 through 24. The national dropout rate for all youth is 7.4 percent.
- The dropout rate for Black youth declined by 2.7 percentage points between 2006 and 2010 and has averaged 11.5 percent over the past decade.[49]
- The U.S. Department of Education has projected a 2 percent decrease in the high school graduation rate for Black students between 2007 and 2020.[50]

The unemployment rate for Black high school dropouts is 47 percent. By comparison, the unemployment rate for White high school dropouts is 26 percent.[51]

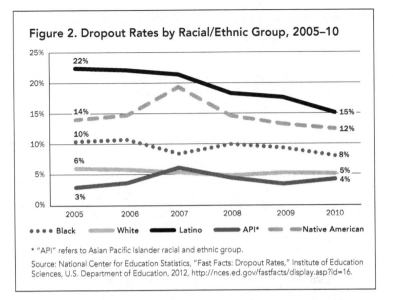

Figure 2. Dropout Rates by Racial/Ethnic Group, 2005–10

● ● ● ● Black　　▬▬ White　　▬▬▬ Latino　　▬▬ API*　　▬▬ Native American

* "API" refers to Asian Pacific Islander racial and ethnic group.

Source: National Center for Education Statistics, "Fast Facts: Dropout Rates," Institute of Education Sciences, U.S. Department of Education, 2012, http://nces.ed.gov/fastfacts/display.asp?id=16.

□ Black high school dropouts are less likely than their Black contemporaries who graduated from high school to keep a job longer than one year. Only 5 percent of Black high school dropouts ages 18 to 25 held a job for two years or more, compared to 8 percent of their Black counterparts with a high school diploma and 13 percent of their counterparts with a bachelor's degree or higher.[52]

BLACK STUDENT PERFORMANCE

How are Black students faring overall and in particular subjects?

□ The average grade point average for African American students is 3.05, compared to 3.36 for all students, 3.52 for Asian students, and 3.45 for White students.[53]

□ Black students make up 16 percent of students in grades 6 through 8 but 42 percent of students in those grades who were held back one year.[54]

□ In 2009, African American students scored an average of 26 points below their White counterparts on reading and math tests.[55]

- 29 percent of Black ninth-grade males have been retained or "held back" at some point between kindergarten and ninth grade, compared with 20 percent of Latino and 11 percent of White ninth-grade males.
- 21 percent of Black ninth-grade females have been retained or "held back" at some point between kindergarten and ninth grade, compared with 10 percent of Latina and 8 percent of White ninth-grade females.[56]

Black fourth graders:

- 83 percent of Black fourth graders score below the proficient level on the National Assessment of Educational Progress (NAEP) reading exam.
- 83 percent of Black fourth graders score below the proficient level on the NAEP mathematics exam.
- 89 percent of Black fourth graders score below the proficient level on the NAEP science exam.[57]

Black eighth graders:

- 85 percent of Black eighth graders score below the proficient level on the NAEP reading exam, compared with 49 percent of Asian students and 43 percent of White students.
- 41 percent of all Black students read below the basic level in eighth grade; however, this number has decreased by 4 percentage points since 2007.[58]
- 87 percent of Black eighth graders score below the proficient level on the NAEP mathematics exam, compared with 42 percent of Asian students and 56 percent of White students.
- 49 percent of Black students perform below the basic level of math in eighth grade; however, this is an improvement since 2007, when 53 percent of Black eighth graders performed below the basic math level.
- 92 percent of Black eighth graders scored below the proficient level in science on the 2011 NAEP exam, as compared with 59 percent of Asian students and 58 percent of White students.[59]

Black twelfth graders:

- 78 percent of Black females and 88 percent of Black males score below the proficient level in reading on the NAEP exam.
- 94 percent of Black youth score below the proficient level in math on the NAEP exam.
- 96 percent of Black youth score below the proficient level in science on the NAEP exam.[60]

Black youth make up 19 percent of students enrolled in districts that offer Gifted and Talented Education (GATE) programs but account for only 10 percent of students enrolled in these programs.[61]

How many Black students are in Advanced Placement (AP) and honors courses?

According to the College Board, a total of 954,070 students took an AP exam in 2012. Student participation in AP courses is often related to the availability of such courses in their schools. For example, Black youth who demonstrate a high probability of success in AP classes are less likely than their White and Asian counterparts to participate in such classes. Therefore, the participation rate of Black students may not be an effective measure of their ability to perform well in such courses.

- In 2012, 30 percent of African American students with a high potential for success in AP math courses (measured by those who perform well on national standardized tests) actually took such classes.
- Black students make up 9.2 percent of all AP test takers, the lowest rate of representation of any group.
- 4 percent of Black AP test takers scored a 3 or higher* on an AP test.
- Since 2011, 32 states have made progress in closing the AP participation gap for Black students, and 38

---

*AP exams are scored on a 5-point scale, 5 being the highest possible score. Students who score a 3 or higher are those considered qualified to receive college credit; however, some institutions may consider a 3 the equivalent of a C.

states and the District of Columbia have improved the success of Black student performance in these courses.

- The five AP exams most often taken by Black students are: English Language and Composition, English Literature and Composition, U.S. History, U.S. Government and Politics, and World History.[62]

Fewer Black students participate in honors courses, compared with their White and Asian counterparts:

- 37 percent of Black students have completed an honors course in precalculus, compared with 52 percent of all students, 67 percent of Asian students, and 55 percent of White students.
- 14 percent of Black students have completed an honors course in calculus, compared with 26 percent of all students, 44 percent of Asian students, and 27 percent of White students.
- 46 percent of Black students have completed an honors course in physics, compared with 53 percent of all students, 63 percent of Asian students, and 53 percent of White students.[63]

How do Black students perform on the SAT?*

- 13 percent of SAT takers identified themselves as Black or African American in 2012, an increase from 9 percent in 2002.

48 percent of Black SAT takers would be first-generation college students.[64]

---

*The validity of standardized, high-stakes tests has been under scrutiny for decades. The lingering gaps in performance are attributed to many factors, including student preparation, experience with and exposure to taking standardized tests, and cultural biases embedded in the testing instrument. For example, recent research (Maria Veronica Santelices and Mark Wilson, "Unfair Treatment?: The Case of Freedle, the SAT, and the Standardization Approach to Differential Item Functioning," *Harvard Educational Review*, spring 2010) has found that the SAT verbal section may present particular biases and challenges for African American test takers, which may inform collegiate admissions practices and responses to performance on this area of the SAT.

- The average reading score on the 2012 SAT for Black youth was 428, which is 99 points below the average score for White youth and 90 points below the average score for Asian youth.
- The average math score on the 2012 SAT for Black youth was 428, which is 108 points below the average score for White youth and 167 points below the average score for Asian youth.
- The average writing score on the 2012 SAT for Black youth was 417, which is 98 points below the average score for White youth and 111 points below the average score for Asian youth.[65]
- Overall, although the performance of Black college-bound seniors on the SAT has fluctuated over the years, it has not changed significantly since 1987:
  - Critical reading: The average score for Black SAT takers is 428, unchanged from 1987.
  - Mathematics: The average score for Black SAT takers is 427, up from 411 in 1987.
  - Writing: The average score for Black SAT takers is 417, down from its peak at 428 in 2006.[66]

Are Black students prepared for college?
- 44 percent of Black students in the ninth grade have a college counselor, compared with 60 percent of Asian ninth graders, 29 percent of Native American ninth graders, and 51 percent of White ninth graders.[67]
- 20 percent of Black students are enrolled in algebra or an advanced course other than algebra by the eighth grade, compared with 92 percent of Asians, 54 percent of Whites, and 51 percent of Latinos.[68]
- Only 5 percent of Black male students and 4 percent of Black female students who took the ACT college readiness exam achieved all four ACT college readiness benchmark scores.[69]
- The percent of Black and White ninth graders who expect to complete college is almost identical—about 50 percent of males and 60 percent of

females; however, fewer than half (42 percent) of all African American college students actually graduate with a bachelor's degree.[70]

BLACK STUDENTS AND HIGHER LEARNING

The lives of Black college students are rarely presented as a dynamic experience. Movies and sitcoms often portray Black college students as peripheral characters who either embody a racial stereotype or else reflect a consciousness that is (sometimes intentionally) detached from Black community and cultural norms. This limited presentation of Black college students—and its accompanying public narrative—masks the growth of the Black student population in colleges and their diverse needs and experiences. The narrative may also make it difficult to recognize strategies that could improve Black student performance, retention, and graduation rates.

How many Black college students are there?

- More than 3 million Black students are enrolled in college nationwide.[71]
- Between 2000 and 2010, the Black proportion of the total college student population increased from 11 percent to 14.5 percent.[72]
- 38 percent of all Black Americans ages 18 to 24 are enrolled in a degree-granting institution—more than double the percentage of Black 18- to 24-year-olds who were enrolled in college in 1970 (15.5 percent).[73]
- Black students make up 13 percent of all students enrolled in higher education.[74]
- African Americans make up 13 percent of the students in community colleges nationwide.[75]

How many Black students are pursuing advanced degrees?

- Black students make up 10 percent of all graduate students.[76]
- Black students account for approximately 7 percent of total student enrollment in medical schools.[77] Two-

thirds of all Black applicants to medical schools are
women.[78]
- There are 10,452 Black students enrolled in juris
  doctorate programs, and they are 29 percent of all
  enrolled law students of color and 7 percent of all
  enrolled law students overall.[79]

**An estimated 42 percent of Black college students are required
to take remedial courses, compared with 31 percent of White
students.[80]**

Where do Black college students receive their degrees?
- 10 percent of college graduates nationwide are
  African Americans.[81]
- 18 percent of the student population at the
  University of Phoenix, the nation's largest degree-
  granting institution, is Black.[82]
- The 105 Historically Black Colleges and Universities
  (HBCUs) in the United States are responsible for
  11 percent of the degrees conferred on Black
  Americans.
- HBCUs in the District of Columbia are responsible for
  46 percent of African American degrees awarded in
  the nation's capital.
- In five states, HBCUs are responsible for more
  than 30 percent of the degrees awarded to African
  Americans: Arkansas (31 percent), Delaware (38 percent), Louisiana (36 percent), Mississippi (37 percent),
  and North Carolina (34 percent).[83]

Are Black students working while enrolled in college?
- 63,000 Black college students are employed.
- 23 percent of Black college students 16 to 24 years
  old are employed, lower than the proportion of Black
  16- to 24-year-olds who are employed and not enrolled in college (31 percent).[84]

To understand the global ecological crisis, it is important to understand that the poisoning of African Americans . . . [is rooted in] . . . economic exploitation, racial oppression, and devaluation of human life. The quest for solutions to environmental problems and for ways to achieve sustainable development in the United States has considerable implications for the global environmental movement.

—Robert Bullard

In 2005, a hurricane ripped through the Gulf Coast of the United States, bringing to the fore many of the hidden truths about how race, socioeconomic status, and environmental concerns intersect. Where we live often has an impact on how we live—on our quality of life. Our environment is affected not only by the natural resources in our lands, but also by decisions made by our businesses, neighbors, and fellow citizens that affect the air we breathe, the food we eat, the water we drink, and the safety of our communities. African Americans may wonder how they are affected by climate change and other environmental factors often associated with faraway ecosystems or polar bears in the Arctic. In fact, these issues increase the vulnerabilities of African Americans.

To this day, a significant number of African Americans originally from the Gulf Coast remain permanently displaced from their homes as a result of failed policy responses to Hurricanes Katrina and Rita and also of the subsequent hardships caused by the 2010 Deepwater Horizon oil spill.*

---

*Commonly known as the BP oil spill, this was an environmental disaster for the Gulf of Mexico. The explosion and sinking of the Deepwater Horizon oil rig led to human deaths, severe marine damage, and the discharge into the Gulf of nearly 5 million barrels of oil.

The carbon footprint of African Americans is only a fraction of that of other groups, yet they have lived and are more likely to live in racially homogenous communities subjected to a high incidence of toxic emissions or near toxic landfills that are known to cause serious respiratory disorders (such as asthma), increased rates of certain cancers, and other chronic illnesses.

However, amid these disturbing statistics there is some good news. More and more "green jobs" are emerging, and African Americans are a part of this growing sector. Black organizations are increasingly involved in the public and policy discourses on environmental and climate justice, advocating for accountability to Black citizens and communities who are at increased health and economic risk from environmental hazards. This section presents a summary of statistics on important environmental concerns and opportunities affecting Black individuals and communities in the United States.

How could Black Americans be affected by the creation of green jobs?

According to the Bureau of Labor Statistics, green jobs, or green-collar jobs, are those jobs that benefit the environment, conserve natural resources, and improve the ability of institutions to be environmentally friendly or use fewer natural resources.[1] In response to the Great Recession of 2007–2010, the Obama administration produced a $787 billion economic stimulus package, the American Recovery and Reinvestment Act of 2009, that included among its components more than $22 billion worth of investment in green jobs.[2] Of great concern to many civil rights and employment justice advocates was the extent to which these investments would reach communities of color, including African American communities.

- Because Black Americans have the second-highest share of transportation and materials moving occupations (10 percent), an investment in transportation and green infrastructure projects (for example, modernizing transportation) would disproportionately benefit African Americans.[3]
- In general, three to five times more people are employed in the generation of renewable electricity

than in fossil fuel extraction, a field in which relatively few African Americans are employed (3.4 percent).

- Shifting 1 percent of electricity to renewable sources would create between 61,000 and 84,000 jobs for African Americans by 2030.[4]
- African Americans are more vulnerable to the negative economic effects sparked by oil price shocks,* including decreased financial resources and the increased unemployment that characterizes recessions.[5]

What are the intersections among Black businesses, energy, and the green economy?

- African American farmers are among the populations most vulnerable to the economic impact of energy policy.[6]
- Although 3 percent of African Americans work in the coal industry, 9 percent are employed in industrial categories that include renewable industries. These figures reflect African American employment in the energy sector in general.[7]

Figure 3. Distribution of Black-Owned Firms in the United States by Industry Division, 2007

Industries not classified, 5%

Administrative support, waste management, and remediation services, 10%

Professional, scientific, and technical services, 4%

Transportation and warehousing, 13%

Retail trade, 6%

Wholesale trade, 3%

Manufacturing, 3%

Construction, 4%

Utilities, 6%

Agriculture, forestry, fishing, and hunting, 2%

Type of Business Owned

0%   10%   20%   30%   40%   50%   60%

Source: U.S. Census Bureau. "2007 Survey of Business Owners." February 8, 2011. www2.census.gov /econ/sbo/07/final/tables/black_table5.pdf.

---

*Price shocks are defined as sudden variations in the price of oil.

- African Americans own 2 percent of the businesses in the agriculture, forestry, and fishing and hunting industries; 4 percent of the businesses in the construction field; and 13 percent of the firms in transportation and warehousing. Each of these sectors is expected to grow in a green economy.[8]

Will Black Americans benefit if the green jobs movement is successful?

- 50 to 60 percent of green jobs are expected to generate "good" wages:
  - 40 percent of green jobs are expected to be in the construction industry, where 4.1 percent of the workers are Black.
  - If nearly 750,000 green jobs are created, and Black workers are hired in accordance with their share of the labor market, Black employment could be increased by about 85,000 jobs.[9]
- The Kyoto Protocol is an international agreement on climate change, linked to the United Nations, which calls for emissions reductions. By 2030, 430,000 jobs would be created for African Americans if a comprehensive climate plan could achieve emissions reductions required by the Kyoto Protocol.[10]

What is the African American carbon footprint?

A carbon footprint is understood to be the amount of greenhouse gases (for example, carbon dioxide) emitted by human or manufacturing entities, including those involving transportation, during a specific period. The carbon footprint is often used as a measure of how human and industrial activity is influencing global climate change. Because a disproportionately high percentage of Black communities are situated in areas prone to the negative effects of climate change, it is worth noting the group's impact on the environment.

- African Americans are responsible for only 9 percent of carbon dioxide emissions, compared with the 26 percent attributed to Whites.
- African Americans produce lower rates of emissions

largely because emissions (per capita) decrease by 19 percent with each descending income level. African Americans are disproportionately concentrated in the lower and middle income deciles, which cause the least pollution.[11]

□ 24 percent of African American households do not own a car, a considerably higher ratio than White (7 percent), Latino (17 percent), and Asian (13 percent) households.[12]

□ African Americans emit, on average, 20 percent less greenhouse gas than their White counterparts.[13]

How much energy do Black Americans consume?

□ African Americans spend more money on energy than non–African Americans at almost all income levels.

□ Electricity expenditures are higher for African Americans than for non–African Americans at almost all income levels.

□ African American expenditures on home heating are higher than those of non–African Americans at almost all income levels.

- Black Americans living at or below the poverty line report that about 13 percent of their total expenditures are made on direct energy purchases, compared with 9 percent reported by poor non-Black people.

□ African Americans spend less money on gasoline and motor oil than their non–African American counterparts.

□ African Americans disproportionately benefit from the Low Income Home Energy Assistance Program (LIHEAP), a federal program designed to help poor households defray the costs of heating, cooling, and weatherization. Between 23 percent and 25 percent of LIHEAP funds go to Black households.[14]

How many Black communities are in close proximity to coal plants?

Coal-fired plants produce dangerous CO_2 emissions that affect not only the environment but also the health of the people most exposed to the fine particulate matter and toxins produced by these facilities.

- □ African Americans are more likely than White Americans to live within two miles of multiple industrial emissions sources.[15]
- □ African Americans are 79 percent more likely than their White counterparts to live in neighborhoods that pose the greatest health dangers.[16]

78 percent of Black Americans live within 30 miles of a coal-fired power plant, compared with 56 percent of White Americans.[17]

How does Black America experience air pollution, related respiratory problems, and negative environmental conditions?

- □ Over 70 percent of African Americans live in counties that fail to meet federal air pollution standards.[18]
- □ Black people are "consistently overrepresented" and over twice as likely to live in the areas with the worst air quality, compared with their proportion of the population in areas with the best air quality.
- □ U.S. counties with the worst fine particulate air pollution tend to have larger percentages of African American residents, smaller percentages of people ages 65 and over, and larger percentages of people in poverty.[19]
- □ 61 percent of African American children live in areas that exceed the official standards for ozone pollution.
- □ In 19 states, Black people are more than twice as likely as Whites to live in areas where industrial pollution is considered the greatest health danger.[20]
- □ Maryland census tracts with the highest concentration of African Americans are three times more likely than predominantly White census tracts to be at risk of cancers believed to be linked to air pollution.[21]
- □ African American children in Atlanta were found to show exacerbated symptoms of asthma following periods of high ozone pollution.[22]

African Americans are 20 percent more likely than Whites to have asthma, a condition that is exacerbated by air pollution.[23]

- Puerto Rican and African American children are 2.4 and 1.6 times more likely, respectively, to have asthma than White children.[24]
- 33 percent of Black Californians say that air pollution is a big problem.[25]
- African Americans are more likely to die from asthma than their White counterparts. In 2006, the age-adjusted death rate associated with asthma was three times higher for Black people (2.8 per 100,000) than for their White counterparts (0.9 per 100,000).[26]
- In Chicago, Black children ages 6 to 12 are more than twice (21 percent) as likely as their White peers (10 percent) to have asthma.[27]
- Exposure to residential allergens is associated with up to 40 percent of the asthma risk confronting Black children and other children of color.[28]
- Only 42 percent of Black Californians have heard of fracking (hydraulic fracturing used to extract oil and natural gas from underground rock formations), compared with 72 percent of Whites in California.[29]
- African Americans have more limited resources to curb air pollution and its effects on their health: the percentage of African Americans without health insurance is 150 percent *higher* than the percentage of the general population without such insurance.[30]

22 percent of African American children living in housing built before 1946 suffer from lead poisoning, compared with 13 percent of Mexican American children and 6 percent of White children living under similar conditions.[31]

How do Black Americans experience climate change and global warming?

- Black Americans cause one-eighth the amount

of global warming pollution caused by White Americans.[32]

- African Americans are disproportionately affected by deaths caused by climate change–related conditions, including heat waves and air pollution. African Americans tend to live in cities, where temperatures are approximately 10 degrees warmer than in surrounding areas, and die from heat-related complications at up to twice the rate for Whites.[33]
- 43 percent of African Americans live in urban "heat islands," which is double the number of Whites who live in such areas.[34]
- In the 1995 Chicago heat wave, the African American death rate was 1.5 times higher than the death rate for Whites.[35]
- A 25 percent reduction in greenhouse gas by 2020 would reduce overall infant mortality, at least one-third of whom would be Black.[36]

How were Black Americans affected by Hurricane Katrina?

Scientific evidence shows that global climate change has increased the frequency of powerful and destructive storms such as Hurricane Katrina, which struck along the Gulf Coast in 2005. The six states that are at greatest risk of hurricanes as a result of climate change are also those in which the largest proportions of Black Americans reside. Hurricane Katrina was among the most significant natural disasters in U.S. history, unveiling the politics of poverty and of disaster recovery.

Hurricane Katrina shrank the Black population in New Orleans by 57 percent.[37]

- The six states with the highest Black populations are all located in the Atlantic hurricane zone.[38]
- 498 African Americans died in Louisiana as a result of Hurricane Katrina.
- In Orleans Parish (New Orleans), the mortality rate

among African Americans was 1.7 to 4 times higher than among Whites.[39]

- 75 percent of Black residents in New Orleans experienced serious flooding.[40]
- 51 percent of displaced Black residents had returned to New Orleans by December 2006, as compared to 71 percent of their non-Black counterparts.[41]
- 81 percent of Black residents of New Orleans reported having a home damaged or destroyed by Katrina, compared with 47 percent of non-Black residents.
- The total number of Black females in the New Orleans metropolitan area decreased from 47 percent to 37 percent of the general population after Hurricane Katrina.
- The rate of poverty among African American women and girls in New Orleans post-Katrina is 23 percent, compared with 47 percent before the hurricane.
- There are 55 percent fewer African American single mothers in New Orleans post-Katrina.[42]

What has been the impact of the 2010 Deepwater Horizon disaster on Black Americans?

President Barack Obama called the Deepwater Horizon incident "the worst environmental disaster America has ever faced."[43] In the aftermath of the spill, many African Americans sought to find employment in the cleanup efforts; however, increased exposure to chemicals and other toxins quickly made these jobs undesirable.[44] The statistics below reveal how some Black individuals, communities, and businesses were affected by the spill.

- There were 50 to 75 Black fishermen in the Gulf Coast in 2010, down from the hundreds working in the region before Hurricane Katrina and the Deepwater Horizon oil spill.
- Advocates in Louisiana say that 90 percent of oyster farms (and boats)—a disproportionate number of them Black-owned—were lost to "unfair policies" from the federal and state governments.[45]

□ African American women, single people, and young unemployed people were the most likely to report experiencing depression following the BP oil spill and Hurricane Katrina, a condition scientists have attributed to greater exposure to the spill and related circumstances.[46]

Through my singing and acting and speaking, I want to make freedom ring. Maybe I can touch people's hearts better than I can their minds, with the common struggle of the common man.

—*Paul Robeson*

The vast and rich tradition of African American participation in and consumption of arts, entertainment, and sports is well documented. From singers and composers to dancers, actors, and filmmakers, African Americans in the arts have left an indelible imprint on American culture. The debate rages on regarding the extent to which television and film provide roles for Black actors that reflect the variety of experiences in the Black community, but groundbreaking roles played by Kerry Washington, Don Cheadle, and others suggest that more opportunities may be on the horizon. However, history has shown that these successes can be sustained only through the development of an infrastructure of Black writers, producers, and directors on staff and thriving in Hollywood, New York City, and other production arenas.

The representation of Black Americans in sports, particularly in basketball and football, is also remarkable. However, as the statistics in this section show, although the number of Black athletes continues to grow, the representation of African Americans in other sports-related professions tells a different story. What follows is a compilation of statistics on the representation and performance trends of Black Americans in professional music, film, and other forms of entertainment and sports.

FILM & TELEVISION

The first African American to host a television variety show was Nat King Cole, who premiered *The Nat King Cole Show* on NBC in November 1956. Another variety program, *Soul Train*, emerged in 1971 and enjoyed tremendous success as one of the longest-running syndicated programs in American television history.[1] Black Americans have led comedies, dramas, talk shows, and other programming on the air, making important contributions to American television.

What are some film, television, and radio trends for African Americans?

- Black Americans attend movies 10 percent more often than the general population.[2]
- 23 percent of African American households have only broadcast TV (as opposed to cable or satellite TV). In Memphis, 60 percent of households with broadcast-only TV are African American.
- With more than 42 million U.S. viewers a week, *The Oprah Winfrey Show* was broadcast TV's highest-ranked talk show for two decades.
- Oprah Winfrey is the only African American on the *Forbes'* list of television's highest paid personalities between June 2012 and June 2013.[3]
- Radio One is the nation's largest radio broadcasting company geared primarily toward African American markets.[4]

Who are Black Hollywood's top moneymakers?

- Four of Hollywood's 25 highest-grossing actors of all time are Black:
  - Eddie Murphy (highest-grossing film to date: *Shrek 2*, $441.2 million),
  - Samuel L. Jackson (highest-grossing film to date: *Star Wars: Episode III—Revenge of the Sith*, $380.3 million),
  - Morgan Freeman (highest-grossing film to date: *The Dark Knight*, $533.3 million), and
  - Will Smith (highest-grossing film to date: *Independence Day*, $306.2 million).[5]
- The five richest Black actors of all time:
  - Tyler Perry, $400 million,
  - Bill Cosby, $350 million,

- Will Smith, $215 million,
- Samuel L. Jackson and Denzel Washington, $150 million each, and
- Martin Lawrence, $110 million.[6]

How inclusive is Hollywood to Black producers and directors?

- Eight television shows in the 2011–12 season hired no Black directors.[7]
- According to *Black Enterprise*, the 10 most "bankable"* Black producers in Hollywood are:

Table 1. Hollywood's Most Bankable Black Producers

Black Entertainment Rank	Producers/ Production Company	Worldwide Gross to Date
1	James Lassiter and Will Smith Overbrook Entertainment	$3 billion
2	Broderick Johnson Alcon Entertainment	$1.4 billion
3	Marlon, Keenen, and Shawn Wayans Wayans Bros. Entertainment	$747.8 million
4	Tyler Perry Tyler Perry Studios	$738.8 million
5	Eddie Murphy Eddie Murphy Productions	$683.1 million
6	Martin Lawrence Runteldat Entertainment	$605.9 million
7	Reuben Cannon Reuben Cannon Entertainment	$577 million
8	Debra Martin Chase Martin Chase Productions	$533.3 million
9	O'Shea "Ice Cube" Jackson Cube Vision Productions	$486.6 million
10	Will Packer Will Packer Rainforest Films	$382.1 million

Source: Kenya N. Byrd and Carolyn M. Brown, "Hollywood's Most Bankable Black Producers: These Power Brokers Wield Clout Behind the Scenes and Generate the Most Green in Film," *Black Enterprise*, December 2012.

---

*This list is based on cumulative gross box office receipts worldwide.

How do Black actors fare in film, television, and theater?

- According to the Screen Actors Guild's latest data, Black actors comprise approximately 13 percent of all actors cast in TV and theatrical roles, excluding animation.
- 12 percent of lead roles and 14 percent of supporting roles were cast with Black actors.
- Between 2002 and 2008, the share of roles awarded to Black actors declined by 2.2 percent.
- Nearly 10 percent of low-budget film-acting roles were awarded to African Americans in 2008—a decline of 6.5 percent from 2007.[8]
- Between 1998 and 2008, the total share of roles awarded to Black actors remained relatively unchanged, about 13 percent.

Where are Black writers in the entertainment industry?

- 108 Black writers (out of a total 1,722 writers) were employed among all 190 broadcast and cable television shows during the 2011–12 season.
- At 6.5 percent of all broadcast and cable television writers, Black writers represent the largest share of writers who are people of color.
- The share of Black television staff employment has increased by only 0.7 percentage points since 2000—from 5.8 percent to 6.5 percent today.
- Black writers are underrepresented as television writers by a factor of 2 to 1, compared with the percentage of Black people in the U.S. general population.
- There were two networks—IFC and Spike—without a single Black writer on staff for the 2011–12 season.
- Networks with the highest representation of Black writers in the 2011–12 season were BET (19), Fox (16), and ABC (13).
- 29 percent of television shows in the 2011–12 season had no Black writer on staff.[9]
- 91 percent of pilot projects in the 2010–11 pilot season did not have a single Black writer.[10]

Are Black Americans recognized by the Academy?

- In 2013, Cheryl Boone Isaacs was elected president of the Academy of Motion Picture Arts and Sciences, making her the first African American to hold the position.[11]
- African Americans compose 2 percent of the Academy of Motion Picture Arts and Sciences.[12]
- 14 major* Academy Awards have been won by Black actors since 1929.[13]
- Black actors, directors, musicians, sound specialists, and writers have won 28 Oscars, or 1 percent of the total Academy Awards given since 1929.[14]
- Black actors have received only 4 percent of the Oscars for best acting since 1929.[15]

How much television does Black America watch?

- The average Black viewer watches nearly 6.5 hours of television each day.
- Older Black viewers (baby boomers) watch nearly 8 hours of live television each day.[16]

THEATER

How are Black Americans represented and celebrated on Broadway?

Since 1898, Black Americans have performed on Broadway. The first play to feature an all-Black cast was *Clorindy, or the Origin of the Cake Walk*, created by the poet Paul Laurence Dunbar and composer Will Marion Cook.[17] Some Black actors have participated in race bending to maximize their ability to work in the performing arts. In 1950, Juanita Hall was the first African American to win a Tony Award, for her role as Bloody Mary, a Polynesian character in *South Pacific*.[18] Since that time, many Black Americans have received praise for outstanding performances in noteworthy projects.

- Over the past five years, Black actors have held 12 percent of all Broadway roles.

---

*"Major" refers to awards in the categories of best actor, best actress, best supporting actor, and best supporting actress.

- Black actors have experienced an increase in representation on Broadway—from 7 percent of all roles in the 2006–7 season to 17 percent in 2010–11.[19]
- There are four Black producers on Broadway and only two Black producers who are currently responsible for taking a project from conceptualization to production on stage, Steven Byrd and Alia Jones of Front Row Productions.[20]
- More than 70 African Americans have received a Tony Award for their performance in a Broadway play.[21]

MUSIC AND ART

How strong are the sales in some traditionally Black music genres?

- R&B is the third most popular music genre (measured by album sales), after rock and alternative rock.
- Albums in the R&B genre moved 49.7 million units in 2012, a 10.2 percent decline from 2011. However, 16.3 million digital R&B albums were sold, a 10.2 percent increase from 2011.
- 24.2 million rap albums were sold in 2012, a decline by 11.4 percent from 2011. Rap sold 10.7 million digital albums, a 14.7 percent increase from the previous year.
- R&B and hip-hop together sold 249.3 million digital tracks in 2012.[22]

Who are the best-selling Black artists from the past decade?

- From 2000 to 2010, seven of the top-ten artists on the Billboard 200 albums chart and the Hot 100 are Black: Usher (2), Nelly (3), Beyoncé (4), Alicia Keys (5), 50 Cent (6), Destiny's Child (9), and Jay-Z (10).[23]
- In 2007, Prince's 21 Nights concert series made him the first artist—and only Black artist—to perform 21 sold-out concerts at the O2 Arena in London. At $22 million, this concert series was the O2 arena's highest-grossing engagement that year. Prince's album *Purple Rain* was the longest-running album to be number one on the Billboard charts (24 weeks) in 1984 and 1985.[24]

- Michael Jackson's *Thriller* (released in 1982) is the bestselling studio album by a single artist in history, with more than $30 million in sales.[25]

What are some of the music and art purchasing trends among Black Americans?

- 19 percent of African Americans listen to jazz through electronic media (television, radio, computer, cell phone, portable devices), a higher rate than that of any other racial or ethnic group.
- African Americans make up 7 percent of adults who listen to classical music through electronic media.
- Only 1.8 percent of Black Americans are recent art buyers, the lowest rate of any group. Black adults make up 5 percent of adults who own art and 3.5 percent of all adults who recently purchased a work of art.[26]

How is Black America exposed to live art performance and instruction?

- Black adults make up 6.6 percent of adults in the United States who play an instrument.
- 21 percent of Black parents report sending their children to live art performances outside of school, compared to 40 percent of White parents who report doing so.
- 5 percent of Black parents report sending their children to art classes.
- Black Americans have the highest rate of participation in choir or choral activities (10 percent).[27]

How do young Black people feel about rap music?

- One study found that 41 percent of Black youth feel that rap music videos should be more political, compared with 23 percent of White youth and 33 percent of Latino youth who think so.[28]
- 70 percent of rap music—a genre considered African American—is purchased by White youth.[29]

OTHER ENTERTAINMENT

- Earning $14 million in 2013 from stand-up perfor-

mances, Kevin Hart is the only African American on the Forbes list of highest-paid stand-up comedians.[30]
- 43 percent of African Americans report reading literature.
- Black adults make up 9 percent of all American adults who read printed books and 9.6 percent of those who read literature in other formats.
- At 8 percent, African Americans have the highest rate of any racial group of accessing nonmusical plays through electronic devices.[31]

PROFESSIONAL SPORTS

What sports programming is most watched on television by Black viewers?
- The top five sports shows watched by African Americans in 2012:
  - Super Bowl XLVI (12.5 million viewers)
  - NFC Championship (7.1 million viewers)
  - NBA Finals–Game 5 (6.7 million viewers)
  - NBA Finals–Game 4 (6.5 million viewers)
  - AFC Championship (6.1 million viewers)[32]

How well are Black athletes represented in professional sports?
Many players listed as Latino may also be of African descent or otherwise classified as Black. The numbers included here represent those players noted as African American.
- Black athletes make up 67 percent of the players in the National Football League (NFL) and hold 21 percent of quarterback positions.[33]
- Black athletes make up 25 percent of the players in Major League Soccer (MLS).[34]
- Black athletes make up 76 percent of the players in the National Basketball Association (NBA).[35]
- Black athletes make up 74 percent of the players in the Women's National Basketball Association (WNBA).[36]
- Black athletes make up 8 percent of the players in Major League Baseball (MLB)—a significant decrease from 19 percent in 1995.[37]

- Black athletes make up 2 percent of the professional players in the National Hockey League (NHL).[38]

How well are Black coaches represented in professional sports?

- There is only one African American head coach in MLS: Robin Frasier of the Chivas USA. Six percent of assistant coaches in MLS are African American.[39]
- There were three Black head coaches in the NFL in 2013. Frederick Douglass "Fritz" Pollard became the first professional Black coach in U.S. history when he led the Akron Pros football team in 1921. Since then, there have been fewer than 20 Black head coaches in NFL history.[40]
- African Americans represent about one-third of defensive coordinators in the NFL.[41]
- 43 percent of head coaches and 43.5 percent of assistant coaches in the NBA are African American.[42]
- 33 percent of head coaches and 40 percent of assistant coaches in the WNBA are African American.[43]
- 14 percent of coaches in MLB are African American.[44]

Are Black Americans owners and presidents of sports franchises?

- There are no Black presidents, CEOs, or owners of teams in MLS.[45]
- There are no Black owners or presidents of an NFL franchise team.[46]
- Michael Jordan is the NBA's only Black majority owner (of the Charlotte Bobcats), but the NBA boasts 13 Black Americans who hold minority ownership of an NBA team, two Black CEOs, and four Black team presidents.[47]
- There are five Black team owners but no Black presidents or CEOs in the WNBA.[48]
- There are two Black owners in MLB: Earvin "Magic" Johnson (Los Angeles Dodgers), who was the first Black owner in MLB, and Paxton Baker (Washington Nationals).

- There were no Black MLB presidents or CEOs in 2012.[49]

How do Black Americans fare in other sports leadership positions (executives, directors, managers, and account executives)?

- African Americans hold 8 percent of all management positions in the NFL, with nine African American vice presidents.[50]
- African Americans represent 6 percent of professional staff in MLS.[51]
- African Americans hold 14 percent of professional staff positions in the NBA.[52]
- African Americans hold 29 percent of professional staff positions in the WNBA.[53]
- In 2013, there was one Black general manager in MLB.[54]
- There are 12 Black vice presidents of NFL teams, and African Americans hold 9 percent of the general manager positions in the NFL.[55]
- 20 percent of general managers in the NBA are Black; there are 35 African Americans who hold team vice president positions in the NBA, including seven Black women.[56]
- In the WNBA, 42 percent of general managers and 19 percent of those in senior administration are African American.[57]
- In 2012, there were 19 African American executive vice presidents, senior vice presidents, and vice presidents in MLB. Additionally, 6 percent of senior team administrators (directors, assistant general managers, senior managers, general counsel, legal counsel, senior advisers, etc.) are Black.[58]

Are Black Americans represented in sports media?

- African Americans compose 6 percent of assistant or deputy sports editors.
- In 2012, 40 African American men and only two African American women were hired as sports columnists at top-tier newspapers and websites.

- African Americans compose about 8 percent of those employed at Associated Press Sports Editors member newspapers.[59]

> **Although African Americans make up just 67 percent of the players in the NFL, Black players received 92 percent of the unsportsmanlike conduct penalties during the 2010–11 season—a statistic that sociologists believe may be linked to a negative reaction to "cockiness" or "self-promotion" when demonstrated by a Black player.[60]**

We plead for health—for an opportunity
to live in decent houses and localities, for a
chance to rear our children in physical and
moral cleanliness.

—*Niagara Movement Declaration of*
Principles, 1905

The health of Black people in the United States has
long been an important priority on the racial equity
agenda. Health care is a core civil and human rights
issue, affecting not only the capacity of individuals
to work and live with dignity but also the quality and
composition of communities. Our physical and mental
health is central to who we are and what we can ac-
complish. Where traditional roads to health care and
health awareness have sometimes been blocked, Black
Americans have a rich history of finding creative ways
to encourage their communities to seek treatment for
disease. For example, in her song "Jitis Blues," Memphis
Minnie emphasized the importance of treating menin-
gitis, which had been considered a disorder prevalent
among Black Americans.

My head and neck was paining me, feel like
    my back was break' in two . . .
My companion take me to the doctor, "Doctor
    please tell me my wife's complaint"
The doctor looked down on me, shook his head,
"I wouldn't mind telling you, son, but I can't
You take her 'round to the city hospital, jus' as
    quick, quick as you possibly can
Because the condition she's in now, you will
    never go home live again"[1]

The health conditions and treatment of Black Americans have also been at the center of efforts to improve
practices in human-subject research. The Tuskegee

syphilis experiment, in which Black men were unethically denied treatment for syphilis, drew attention to the rights of research subjects and changed the way that biological and social scientists interact with individuals in the name of science.

Black Americans have historically been subject to diagnoses that served the political function of pathologizing the Black body, and in fact it is true that Black Americans have suffered disproportionately from pain and disease. However, much of it would have been preventable had they had equal access to quality foods and proper and regular care.

There have been many public discussions about health disparities, yet increased rates of infections, urban food deserts, and unequal access to insurance and to quality medical care remain problems in many Black communities. The severity and prevalence of particular health concerns should prompt us to ask:

- How many liquor stores are in African American communities?
- How many Black doctors and medical students are there?
- What is the rate of drug use among Black American teenagers?
- What are some of the key indicators of mental and physical health and how are African Americans faring compared with the general population in the incidence of infectious disease?
- How do chronic and preventable diseases affect Black Americans?

Trends in these and other related issues are addressed in this compilation of statistics on health and health care in Black America.

HEALTH PROFESSIONALS

Black medical professionals have been a crucial lifeline for the Black community. Throughout history, Black doctors have defied the challenges of racial oppression and poverty to emerge as healers. From the humble, enslaved beginnings of James Derham (1762–c.1802), the first Black doctor recognized in the United States, to the accomplishments of other "first" physicians—including Charles Drew, Daniel Hale Williams, Joycelyn Elders, and others—we now have a cadre of physicians and other health professionals who, among other commitments, are more likely to work in Black communities.

What percentage of health professionals are African American?

- 4 percent of doctors in the United States are Black.[2]
- Approximately 10 percent of registered nurses (RNs) in the United States are Black, and 22 percent of licensed practical nurses (LPNs) and licensed vocational nurses (LVNs) are Black.
- 35 percent of nursing aides, psychiatric aides, and home health aides in the United States are Black.
- 15 percent of physical therapists, medical assistants, and medical aides are Black.[3]
- 10 percent of dental assistants in the U.S. are Black.
- 27 percent of phlebotomists in the U.S. are Black.
- 22 percent of medical health care support workers in the United States, including medical equipment preparers, are Black.[4]

Where have Black doctors been educated?

In 1837, James McCune Smith became the first Black person to earn a medical degree.[5] A suffragist and abolitionist, Smith earned his degree abroad at the University of Glasgow in Scotland. In 1847, David Jones Peck (1826–55) became the first Black doctor to earn a degree from an American medical school, Rush Medical College in Chicago, after which he worked closely with Frederick Douglass, William Lloyd Garrison, and others to promote racial justice, the abolition of slavery, and the full inclusion of Black people in the American democracy.

- In 2012, 3,824 Black/African American undergraduate students applied to medical school, a record number, and 1,416 enrolled, also a record high.[6]
- In 2011, Howard University, a historically Black institution, produced 87 Black graduates who applied to U.S. medical schools, more than any other college

or university in the United States. In that same year, Xavier University in New Orleans, also an HBCU, was a close second with 68.

◻ Spelman College, a historically Black women's college, ranked fourth in the number of Black graduates who applied to medical school in 2011. Other HBCUs that produced 40 or more graduates who applied to medical school included Hampton University and Oakwood University.

◻ In 2011, the University of Florida produced 64 Black medical school applicants, more than any other predominantly White undergraduate institution. Other predominantly White institutions producing the largest numbers of Black undergraduate students applying to medical school include the University of Maryland, the University of Miami, the University of South Florida, Florida State University, Cornell University, Emory University, Rutgers University, and the University of Texas.[7]

Where are Black medical students being educated?

◻ 16 percent of all African American medical school students enroll in the three historically Black medical schools: Meharry, Howard, and Morehouse.[8]

◻ The medical schools with the highest number of Black matriculates in 2011:
  ▪ Meharry Medical College, Nashville (92)
  ▪ Howard University College of Medicine, Washington, D.C. (75)
  ▪ Morehouse School of Medicine, Atlanta (45)
  ▪ University of Texas Medical Branch School of Medicine, Galveston, Texas (43)
  ▪ University of Illinois College of Medicine, Chicago (27)
  ▪ Ohio State University College of Medicine, Columbus (24)
  ▪ Indiana University School of Medicine, Indianapolis (21)
  ▪ Medical University of South Carolina College of Medicine, Charleston (20)
  ▪ University of Texas Medical School at Houston (18)

- Drexel University College of Medicine, Philadelphia (17); Duke University School of Medicine, Durham, North Carolina (17); Medical College of Wisconsin, Milwaukee (17).[9]

How many Black Americans have a hard time accessing health care?

Black Americans' access to health care—a critical factor in the reduction of health disparities—is informed by many factors, from socioeconomic status and affordability to availability of transportation and insurance and trust in health care professionals and institutions. Because of limited access to quality preventive care, Black Americans are more likely to experience serious outcomes from controllable disorders and to rely on emergency care, which is more expensive.

- 20 percent of African Americans are uninsured, compared with 30 percent of Latino Americans, 17 percent of Asian Americans, and 15 percent of White Americans.[10]
- 7 percent of Black children are uninsured.[11]
- 21 percent of Black transgender people report being refused medical care because of bias.
- 34 percent of Black transgender people report having postponed care even if they were injured or sick, for fear of discrimination.[12]

What are some pregnancy and birthing trends among Black Americans?

- There were 636,425 African American births in 2010.
- The rate of African American births per 1,000 women 15 to 44 years old was 66.6 in 2010.
- African Americans produce 14 percent of low-weight births in the United States.
- African American babies are 50 percent less likely to be breast-fed for at least three months than White and Latino babies.
- Black and Latina teens 15 to 19 years old continue to have the highest rates of pregnancy, 52 per 1,000 and 56 per 1,000, respectively. However, African Americans are experiencing fewer teen pregnancies than before:

the pregnancy rates for Black girls 15 to 17 years old decreased by 39 percent between 1998 and 2008.[13]

What are the contraception trends for Black Americans?

Choices with respect to the use and type of birth control are varied and dependent upon a host of factors, including socioeconomic status, satisfaction with the chosen method, attitude toward pregnancy, and other cultural norms.[14] Low-income Black women on public assistance or in correctional facilities were subjected to forced sterilization* as a part of eugenics practices that were legal throughout the United States before the mid-1980s.[15]

- Black women ages 15 to 44 have the highest rate of sterilization, 40 percent. By comparison, the rate for Latinas is 34 percent, and for White women it is 23 percent.
- 2 percent of Black males have been sterilized, compared with 6 percent of Latino males and 14 percent of White males.
- Black women ages 15 to 44 are more than three times as likely as their White counterparts and nearly twice as likely as their Latina counterparts to use an injectable form of birth control (as opposed to oral contraception or other methods).
- 27 percent of Black women ages 15 to 44 use a condom as a form of birth control, compared with 21 percent of White and 19 percent of Latina women.[16]

What is the infant mortality rate among African Americans?

Black people have the highest infant mortality rate in the United States—13 percent.

- Black mothers are more than twice as likely as White

---

*"Forced sterilization" refers to government policies and practices that require individuals to undergo medical procedures to prevent them from reproducing.

mothers to experience the death of a baby within the first 28 days of the infant's life.

◻ The Black infant mortality rate is highest in Hawai'i (21 percent); the White infant mortality rate in that state is 4 percent; for all races combined, it is 6 percent.

◻ The states with the highest rates of Black infant mortality are Hawai'i (21 percent); Indiana (16 percent); Kansas (15.7 percent); Wisconsin (15.5 percent); Michigan (15.4 percent); Ohio, Tennessee, and West Virginia (15.3 percent); North Carolina (15.2 percent); Mississippi (15.1 percent); Louisiana and Pennsylvania (14.5 percent); and Missouri (14.4 percent).[17]

The Black infant mortality rate in the District of Columbia is 19 percent.[18]

What is the life expectancy for African Americans?

◻ Black people are living longer: between 2000 and 2009, life expectancy at birth increased more for the Black population than for the White population, which has narrowed the racial gap in life expectancy. On average, the Black life expectancy is 73.5 years: 77 years for Black females and 70 years for Black males.[19]

MENTAL HEALTH & CHEMICAL DEPENDENCY

The impact of mental illness and chemical dependency on Black lives has been tremendous, and the stigma associated with these conditions has prevented many African Americans from seeking treatment. Although mental illness and addiction are important and real conditions affecting the Black community, Black people who suffer from these conditions tend to seek help from churches, family, other community institutions, or a primary care physician rather than from a specialized mental health professional.[20] In some cases, this has increased the difficulty of overcoming both the illnesses and the problems arising from the self-medication often used to treat them. Cultural incompetence,* lack of access to quality care, and overdiagnosis and misdiagnosis of certain conditions also play a role. In addition, Black people experience at higher rates than other groups conditions that may exacerbate the risk of mental illness, such as homelessness, foster care, and exposure to violence and victimization.

How are Black Americans affected by mental health conditions?

- African Americans are 20 percent more likely than Whites to report feeling serious psychological distress.
- African Americans make up 4 percent of all adults reporting serious psychological distress, but that percentage doubles for African Americans below the poverty line.[21]
- Black children in households below the poverty line are more likely to be diagnosed with Attention Deficit Hyperactivity Disorder (ADHD): 17 percent of Black children ages 5 to 17 living in poverty are diagnosed with ADHD, compared to 13 percent of all youth living in poverty.
- Black Americans make up 12 percent of single-race adults who experience feelings of sadness, worthlessness, and hopelessness. Multiracial Black adults make up 19.6 percent of all people of two or more races who report such feelings.[22]
- 9 percent of Black adults feel that everything is an effort, compared with 5 percent of White adults.[23]
- Black full-time college students and their similarly situated Black counterparts out of college experienced a major depressive episode in the past year at similar rates, 7 percent and 6 percent, respectively.[24]

---

*"Cultural incompetence" refers to the absence of what the U.S. Office of Minority Health calls "a set of congruent behaviors, attitudes, and policies that come together in a system, agency, or among professionals that enables effective work in cross-cultural situations" (Office of Minority Health, U.S. Department of Health and Human Services, "What Is Cultural Competency?," May 9, 2013, minorityhealth .hhs.gov/templates/browse.aspx?lvl=2&lvlID=11).

What are the suicide trends and treatment patterns among Black Americans?

- The suicide rate for African Americans is 60 percent lower than that of Whites.[25]

> **Although the suicide rate for all Black Americans is only 5 percent, a recent national survey shows that 49 percent of Black transgender people report having attempted suicide.[26]**

- The suicide rate for African American men is 9 percent, as compared with 23 percent for White men and 2 percent for Black women.[27]
- Black men ages 25 to 44 years old have the highest rate of suicide (13 percent) among all African American men.[28]
- 8 percent of Black high school students have attempted suicide.[29]
- 9 percent of Black adults receive mental health treatment or counseling. By comparison, 16 percent of Whites receive mental health treatment or counseling.[30]
- The suicide rate of Black males ages 15 to 19 is 7 percent.[31]
- 6 percent of Black men receive mental health treatment or counseling, compared with 11 percent of White men.
- 6 percent of Black adults receive prescription medications for mental health treatment, compared with 14 percent of White adults.
- 4 percent of Black men receive prescription medications for mental health treatment, compared with 9 percent of White men.[32]

What is the impact of drug use and addiction on Black Americans?

- African Americans, who make up 14 percent of the U.S. population, account for 12 to 14 percent of all regular drug users.[33]
- Black Americans ages 12 and older have the second-

lowest (behind Asian Americans) rate of substance dependence or abuse, 7.2 percent.[34]

Black high school students currently report using marijuana at percentages comparable to those of their White and Latino counterparts: 22 percent for each group.[35]

- At the turn of the current century, alcohol and cocaine were the two substances most commonly abused by Black Americans. In 2000, 55 percent of African Americans seeking treatment were addicted to cocaine; however, by 2010, the ratio had decreased to 40 percent.[36]
- 32 percent of crack cocaine users are African American.
- 6.6 percent of Black Americans report having used hallucinogens in their lifetime.
- 7.5 percent of Black Americans report having used an inhalant in their lifetime.[37]

What percentage of Black Americans struggle with alcohol consumption?

- 17 percent of Black Americans report that they drink more alcoholic beverages than they should, compared with 23 percent of White Americans.[38]
- 25 percent of Black youth report drinking alcohol before the age of 13, compared with 18 percent of White youth and 27 percent of Latino youth who report the same.[39]
- 22 percent of Black people report that their binge drinking has been a cause of trouble in their family, compared with 32 percent of Whites reporting the same problem.[40]
- More Black Americans report abstaining from drinking alcohol (42 percent) than White Americans who report the same (30 percent).[41]
- 30 percent of Black high school students report riding with a driver who had been drinking alcohol, compared with 26.2 percent of White high school

students and 34.2 percent of Latino high school students.[42]

What are trends in nicotine use among Black Americans?

- ▫ 24 percent of Black men smoke cigarettes, the same rate as that of White men.
- ▫ 18 percent of Black women smoke cigarettes, a lower percentage than that of White women (21 percent).[43]

DISEASE AND CHRONIC ILLNESS

Black Americans sometimes use coded language to describe disease and chronic illness (for example, "having sugar" to describe diabetes). Such codes may serve to mask pain; they also reduce the likelihood that the patient will receive proper treatment. In the case of HIV, AIDS, and other sexually transmitted and/or fatal diseases, the infection rates for Black Americans are sometimes used to judge community behaviors in ways that affect not only private human interactions but also public policy. For more than 30 years, ever since the AIDS epidemic was first identified, Black individuals and communities have felt its impact strongly—and still too many Black Americans are suffering as a result of unequal access to care, prevention information, and culturally competent responses.

What are the trends among Black Americans regarding HIV status?

- ▫ Only 54 percent of African Americans report being aware of their HIV status, compared with 86 percent of White Americans.[44]
- ▫ African Americans are disproportionately infected with HIV: Black people account for 44 percent of newly acquired HIV infections.[45]
- ▫ Black men account for 70 percent of all new HIV infections among African Americans. The rate of new infection for Black males is seven times higher than the rate of new infection for White males, twice as high as that for Latino men, and nearly three times as high as the rate for Black women.[46]
- ▫ Although African Americans have the highest HIV

testing rate (62 percent), they are more likely to get tested for HIV late in the course of their infections and are less likely to receive Highly Active Antiretroviral Therapy (HAART).[47]

☐ Over a quarter million African Americans with an AIDS diagnosis had died in the United States by the year 2009.[48]

☐ 20 percent of Black transgender people are HIV positive; an additional 10 percent are not aware of their status.[49]

☐ In 2010, among Black men who have sex with men (MSM) ages 13 to 24 had more new HIV infections (4,800) than any other racial or age group.

☐ In 2010, Black gay, bisexual, and other MSM represented about 72 percent of new HIV infections among all Black Americans and 36 percent of new HIV infections among all MSM.

☐ 87 percent of HIV infections among Black women are attributed to heterosexual sex.

☐ Racial disparities in HIV infection rates are more pronounced among women: the estimated rate of new HIV infections for Black women is 20 times higher than the rate for White women, and almost 5 times as high as the rate for Latinas.[50]

☐ Black women account for 29 percent of new HIV infections among all African Americans, a 21 percent decrease since 2008.

One in 16 Black men and one in 32 Black women in the United States will be diagnosed with HIV in their lifetime.[51]

☐ A 2012 study found that African-born men in the United States were diagnosed with HIV at later stages of the disease than were African-born women.[52]

What are the trends among Black Americans regarding cancer?

☐ African Americans are more likely than Whites to be diagnosed with cancer at a later stage of the disease.

☐ Colorectal cancer is the third most common cancer

and the third leading cause of cancer deaths among African Americans.

□ Black Americans are 55 percent more likely than White Americans to develop lung cancer from light to moderate cigarette smoking.[53]

□ The incidence rate of prostate cancer is significantly higher in African American men (234.9 cases per 100,000) than in White American men (150.4 cases per 100,000).[54]

□ African American men and Jamaican men of African descent have the highest prostate cancer incidence in the world.[55]

□ African American men are 2.7 times more likely to begin treatment for end-stage renal disease related to diabetes than White men.[56]

□ More Black women die from breast cancer even though more White women are diagnosed with the disease. Black women tend to be diagnosed at later, harder-to-treat stages of breast cancer and also tend to have more aggressive forms of breast cancer.[57]

What are the trends among Black Americans regarding liver disease?

□ Chronic liver disease is the eighth leading cause of death for Black Americans ages 45 to 54 years old.[58]

□ 1 percent of Black adults have been told by a physician that they have chronic liver disease, the same percentage as White adults.[59]

What are the trends among Black Americans regarding diabetes?

□ 13 percent of African Americans have been diagnosed with diabetes. Black adults are twice as likely as White adults to have been diagnosed with diabetes.[60]

□ Diabetic Black Americans are 1.7 times as likely as diabetic Whites to be hospitalized.

□ African Americans are 2.2 times as likely as Whites to die from diabetes.[61]

□ 22 percent of African Americans with diabetes experience visual impairment.[62]

□ The rate of African American diabetes-related lower

extremity amputation is 4.5 per 1,000 diabetics, about double the rate for Whites, 2.3 per 1,000.[63]

□ 23 percent of Black women with diabetes experience visual impairment, a slightly higher rate than Black men with diabetes (20 percent).[64]

What are some obesity trends among Black Americans?

□ Approximately one-third of Black and White Americans ages 18 and over are overweight but not obese.[65]

□ There are more than 10 million obese African American adults in the United States—36 percent of all Blacks ages 18 and over and nearly a quarter of the total Black population.[66]

□ 25 percent of Black youth ages 6 to 17 are over-weight, compared to 15 percent of White youth.[67]

□ 16 percent of Black high school students are over-weight but not obese.

□ 18 percent of Black high school students are obese.[68]

How are Black communities affected by liquor stores and food deserts?

"Food deserts" are locations with limited access to fresh foods and groceries. In these areas, there tends to be a con-centration of fast food outlets, liquor stores, and less healthy options for purchasing food in general. Poor diet has been linked to obesity and other preventable illnesses.

□ In 2009, Black Americans spent over $1,800 less on food than all other consumers.[69]

□ Black communities nationwide have more liquor stores than White communities.[70]

□ Among African Americans who drink, those who live in neighborhoods with a greater concentration of liquor stores are more likely to be classified as at-risk drinkers than are those living in neighborhoods with fewer liquor stores.[71]

□ Most of the nation's worst food deserts are dispropor-tionately located in cities with a high percentage of Black Americans. The nine worst food deserts are lo-cated in the following cities (percent African American):

- New Orleans (60 percent)

- Chicago (33 percent
- Atlanta (54 percent)
- Memphis (63 percent)
- Minneapolis (19 percent)
- San Francisco, in the historically Black communities Bayview, Hunters Point, and Visitacion Valley (33 percent and 13, respectively)
- Detroit (83 percent)
- New York City (26 percent)
- Camden, New Jersey (48 percent).[72]

▫ The proportion of Black Americans is more than twice as large in urban food deserts as it is in other urban areas.[73]

▫ Black adults over the age of 20 consume more fast food than their White and Latino counterparts. Between 2007 and 2010, fast food made up 21 percent of the daily caloric intake of Black adults ages 20 to 39 and 13 percent of the daily caloric intake for Black adults ages 40 to 59 years old.[74]

What are the trends among Black Americans regarding heart disease?

▫ 6 percent of African Americans ages 18 and over are diagnosed with coronary heart disease.[75]

▫ Black adults are 40 percent more likely to have high blood pressure than White adults, and they are 10 percent less likely than their White counterparts to have their blood pressure under control.[76]

▫ The death rate from heart disease among African Americans is 239.2 per 100,000, compared with 180.9 per 100,000 for Whites.

▫ In 2009, Black men had the highest death rate from heart disease, 302.4 per 100,000. By comparison, Black women died from heart disease at a rate of 195.4 per 100,000, with White men and women dying from heart disease at rates of 231.1 and 142.1 per 100,000, respectively.[77]

34 percent of Black Americans have high blood pressure.[78]

Race has always played a central role in constructing presumptions of criminality.

—Angela Y. Davis

The penal systems* in the United States have had a profound impact on the lives of millions of African Americans since the nineteenth century, when Black Americans were first steered toward the criminal justice system at increasing rates by racially biased police and judicial practices. In 1901, W.E.B. Du Bois penned an article, "The Spawn of Slavery," in which he asserted that the American criminal justice system was in many ways an extension of the social control mechanisms put in place during the practice of slavery. Addressing the specific overrepresentation of African Americans among the prison population, as well as the penal practices and conditions of confinement in the American South, Du Bois wrote, "The greatest difficulty today in the way of reform is this race question . . . we must remember that crime is not normal; that the appearance of crime among . . . Negroes is a symptom of wrong social conditions—of a stress of life greater than a large part of the community can bear."[1]

Today, the contentious relationship between many African American communities and law enforcement continues, through questionable policies such as the increased use of stop-and-frisk** in some communities and more explicit police misconduct in others. This has caused many in the Black community and beyond to

---

*The criminal and juvenile justice systems, although often convoluted in the public domain, are two separate court systems—one for adults and one for youth ages 15–17 and under, depending on the jurisdiction in a state. Because criminal and juvenile justice are largely administered at the state and local levels, in most jurisdictions, the criminal justice system is reserved for people who are at least 18 years old. In some cases, juveniles will receive a waiver to adult court and be tried as an adult.

**A controversial law enforcement policy allowing police officers to stop and search anyone who they "reasonably suspect" has committed, is commit-

question the legitimacy of several law enforcement agencies and other key decision makers in the criminal and juvenile justice systems.

Since Reconstruction and the modern civil rights movement, the reach of the justice system has spread into African American communities, schools, and homes—often perpetuating the separate and unequal treatment of Black Americans in social, political, and economic life. In her book *The New Jim Crow: Mass Incarceration in the Age of Colorblindness*, legal scholar Michelle Alexander describes in detail the human rights conundrum produced by today's systematic discrimination against persons with a history of criminal conviction, a form of discrimination that effectively raises barriers to housing, voting, education, and employment. As Alexander writes, "a new social consensus must be forged about race and the role of race in defining the basic structure of our society" if we are to abolish what she describes as a "racial caste" system in the United States.[2]

The American justice system is vast and complex, operating along a continuum from referral and arrest through sentencing and community reentry—African American participation in the system extends beyond being physically or otherwise confined by it. In fact, because of racial disparities associated with incarceration and other points of contact with the justice system, there are many Black advocates, professionals, and opinion and thought leaders working on a variety of criminal and juvenile justice issues. This multifaceted involvement is captured, in part, in the following collection of national statistics showing how and where Black people have been situated in this country's criminal and juvenile justice systems.

---

ting, or is about to commit a crime. Several lawsuits were filed against the New York Police Department, charging the department with engaging in racial profiling and unjustifiable stop-and-frisks of law-abiding New York City residents, primarily in communities of color. In 2013, U.S. District Court Judge Shira Scheindlin ruled in *Floyd v. the City of New York* that the stop-and-frisk practice violated the Fourth Amendment protection against unreasonable search and seizure, and was therefore unconstitutional. In *Ligon v. City of New York*, Judge Scheindlin also ordered the NYPD to end its practice of unlawfully stopping people as part of its Clean Halls program.

LAW ENFORCEMENT, CRIME, AND SAFETY

How are Black Americans represented in the field of law enforcement?

- ▢ Black people make up 12 percent of full-time, sworn personnel in local police departments nationwide.[3]
- ▢ In large city police departments, Black people make up 20 percent of full-time sworn personnel.[4]

Table 2. Percentage of Black, Full-Time Sworn Officers in Cities with a Population of 1 Million or More, 2000

City	Percent of Black Officers
Philadelphia	35%
Chicago	26%
Dallas	21%
Houston	19%
Los Angeles	14%
New York City	13%
Las Vegas	9%
San Diego	9%
San Antonio	6%
Phoenix	4%

Source: Matthew J. Hickman and Brian A. Reaves, "Police Departments in Large Cities, 1990–2000," NCJ 175703, Bureau of Justice Statistics, May 5, 2002, 11. Table adapted by the author.

- ▢ The proportion of Black full-time sworn personnel is over 10 percent in 13 states, according to the most recent data available:
  - Mississippi: 31 percent
  - Alabama: 28 percent
  - Maryland: 19 percent
  - Arkansas, Georgia, and North Carolina: 15 percent
  - Florida, Louisiana, and South Carolina: 14 percent
  - Illinois: 13 percent
  - Massachusetts, Ohio, and Texas: 11 percent[5]

Table 3. Black, Full-Time Federal Officers (in Select Agencies That Employ 50 to 499 Officers) with the Authority to Arrest and Carry Firearms, 2008

Federal Agency	Percent of Black or African American Officers
Pentagon Force Protection Agency	43%
U.S. Capitol Police	30%
Federal Bureau of Prisons	24%
Veterans Health Administration	24%
U.S. Postal Inspection Service	20%
Administrative Office of the U.S. Courts	14%
Internal Revenue Service	11%
Bureau of Alcohol, Tobacco, Firearms and Explosives	9%
Drug Enforcement Administration	7%
Federal Bureau of Investigation	5%
National Park Service, U.S. Park Police	2%

Source: Brian A. Reaves, "Table 4: Gender and Race or Ethnicity of Federal Officers with Arrest and Firearm Authority, Agencies Employing 500 or More Full-Time Officers, September 2004" and "Table 5. Female and Minority Representation Among Personnel with Arrest and Firearm Authority in Non–Inspector General Agencies with at Least 100 but Fewer Than 500 Full-Time Officers, September 2004," in "Federal Law Enforcement Officers, 2004," NCJ 212750, Bureau of Justice Statistics Bulletin, July 2006, 6, 7. Tables adapted by the author.

- Between 2002 and 2011, Black people accounted for 12 percent of officers killed on the job and for 44 percent of persons identified as responsible for the killing of law enforcement officers between 2001 and 2010.[6]

What is the Black public's opinion on law enforcement in this country?

- Only 14 percent of Black Americans have a great deal of confidence in local police officers to treat Black and White Americans equally, compared with 38 percent of Whites.[7]
- Only 44 percent of Black Americans agree that there

are situations in which they could "approve of a policeman striking an adult male citizen," compared with 71 percent of White Americans.[8]

- The percentage of African Americans who approve of a policeman striking a citizen who:
  - Was attacking the policeman with his fists: 76 percent (compared with 92 percent of Whites)
  - Was attempting to escape from custody: 50 percent (compared with 72 percent of Whites)
  - Had said vulgar and obscene things to the policeman: 6 percent (compared with 7 percent of Whites)
  - Was being questioned in a murder case: 11 percent (compared with 8 percent of Whites).[9]

- 26 percent of Black high school seniors report having a "good" or "very good" attitude about the performance of law enforcement agencies, compared with 44 percent of White high school seniors.[10]

- 67 percent of Black people report that racial profiling is widespread in stops of motorists on roads and highways, and only 23 percent of Black people feel that such profiling is justified.

- 65 percent of Black people report that the racial profiling of shoppers in malls or stores is widespread, but only 19 percent of Black people feel that it is justified.[11]

- 67 percent of Black Americans report that there is police brutality practiced in the area where they live, compared with 25 percent of White Americans.[12]

- 39 percent of Black people rate the honesty and ethical standards of the police as "very high" or "high," compared with 59 percent of Whites.[13]

- 32 percent of Black people report having a "great deal or quite a lot" of confidence in the police, compared with 57 percent of Whites. By contrast, 23 percent of Black people report having "very little" confidence in the police, compared with 14 percent of Whites and 13 percent of Latinos.[14]

How many Black Americans are arrested?

Black communities in the United States have been subjected to increased surveillance and patrolling, which may have an impact on rates of arrest. Therefore, arrest rates should not be equated with levels of criminal or delinquent behavior, but rather taken as a measure of behaviors that have been discovered, interrupted, and reported by law enforcement.

28 percent of all persons arrested are Black.[15]

- 14 percent of Black adults have had contact with police, compared with 15 percent of Latino adults and 18 percent of White adults; however, Black motorists are nearly twice as likely to be arrested and nearly three times as likely as White motorists to experience force during interactions with law enforcement.
- Nationwide, Black motorists are stopped at about the same rate as Whites and Latinos; however, Black motorists are three times as likely (12 percent) as White motorists (4 percent) and twice as likely as Latino motorists (6 percent) to be searched during a traffic stop.[16]
- Black Americans (including those who are multiracial) make up 14 percent of the general population but account for 28 percent of total arrests nationwide.
- Black Americans account for 50 percent of total arrests for murder and nonnegligent manslaughter and 56 percent of arrests for robbery.
- Black Americans make up 22 percent of the population in cities, but account for 31 percent of total arrests in cities nationwide and 41 percent of persons arrested for violent crimes in these cities.[17]
- Black people make up 10 percent of the population in suburban areas, but account for 25 percent of suburban arrests nationwide and 32 percent of suburban arrests for violent crimes.[18]
- Black people make up 9 percent of the population in rural areas but account for 14 percent of

nonmetropolitan* arrests nationwide and 20 percent of nonmetropolitan arrests for violent crimes.[19]

How many Black youth are arrested?

In 1933, more than 10,000 Black boys and 1,800 Black girls were arrested and had cases disposed in 67 U.S. courts and federal authorities.[20] In 2011, more than 350,000 Black youth were arrested nationwide.[21] Concentrated poverty, law enforcement practices at the neighborhood level, health, education, and family characteristics are associated with an increased risk of delinquency and arrest. Also increasing the risk are school-based zero tolerance policies that emerged from the Federal Gun Free School Act (1994). This act established predetermined consequences for a list of negative student behaviors, mostly behaviors associated with guns, controlled substances, and sexual assaults. Out of these policies grew a climate that facilitated the use of surveillance instruments and punishment practices. These in turn have fueled the "school to confinement" phenomenon, which has disproportionately affected Black girls and boys.

- Nationwide, 16 percent of persons under the age of 18 are Black, and 32 percent of total juvenile arrests are of Black youth.[22]
- Among school systems with 50,000 or more students enrolled, Black youth represent 24 percent of enrollment but 35 percent of school arrests. In Chicago, Black youth account for 76 percent of school-based arrests.
- Nationwide, Black youth account for 35 percent of school-related arrests and 42 percent of school-based referrals to law enforcement.[23]

---

*Nonmetropolitan areas are not synonymous with "rural" counties, as over half of nonmetropolitan areas are located in larger metropolitan counties. According to the USDA, nonmetropolitan areas include some combination of "open countryside, rural towns (places with fewer than 2,500 people), and urban areas with populations ranging from 2,500 to 49,999 that are not part of larger labor market areas (metropolitan areas)" (Economic Research Service, USDA, "Rural Classifications: Overview," www.ers.usda.gov/topics/rural-economy-population/rural-classifications.aspx #.Ua5ESjkZ60s).

- 54 percent of all persons under 18 arrested for murder and nonnegligent manslaughter are Black, and Black youth account for 69 percent of juvenile arrests for robbery.[24]
- Black youth account for 33 percent of total juvenile arrests in cities and 53 percent of youth arrests for violent crimes in these cities.[25]
- Black youth account for 28 percent of total juvenile arrests in suburban areas and 46 percent of arrests for violent crimes in these areas.[26]
- Black youth account for 14 percent of the total arrests and 27 percent of arrests for violent crimes in nonmetropolitan areas nationwide.[27]

How does police harassment and misconduct affect Black Americans?

- 3 percent of Black people report experiencing a threat or the use of excessive force during their most recent contact with police, compared with 1 percent of Whites and 2 percent of Latinos.
- 70 percent of Black people who have experienced the use of police force against them feel that the force was excessive.[28]
- Black people are three to five times more likely than Whites to believe that police misconduct frequently occurs in their city, and Black Americans are three times more likely to say that it occurs very often in their neighborhood.[29]

About one-third of African Americans and one-fifth of Latinos report having been stopped by police in their city without good reason.[30]

- 38 percent of Black transgender people who have interacted with the police report having experienced harassment.
- 15 percent of Black transgender people who have interacted with the police report having experienced physical assault.

□ 35 percent of Black transgender people who have been arrested or held in a cell believe that they were arrested or held "due to bias" associated with their perceived race, gender, or sexual orientation.[31]

How are Black Americans affected by crime and victimization?

□ 47 percent of Black people in the United States report that there is an area within a mile of their home where they are afraid to walk alone at night.[32]

□ The rate of reported intimate partner violence among Black Americans is 8 percent, a decline by 62 percent since 1994.[33]

□ 55 percent of Black Americans report avoiding certain places or neighborhoods because of a concern over crime, compared with 46 percent of White Americans.

□ 17 percent of Black people report carrying a gun because of a concern over crime, compared with 12 percent of Whites.[34]

African Americans make up 25 percent of all human sex trafficking victims in the United States and its territories.[35]

□ Black adults ages 20 to 24 are the victims of rape or sexual assault at a rate of 6 percent, as compared with a 1 percent sexual victimization rate for White adults in the same age group.[36]

□ There were 6,470 Black victims of murder and non-negligent manslaughter known to the police in 2010, a figure that represents approximately 48 percent of that year's murders nationwide.[37]

□ Black people experience violent victimization (aggravated and simple assault) at a rate of 26 percent.

□ Black people experience serious violent victimization (rape or sexual assault, violent or armed robbery, and aggravated assault) at a rate of 11 percent.[38]

□ 17 percent of Black people report that they or another member of their household had been the victim of identity theft within the past 12 months, compared with 9 percent of Whites and 13 percent of Latinos.[39]

How many Black youth are victimized by crime and violence?

◻ Black youth ages 12 to 15 are the victims of violent crime at a rate of 56 percent, compared to a rate of 40 percent for White youth.[40]

◻ 77 percent of Black high school seniors report being concerned about crime and violence "sometimes" or "often."[41]

◻ 14 percent of Black high school students report being deliberately physically hurt by a boyfriend or girlfriend, compared with 8 percent of White and 12 percent of Latino high school students.[42]

◻ 96 percent of Black high school seniors report that no one has ever injured them with a weapon (for example, a knife, gun, or club) at school, comparable to 97 percent of White youth who report the same.[43]

◻ 38 percent of Black youth ages 12 to 18 report the presence of street gangs in their school, compared with 36 percent of Latino youth, 16 percent of White youth, 17 percent of Asian youth, and 26 percent of youth identifying as "Other, non-Hispanic" who report the same.[44]

◻ Nationwide, 38 percent of Black teens report being bullied, compared with 54 percent of Asian teens, 34 percent of Latino teens, and 31 percent of White teens. Reported reasons for which Black students are teased and/or bullied include performing well academically, the color of their skin, having a frail physique, and not being "Black enough."[45]

◻ 50 percent of Black high school and college students fear gun violence, compared with only 31 percent of their White counterparts. Fewer African American students than White students say that they plan to own a gun in the future.[46]

- 41 percent of the high school students who report that they have been in a physical fight are Black, compared with 28 percent of White students and 36 percent of Latino students.
- 10 percent of high school students reporting that they have been forced to have unwanted sexual intercourse are Black, 6 percent are White, and 8 percent are Latino.[47]

What is the Black public opinion on crime and safety?

- 36 percent of Black people report having "very little to no" confidence in the criminal justice system, compared with 30 percent of Whites and 21 percent of Latinos who feel the same.[48]
- The overwhelming majority of Black people— 85 percent—believe that in order to curb crime, "more money and effort should go to attacking the social and economic problems that lead to crime, such as better education and job training," compared with 60 percent of Whites who feel the same.[49]
- Black people make up 14 percent of the U.S. population but account for:
  - 71 percent of those who frequently or occasionally worry about being the victim of identity theft;
  - 43 percent of those who frequently or occasionally worry about their home being burglarized when they are not there;
  - 43 percent of those who frequently or occasionally worry about having their car stolen or broken into;
  - 38 percent of those who frequently or occasionally worry about having their child physically harmed at school;
  - 36 percent of those who frequently or occasionally worry about getting mugged;
  - 35 percent of those who frequently or occasionally worry about being a victim of terrorism;
  - 29 percent of those who frequently or occasionally worry about being the victim of a hate crime;
  - 28 percent of those who frequently or occasionally

worry about their home being burglarized when they are there;

- 26 percent of those who frequently or occasionally worry about being attacked while driving their car;
- 16 percent of those who frequently or occasionally worry about being sexually assaulted; and
- 6 percent of those who frequently or occasionally worry about being assaulted or killed by a co-worker or other employee where they work.[50]

How were Black Americans affected by the September 11, 2001, terrorist attacks?

On September 11, 2001, an extremist group referred to as al-Qaeda hijacked four U.S. planes and used two of them as weapons to destroy the north and south towers of the World Trade Center. A third plane crashed into the Pentagon, and a fourth, intended for the U.S. Capitol, crashed in Pennsylvania when passengers attempted to recover the plane from its hijackers. These events represent the most destructive acts of foreign terrorism on U.S. soil to date.

- 286 Black people were killed by the September 11, 2001, terrorist attacks.
- Black people made up 8 percent of those killed at the World Trade Center as a result of the September 11, 2001, terrorist attacks.[51]

> Black people made up 27 percent of those killed at the Pentagon as a result of the September 11, 2001, terrorist attacks.[52]

- Black people were 8 percent of those killed in Somerset County, Pennsylvania, as a result of the September 11, 2001, terrorist attacks.[53]

How many Black Americans practice law?

- Approximately 5 percent of attorneys identify as Black or African American.[54]
- African Americans account for 3 percent of the American Bar Association membership.[55]

- 13 percent of judges, magistrates, and other judicial workers are African American.
- 11 percent of paralegals and legal assistants are African American.[56]
- There are 183 African American judges on the federal bench (as of January 2013).[57]

How do African Americans fare in presidential appointments to the bench?

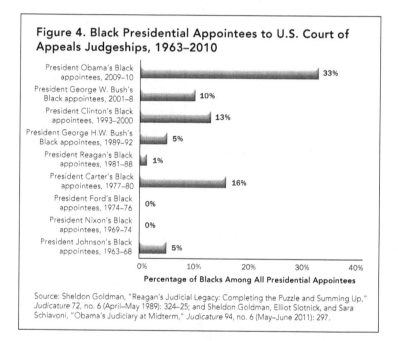

Figure 4. Black Presidential Appointees to U.S. Court of Appeals Judgeships, 1963–2010

Percentage of Blacks Among All Presidential Appointees

Source: Sheldon Goldman, "Reagan's Judicial Legacy: Completing the Puzzle and Summing Up," *Judicature* 72, no. 6 (April–May 1989): 324–25; and Sheldon Goldman, Elliot Slotnick, and Sara Schiavoni, "Obama's Judiciary at Midterm," *Judicature* 94, no. 6 (May–June 2011): 297.

- 33 percent of the judges appointed to U.S. courts of appeals by President Barack Obama in the first year of his first term (2009–10) were Black—a proportion that is higher than that of any previous U.S. president.
- 25 percent of the judges appointed to U.S. district courts by President Obama in the first year of his first term were Black—another proportion higher than that of any U.S. president since the modern civil rights movement.[58]

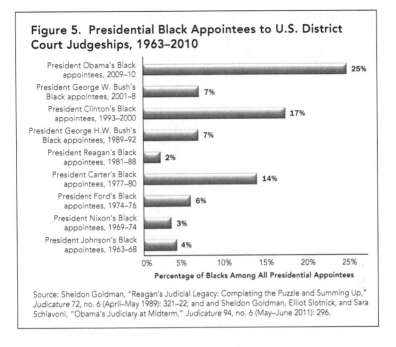

Figure 5. Presidential Black Appointees to U.S. District Court Judgeships, 1963–2010

President	Percentage
President Obama's Black appointees, 2009–10	25%
President George W. Bush's Black appointees, 2001–8	7%
President Clinton's Black appointees, 1993–2000	17%
President George H.W. Bush's Black appointees, 1989–92	7%
President Reagan's Black appointees, 1981–88	2%
President Carter's Black appointees, 1977–80	14%
President Ford's Black appointees, 1974–76	6%
President Nixon's Black appointees, 1969–74	3%
President Johnson's Black appointees, 1963–68	4%

Percentage of Blacks Among All Presidential Appointees

Source: Sheldon Goldman, "Reagan's Judicial Legacy: Completing the Puzzle and Summing Up," *Judicature* 72, no. 6 (April–May 1989): 321–22; and and Sheldon Goldman, Elliot Slotnick, and Sara Schiavoni, "Obama's Judiciary at Midterm," *Judicature* 94, no. 6 (May–June 2011): 296.

How are African Americans affected by jury selection and composition?*

African American jurors appear in historical accounts of U.S. judicial practices as early as 1860.[59] For decades, peremptory challenges were routinely used in U.S. courts to remove Black jurors from juries. In 1986, this practice became illegal with the U.S. Supreme Court decision in *Batson v. Kentucky*, which ruled that prosecutors must show a legitimate reason for excusing a potential Black juror.[60] However, there is still evidence of racial discrimination in the selection and assignment of jurors.[61]

---

*The historical exclusion of African Americans from jury service has been examined and discussed since the 1800s. It has been noted that the first African American juror in a criminal case served in 1860 in Massachusetts. Not until the U.S. Supreme Court adopted a "fair cross-section" standard in the 1960s and 1970s, requiring jury and grand jury pools to reflect the demographics of the community, did representation of people of color in jury pools improve (Equal Justice Initiative, *Illegal Racial Discrimination in Jury Selection: A Continuing Legacy* [Montgomery, AL: Equal Justice Initiative, 2010], 9).

- When there is an absence of potential Black jurors in a jury selection pool, Black defendants are significantly more likely than White defendants to be convicted of at least one crime (81 percent for Black people versus 66 percent for Whites).
- There is a 16-point gap between the conviction rates for Black defendants and White defendants when there are no Black people in the jury pool.
- One Black juror is needed to raise the conviction rate for Whites (11 percent) from the relatively low conviction rate for all-White juries in cases involving a White defendant.[62]

Between 2005 and 2009, prosecutors in Houston County, Alabama, used peremptory strikes to remove 80 percent of the African Americans qualified for jury service in capital cases.[63]

- Black Americans make up 30 percent of the population in Tuscaloosa County, Alabama, but they are underrepresented by 70 percent on juries in criminal trials.
- Three days of rioting, 18 people dead, and $200 million in property damage: what occurred in Miami in 1980 after an all-White jury acquitted four police officers charged with shooting an African American man.[64]
- Three days of protesting, 60 people dead, 16,000 arrests, and almost $1 billion in property damage: what happened in Los Angeles in 1992 after a jury without any African Americans acquitted officers charged with the severe beating of Rodney King, a Black man.[65]

What is the Black public opinion on the fairness of courts and the U.S. Judicial system?

- 16 percent of Black people think that courts in their area deal "too harshly" with criminals, compared with 8 percent of Whites who think so.[66]
- 36 percent of Black people have "very little" or "no" confidence in the U.S. Supreme Court, compared with 22 percent of Whites who feel the same.[67]

- More than one-third of both Black and White Americans rate the honesty and ethical standards of lawyers as "low" or "very low."[68]

SENTENCING

What are the offense and sentencing trends for Black Americans?

- Black people make up 20 percent of all individuals sentenced in U.S. district courts under the U.S. Sentencing Commission guidelines. Specifically, Black Americans, including those who are Black multiracial, make up 14 percent of the U.S. population, but
  - 26 percent of those sentenced for drug trafficking offenses,
  - 40 percent of those sentenced for robbery offenses,
  - 42 percent of those sentenced for forgery and counterfeiting, and
  - 50 percent of those sentenced for firearms offenses.[69]
- Black people account for 55 percent of those held in state prison for violent offenses.[70]
- In 2006, Black people made up 45 percent of felony defendants in the nation's 75 largest counties. In Shelby County, Tennessee, where 52 percent of the population was Black, 85 percent of felony defendants in court were Black.[71]
- Black-on-White crime tends to be sentenced more severely than either Black-on-Black or White-on-White crime.[72]

What are the offense and sentencing trends for Black youth?

Between 1985 and 2009, the case rate for person offenses such as assault, robbery, rape, and homicide increased by 62 percent for Black youth, and the case rate for public order offenses, such as graffiti or disorderly conduct, increased by 177 percent.[73]

- Between 1996 and 2009, the drug offense case rate for Black youth decreased by 41 percent nationwide.[74]
- Black youth were defendants in 34 percent of all cases closed by juvenile courts in 2008.[75]
- Between 1985 and 2007, the delinquency case rate for Black youth declined by 15 percent.[76]
- Black youth make up 35 percent of youth sent to adult criminal court.[77]

54 percent of Black people, 59 percent of White people, and 58 percent of people of color overall believe that juveniles between the ages of 14 and 17 who commit violent crimes should be treated the same as adults.[78]

INCARCERATION AND DETENTION

How many Black Americans are employed by prisons and jails?

- Over one-fifth of Federal Bureau of Prisons staff are Black.[79]
- Black people compose 22 percent of all staff and 24 percent of correctional officers in jails.[80]

How many Black Americans are incarcerated in prisons and jails?

Black males account for 36 percent of all male prisoners, and Black females account for 25 percent of all female prisoners under federal and state jurisdiction.[81]

- Black people are 14 percent of the total U.S. population but account for 38 percent of all inmates in local jails nationwide.[82]
- Black and Latino prisoners in federal and state facilities are typically younger than their White counterparts.[83]
- Black people account for 39 percent of all prisoners under the jurisdiction of the Federal Bureau of Prisons.[84]

- The average time that Black Americans serve in state prison for all offenses is 32 months (2.7 years), compared with an average of 26 months (2.2 years) served by White Americans in state prisons.[85]
- Black veterans account for 32 percent of veterans in state prisons and 38 percent of veterans in federal prisons.[86]
- 7,017 Black prisoners died in state correctional facilities between 2001 and 2006.[87]

What are the trends for incarcerated Black youth?

- 58 percent of youth admitted to adult state prisons are Black.[88]
- 41 percent of youth in public and private residential custody facilities nationwide are Black. The most serious offenses for which Black youth are incarcerated are:
  - Violent offenses: 45 percent
  - Property offenses*: 41 percent
  - Public order offenses**: 41 percent
  - Drug offenses: 36 percent
  - Technical violations†: 36 percent
  - Status offenses††: 34 percent[89]
- California places more Black children in residential custody facilities than any other state in the nation. Florida and Pennsylvania round out the top three states with the largest number of Black youth in residential correctional facilities.[90]
- With a detention rate of 28 percent, Black youth are

---

* Property offenses include burglary, larceny-theft, motor vehicle theft, and arson.

** Public order offenses include acts that are deemed criminal because they are considered disruptive or harmful to the common good. Examples include, but are not limited to, prostitution, pornography, and victimless crimes.

† Technical violations include the violation of any court-ordered condition of probation or parole. If, for example, it is a court-ordered condition of release or probation for a juvenile to go to school or refrain from using illicit drugs, chronic absenteeism and testing positive for a controlled substance would be technical violations.

†† Status offenses are crimes that would not be crimes if the person committing the act were not a juvenile. For example, not going to school, running away from home, or breaking curfew are status offenses.

twice as likely as White youth (14 percent) to be detained in correctional facilities for cases involving drug offenses.[91]

How are Black inmates affected by inmate violence, victimization, and death?

- 3 percent of Black male inmates and 15 percent of Black female inmates report inmate-on-inmate sexual victimization.
- 7 percent of Black male inmates and 4 percent of Black female inmates report staff sexual misconduct.[92]
- 29 percent of Black transgender people report having been physically assaulted in prison or jail.
- 32 percent of Black transgender people report having been sexually assaulted while in custody.[93]
- 18 Black youth died in state juvenile correctional facilities between 2002 and 2005, representing 42 percent of all young people across the country who died in such facilities during that period.[94]
- Over the past decade, 3,291 Black inmates have died in local jails. Of these deaths, 76 percent were attributed to illness, 14 percent were suicides, 5 percent were the result of drug and alcohol intoxication, and 3 percent were homicides.
- During this same period, there were 11,701 Black inmate deaths in state prisons—37 percent of the total state prison deaths over that decade.
- During this same period, Black inmates suffered from an AIDS-related mortality rate that was at least double that of any other racial or ethnic group in state prisons.[95]

Juvenile Life Without Parole (JLWOP)*

- Between 2010 and 2011, Black youth made up

---

*In its 2012 decision on *Miller v. Alabama*, the U.S. Supreme Court held that sentencing scenarios requiring life without parole for juvenile offenders are unconstitutional, including for youth convicted of homicide.

23 percent of juvenile offenders whose victims were White but 43 percent of such offenders sentenced to life without parole. By contrast, White youth accounted for 77 percent of juvenile offenders against White victims but only 57 percent of those sentenced to life without parole for such crimes.

□ Between 2010 and 2011, Black youth made up 94 percent of juvenile offenders whose victims were Black and 96 percent of such offenders sentenced to life without parole.[96]

How many Black Americans face the death penalty?

□ California leads the nation in the number of African Americans on death row (261), followed by Florida (146) and Texas (126).[97]

□ In 2010, 13 Black prisoners were executed in the United States for murder.[98]

□ Black people account for 49 percent of the prisoners under the sentence of death in the United States.[99]

What is the Black public opinion on the death penalty?

□ 71 percent of Black people are not in favor of the death penalty for a person convicted of murder.[100]

□ 73 percent of Black people do not believe that the death penalty is a deterrent to the commission of murder or that it lowers the murder rate.[101]

□ 67 percent of Black people believe that the death penalty is applied unfairly. By comparison, 36 percent of White Americans and 58 percent of non-White Americans believe the same.[102]

ACCUMULATED DISADVANTAGE

"Accumulated disadvantage" is defined as the increased and compounded vulnerability of certain populations to being overrepresented in secure confinement and disproportionately subjected to other serious sanctions associated with the criminal and juvenile justice systems.[103] The likelihood of incarceration (or other "back-end" justice interventions) may escalate depending on the rate of contact at earlier decision points (e.g., arrest) along what is known as the justice continuum. What follows is a snapshot of the racial disparity, overrepresentation, and accumulated disadvantage experienced by Black people in the U.S. criminal and juvenile justice systems.

Wages grow at a 21 percent slower rate for Black formerly incarcerated people than for White formerly incarcerated people.[104]

Criminal Justice System

Black Americans (including those who are multiracial) represent 14 percent of the total U.S. population, but account for:
- 32 percent of all arrests.
- 45 percent of felony defendants in court among the largest 75 U.S. counties.
- 38 percent of the jail population.
- 37 percent of the federal prison population.
- 49 percent of prisoners on death row.

Juvenile Justice System

Black youth make up 16 percent of all youth under age 18 in the United States but account for:
- 28 percent of juvenile arrests.
- 34 percent of all cases disposed by juvenile court.
- 70 percent of all youth formally referred to juvenile court in delinquency drug cases.
- 59 percent of all youth formally referred to juvenile court for drug offenses.
- 35 percent of juvenile drug cases found delinquent that result in offending youth being placed out of their homes.
- 56 percent of delinquent cases that were placed on probation for person offenses and 52 percent of delinquent cases placed on probation for property offenses.
- 41 percent of youth in public and private residential custody facilities.

- 35 percent of youth judicially waived to adult criminal court.
- 58 percent of youth admitted to an adult state prison.

THE WAR ON DRUGS

How has the war on drugs affected Black Americans?[105]

In 2010, Congress passed the Fair Sentencing Act, which reduced the crack–cocaine sentencing disparity from a ratio of 100:1 to 18:1. This was intended to have an impact on the disproportionate incarceration of Black Americans for related offenses.[106]

- The rate of drug use among Black people ages 12 and older is 10 percent, yet Black people account for 32 percent of those arrested for "drug abuse violations" in the United States.[107]
- 35 percent of all persons arrested for "drug abuse violations" in U.S. cities, 26 percent of those arrested for such violations in metropolitan counties, and 25 percent of those arrested for such violations in suburban areas are Black.[108]
- Though Black and White rates of marijuana use are comparable, a Black person is 3.73 times more likely to be arrested for marijuana possession than a White person, a disparity that increased by 32.7 percent between 2001 and 2010.
- In the majority of U.S. counties, Black Americans are between two and five times more likely than White Americans to be arrested for marijuana possession.[109]
- More than 80 percent of people convicted of federal crack cocaine offenses are Black.[110]
- 27 percent of people convicted of powder cocaine offenses are Black.[111]
- The percentage of African Americans arrested for federal drug offenses (excluding marijuana possession) declined by 17 percent between 1999 and 2005, and the percentage of African Americans arrested for state and local drug offenses (excluding

marijuana possession) declined by nearly 22 percent in the same period.[112]

◻ The number of African Americans in federal prison for drug offenses increased by 31 percent between 1999 and 2005, even while the proportion of Black drug offenders remained the same.[113]

◻ During that same period, the number of African Americans in state prisons for drug offenses declined by 21 percent. Since more African Americans were imprisoned in the federal system, caution must be used in interpreting the decline.[114]

What do Black Americans think about how the judicial system responds to drug use?

◻ 50 percent of Black people in the United States support the legalization of marijuana use.[115]

◻ 65 percent of Black people in the United States reported feeling that too little is being spent on dealing with drug *addiction*.[116]

How do Black Americans feel about pornography?

◻ 32 percent of Black Americans feel that there should be laws against the distribution of pornography to people of any age.[117]

How do Black Americans feel about the legality of abortion?

◻ 30 percent of Black Americans think that abortions should always be legal, about the same number as White Americans (29 percent).

◻ 20 percent of Black people think that abortions should never be legal.[118]

How are Black Americans affected by unauthorized immigration and how do they feel about it?

◻ 47 percent of Black Americans think that in dealing with unauthorized immigration, the United States should prioritize better border security and stronger enforcement of existing immigration laws *as well as* creating a path to citizenship.[119]

- Black people make up 1 percent of all federal defendants in criminal immigration cases, 2 percent of those charged with illegal entry into the United States, and 4 percent of those charged with misuse of a visa.
- The number of Black people in federal prison for immigration offenses declined by 1.8 percent between 2000 and 2010.
- Black people make up 6 percent of the population of "immigration offenders" under federally supervised release or probation.[120]

What do Black Americans think about gun control?

In Florida in 2013, George Zimmerman, a 33-year-old Latino biracial man, was found not guilty for the murder of 17-year-old Travyon Martin, an unarmed African American boy. This case and others like it continue to fuel a debate about gun control, Stand Your Ground (SYG) laws,* and the killing of African Americans deemed "justifiable by law." A national poll found that 86 percent of Black Americans and only 35 percent of White Americans felt that the shooting of Trayvon Martin was unjustified.[121]

- 33 percent of Black people report having a gun at home, compared with 29 percent of all people of color and 51 percent of Whites.[122]
- 67 percent of Black people feel that the laws governing the sale of firearms should be made more strict, compared with 58 percent of all people of color and 39 percent of Whites.[123]
- 66 percent of Black people feel that it is more important to control gun ownership than to protect the right of Americans to own guns, compared with 75 percent of Latinos and 42 percent of Whites.[124]
- Between 2005 and 2010, White-on-Black homicides

---

*Stand Your Ground laws grant an individual the right to use deadly force in self-defense, without a requirement to retreat or avoid confrontation. To date, more than 25 states have some form of a Stand Your Ground law. In SYG states, a finding of justifiable homicide is 65 percent more likely.

were most likely among all homicides in SYG states to be ruled justified (11.4 percent); Black-on-White homicides were least likely (1.2 percent) to be ruled justified in those states.

□ Between 2005 and 2010, nearly 17 percent of White-on-Black homicides in non-SYG states were ruled justified, compared with 9.5 percent homicides ruled justified in those states.

□ As in the case of Trayvon Martin, when there is a firearm, a single victim, a single shooter, and both victim and shooter are male and strangers, racial disparities are more pronounced:

- White-on-Black homicides have justifiable findings 33 percentage points more often than Black-on-White homicides.
- White-on-Black homicides are 281 percent more likely than White-on-White homicides to be found justifiable.[125]

Body and soul, Black America reveals the extreme questions of contemporary life, questions of freedom and identity: How can I be who I am?

—June Jordan

The collective and individual identities of Black America are constantly evolving—changing as barriers are removed and new opportunities revealed. Where Black people live and how they spend their time depend on a host of variables that help to define the quality and texture of Black life in America. A people whose dominant expression has been informed by an unshakable faith in God and ritual, African Americans have responded to conditions designed to undermine their equal access to public services with a faithful determination to live free of racial oppression. Important civil and human rights victories have dismantled legal segregation and opened the door to opportunity and an improved quality of life, but there remain aspects of Black life that carry the tinge of segregation. Yet despite this legacy of racial inequality, the contemporary experiences of Black Americans are being reshaped by modern amenities and innovation—creating a cultural quilt that is diverse and intricate.

The statistics presented here show where Black people live in the United States and present trends associated with African American daily activities, priorities, and households. Also included are survey statistics that reveal African Americans' opinions on current cultural topics associated with lifestyle and identity.

DAILY ACTIVITIES & PRIORITIES

What daily activities are important to Black Americans?

- 92 percent of Black women feel that having free time to do what they want is important, compared with 61 percent of Black men who feel that this is important.

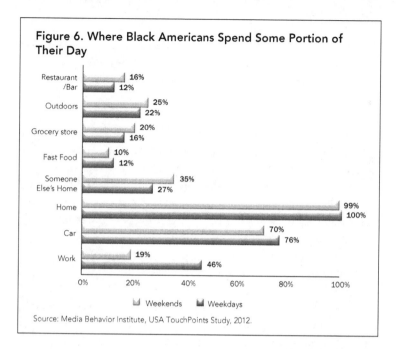

Figure 6. Where Black Americans Spend Some Portion of Their Day

	Weekends	Weekdays
Restaurant/Bar	16%	12%
Outdoors	25%	22%
Grocery store	20%	16%
Fast Food	10%	12%
Someone Else's Home	35%	27%
Home	99%	100%
Car	70%	76%
Work	19%	46%

Source: Media Behavior Institute, USA TouchPoints Study, 2012.

- 89 percent of Black men think that a good romantic relationship is important, compared with 76 percent of Black women who feel the same.[1]

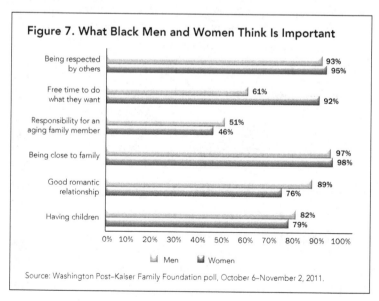

Figure 7. What Black Men and Women Think Is Important

	Men	Women
Being respected by others	93%	95%
Free time to do what they want	61%	92%
Responsibility for an aging family member	51%	46%
Being close to family	97%	98%
Good romantic relationship	89%	76%
Having children	82%	79%

Source: Washington Post–Kaiser Family Foundation poll, October 6–November 2, 2011.

- Younger Black Americans—Generation Y—are more likely to spend time socializing and consuming media on mobile and gaming devices than are Black baby boomers, and Black baby boomers are more likely than younger African Americans to cook and do chores or community-related activities.[2]

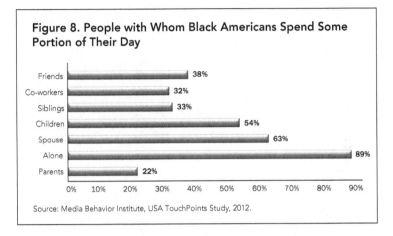

Figure 8. People with Whom Black Americans Spend Some Portion of Their Day

Source: Media Behavior Institute, USA TouchPoints Study, 2012.

89 percent of Black Americans spend some portion of their day alone.[3]

Where do Black Americans live?

- The U.S. cities with the largest Black populations are New York (2.2 million) and Chicago (913,000).[4]
- The American South today is home to 21,894,000 African Americans—more than half of the Black population in the United States—the highest number since 1960.[5]
- More than 1 million multiracial Black Americans live in the South.[6]
- 17 percent of Black people live in the Northeast.
- 17 percent of Black people live in the Midwest.
- 9 percent of Black people live in the West.[7]
- During the late 1990s, more college-educated African Americans migrated to the South, particularly

Table 4. 10 Places with the Largest Number of Black Americans, 2010

Places with a Population of 100,000 or More	Total Population	Rank	Number of Black or African Americans Alone or in Combination*	Number of Black or African Americans Alone
New York, NY	8,175,133	1	2,228,145	2,088,510
Chicago, IL	2,965,598	2	913,009	887,608
Philadelphia, PA	1,526,006	3	686,870	661,839
Detroit, MI	713,777	4	601,988	590,226
Houston, TX	2,009,451	5	514,217	498,466
Memphis, TN	646,899	6	414,928	409,687
Baltimore, MD	620,961	7	403,998	395,781
Los Angeles, CA	3,792,621	8	402,448	365,118
Washington, DC	601,723	9	314,352	305,125
Dallas, TX	1,197,816	10	308,087	298,993

Source: Table modified and reproduced from Sonya Rastogi, Tallese D. Johnson, Elizabeth M. Hoeffel, et al., "The Black Population, 2010," 2010 Census Briefs, U.S. Census Bureau, September 2011, Table P1; U.S. Census Bureau, "Table P1. Race," in "2010 Census Redistricting Data (Public Law 94-171) Summary File," 2010 Census of Population and Housing, January 2011, 6-22–6-23. According to the U.S. Census, of the 282 places in the United States with a population of 100,000 or more, 273 were incorporated places (including five city-county consolidations) and nine census designated places (CDPs), which were not legally incorporated.

to metropolitan areas such as Atlanta, than to any other region of the United States, reversing a 35-year trend. By contrast, New York, Chicago, Los Angeles, and San Francisco experienced the greatest out-migration of Black people during the same period.[8]

□ Approximately 60 percent of all African Americans live in nine states: New York (3.3 million), Florida

---

*Black in combination with another racial category.

(3.2 million), Georgia (3.1 million), California (2.7 million), North Carolina (2.2 million), Illinois (2 million), Maryland (1.8 million), Virginia (1.7 million), and Ohio (1.5 million).

◻ California is the state with the highest percentage of multiracial (mixed-race) Black or African American people (12 percent), followed by New York (8 percent), Florida and Texas (6 percent each), and Ohio (4 percent).

◻ There are five states in which the population is more than 25 percent Black: Mississippi (33 percent), Georgia (32 percent), Maryland (31 percent), South Carolina (29 percent), and Alabama (27 percent).

◻ There are 12 states in which less than 3 percent of the total population is Black: Hawai'i, New Mexico, and Oregon (3 percent each); Utah, South Dakota, North Dakota, New Hampshire, and Maine (approximately 2 percent each); and Wyoming, Idaho, Montana, and Vermont (approximately 1 percent each).

◻ 52 percent of the people in Washington, D.C., are Black or African American.

◻ Black people who live outside the South tend to be located in metropolitan areas—of the 317 counties in which Black people compose between 25 percent and 50 percent of the population, only 17 are *not* in the South. Of those 17 counties, 15 are located in metropolitan areas.

◻ Among U.S. cities with a population of 100,000 or more, Detroit has the highest proportion of Black Americans: 84 percent.

◻ The top five metropolitan areas with the highest percentages of African Americans living in their respective largest principal cities are:
- New York–Northern New Jersey–Long Island (61 percent);
- Detroit-Warren-Livonia (60 percent);
- San Diego–Carlsbad–San Marcos (56 percent);
- Chicago-Joliet-Naperville (54 percent);
- and Philadelphia-Camden-Wilmington (53 percent).[9]

Are Black Americans still affected by segregation?

- Between 2005 and 2009, 30 percent of African Americans lived in census block groups that were at least 75 percent African American.[10]
- The 10 cities, by rank, where Black Americans experience the most residential segregation are:
  - Milwaukee
  - New York City
  - Chicago
  - Detroit
  - Cleveland
  - Buffalo, New York
  - St. Louis
  - Cincinnati
  - Philadelphia
  - Los Angeles[11]
- Approximately half of the Black population in the United States still lives in neighborhoods that have no White residents.[12]

HOUSEHOLD AND MARITAL STATUS

How many Black Americans are married and whom do they marry?

- 31 percent of Black Americans are married, compared with 55 percent of Whites and 49 percent of people from other racial and ethnic groups (Native American, Asian, and Latino).
- 11 percent of Black people are divorced.
- 6 percent of Black people are widowed.
- 47 percent of Black people have never been married, compared with 26 percent of Whites and 37 percent of people from other racial and ethnic groups.[13]
- Approximately 24 percent of Black male newlyweds are married to someone of another race or ethnicity, compared with 17 percent of Asian male newlyweds, 26 percent of Latino male newlyweds, and 9 percent of White male newlyweds.[14]
- Approximately 9 percent of Black and White female newlyweds are married to someone of another race or

ethnicity, compared with about 36 percent of Asian female newlyweds and 25 percent of Latina newlyweds.[15]

▫ Black Americans have always been more approving than White Americans of interracial marriage, going back to 1968 when Gallup was first able to report reliable estimates of each group's opinions. The gap in approval has narrowed considerably over the past two decades, averaging 13 percentage points since 1997, down from an average 32-point gap from 1968 to 1994.[16]

Who (and what) constitutes Black households?

▫ 30 percent of Black households are headed by single women, three times as many as White and Asian households.[17]

▫ 24 percent of African Americans live alone—a higher proportion than any other racial group in the United States.[18]

▫ 44 percent of Black families live in homes they own, compared with 74 percent of White families.

▫ 51 percent of Black households are in rented homes, compared with 18 percent of White households.[19]

▫ 68 percent of Black married-couple families live in homes they own, compared with 87 percent of White married-couple families.[20]

Which Black people are raising Black children?

▫ 54 percent of Black children live in a single-parent household.[21]

▫ Black Americans in heterosexual relationships are 1.3 times more likely than White American heterosexual couples to be raising children.[22]

▫ 24 percent of grandparents (more than 600,000) who live with and are responsible for the care of grandchildren under age 18 are Black.[23]

▫ Only 34 percent of Black women say that having a child without being married is acceptable, compared with 65 percent of Black men and 60 percent of White women who say so.[24]

- African Americans in same-sex couples are 2.4 times more likely than their White counterparts to be raising children (40 percent and 16 percent, respectively).[25]

What are the conditions of Black children in foster care?

Children are placed into foster care for a host of reasons. Some have suffered physical, emotional, and sexual abuse; in other cases, the original caregiver is unable to care for a child properly. The placement of Black children into foster care has been a controversial issue, because of the subjectivity of the decision-making process and cultural differences in perceptions about the "quality" of Black homes. Studies have found that Black families are no more likely than other racial groups to abuse and neglect their children, yet racial disparities persist with respect to the number of Black children who are removed from their homes and placed into the child welfare system.[26] These factors and the difficulty of placing Black foster youth in permanent homes in a timely manner contribute to the disproportionately high number of Black youth lingering in foster care.[27]

- Today, 28 percent of all children in foster care are Black—a significant decrease from 38 percent in 2001.[28]
- In three states, Black children compose more than 50 percent of the children in foster care: Delaware (53 percent), Illinois (54 percent), and Maryland (64 percent).[29]
- Black children also account for 28 percent of all children who are waiting to be adopted.[30]
- Once Black children are removed from their homes, their stay in foster care is, on average, nine months longer than the average stay of White children.[31]
- More than 8 percent of all foster care youth have received antipsychotic medication (such as Adderall or Ritalin), about twice the rate for youth who are not in foster care. Black youth are 27 percent more likely than White youth to be given two or more antipsy-

chotic medications at once—a practice that is associated with greater adverse effects.[32]

□ Several states view the following factors as having a "very great" or "great" impact on family reunification efforts for Black children in foster care:
  - Lack of affordable housing options—18 states
  - Distrust of the child welfare system—9 states
  - Lack of substance abuse treatment for parents—14 states[33]

How do Black youth leave foster care?

□ Nationwide, 26 percent of all youth discharged from foster care are Black.[34]

□ 23 percent of all adopted children are Black.[35]

□ The proportion of Black youth in foster care dropped from 38 percent in 2001 to 27 percent in 2011.[36]

ADDITIONAL LIFESTYLE INFORMATION

What are the religious practices of Black Americans?

□ Black Americans are the most likely of all major racial groups in the United States to report a formal religious affiliation.

□ 75 percent of Black Americans who report belonging to the category "religious [but] unaffiliated" say that religion is either somewhat or very important in their lives, compared with slightly more than one-third of the "religious [but] unaffiliated" population overall.[37]

□ 59 percent of Black Americans attend historically Black Protestant churches.[38]

□ 85 percent of adults attending historically Black Protestant churches in the United States say that religion is very important in their lives.[39]

□ 15 percent of Black Americans attend evangelical Protestant churches. By comparison, 26 percent of the total U.S. population attend such churches.

□ 5 percent of Black Americans are Catholic, compared with 24 percent of the U.S. population.[40]

- 1 percent of the Black population in the United States self-identifies as Muslim; however, African Americans constitute at least one-third of the U.S. Muslim community.[41]

What is the sexual identity of Black Americans?

- The majority of Black Americans (95 percent) identify as heterosexual; however, a 2012 Gallup Poll shows that in the United States, Black adults are more likely than White adults to identify as lesbian, gay, bisexual, or transgender (LGBT), 5 percent and 3 percent, respectively.[42]
- It is estimated that there are 85,000 Black same-sex couples in the United States.[43]

What is Black public opinion on marriage equality?

- Since 2003, the proportion of African Americans favoring gay marriage has increased from 27 percent to 40 percent. However, 48 percent of Black Americans still directly oppose gay marriage, compared with 43 percent of White Americans and 43 percent of Latinos.[44]
- 53 percent of Black people report feeling that "gay or lesbian relations between consenting adults should not be legal," compared with 29 percent of Whites who feel the same.[45]
- 25 percent of African Americans say they feel less favorably toward President Obama because of his support for gay marriage, and 19 percent feel more favorably toward him because of his stand on the issue.[46]

Around 1723, Crispus Attucks was born into slavery. After his escape from slavery, Attucks worked for two decades coming in and out of New England on trading ships and whaling vessels. In 1770, following an altercation between British redcoats and a group of colonist seamen, a larger riot erupted—what came to be known as the Boston Massacre—resulting in the death of five men from British gunfire. Crispus Attucks was the first to die in that unrest, making him a casualty of the American Revolution.

—Adapted from "Crispus Attucks," Bio.com

For elementary school students nationwide, this story is often the earliest example of African American patriotism. Crispus Attucks is frequently used as a symbol of the long tradition of African American service and participation in the U.S. military. Yet many more heroes have emerged from the African American service tradition—from Colonel Charles Young to General Colin Powell, the military has provided for many Black Americans an opportunity to serve their country, to learn, and to lead.

The U.S. military comprises four major branches: the army, the navy, the marines, and the air force. Barack H. Obama, as president of the United States, is the commander in chief of all four. The U.S. Department of Defense (also known as the Pentagon) is responsible for coordinating and supervising agencies and functions associated with national security and the armed forces.[1] These institutions each have their own history with respect to the inclusion and advancement of Black men and women who devoted their lives to military service. For example, the Tuskegee Airmen, a group of Black air force aviators in World War II, became one of the earliest "top guns" in that combat and were ultimately celebrated around the world for their heroism and sacrifice. However, the path to military advancement has not been an easy road for many African Americans.

In 1948, the U.S. military became the first public institution to end segregation, serving as an important institutional model for integration and civil rights nationwide. This crucial step opened the door for many African Americans to quality education, housing, and the prestige of having served as a soldier. As this collection of statistics reveals, the U.S. armed forces have represented both a chance to succeed and been a painful reminder of social inequalities that prevent the full inclusion and participation of African Americans in our democracy.

THE U.S. ARMED FORCES

How many Black Americans are enlisted in the U.S. armed forces?

- There are 148,200 African Americans in the military reserve.[2]
- African Americans make up 17 percent of the armed forces.[3]
- 18 percent of the total U.S. Army population is African American.[4]
- 19 percent of new recruits to the U.S. Air Force are African Americans.[5]
- 14 percent of all U.S. Air Force members are African American.[6]
- There are 48,000 African Americans in the National Guard.[7]

How many cadets in military academies are Black?

According to the director of admissions at West Point, there were 2,784 Black students nationwide who qualified for admission to West Point in 2006, based solely on SAT scores. Although other factors are considered for admission, performance on this test has been a barrier to the inclusion of Black cadets.

- 6 percent of cadets in the U.S. Military Academy (West Point) are Black.

- 12 percent of all ROTC cadets, excluding private military academies, are Black.[8]

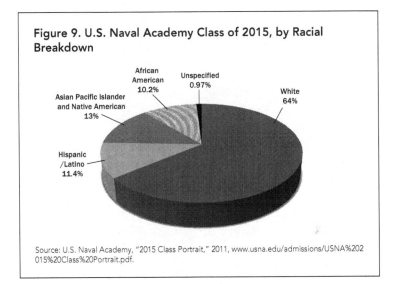

Figure 9. U.S. Naval Academy Class of 2015, by Racial Breakdown

African American 10.2%

Unspecified 0.97%

White 64%

Asian Pacific Islander and Native American 13%

Hispanic /Latino 11.4%

Source: U.S. Naval Academy, "2015 Class Portrait," 2011, www.usna.edu/admissions/USNA%202015%20Class%20Portrait.pdf.

How many officers are African American?

- 14 percent of officers in the U.S. Army are Black.
- 8 percent of officers in the U.S Navy are Black.
- 6 percent of officers in the U.S. Marine Corps and U.S. Air Force are Black.[9]
- Overall, approximately 6 percent of general officers or admirals are African American.
- Ten Black men have ever gained four-star rank in the U.S. armed forces to date: five in the army, four in the air force, and one in the navy.
- There are 8 African American three-star officers (lieutenant generals or vice admirals).
- There are 17 African American two-star officers (major generals or rear admirals).
- There are 26 African American one-star officers (brigadier generals or rear admirals); this group includes three women.[10]
- 17 percent of chief master sergeants on active duty in the air force are Black.[11]

How many Black Americans are in combat?

- African Americans make up 20 percent of those on active duty in the U.S. Army.
- African Americans make up 17 percent of those on active duty in the U.S. Navy.
- African Americans make up 10 percent of those on active duty in the U.S. Marine Corps.
- African Americans make up 15 percent of those on active duty in the U.S. Air Force.[12]
- Black Americans account for nearly 10 percent of armed service members who have died in combat in Operation New Dawn and Operation Iraqi Freedom, and for 8 percent of military casualties in Operation Enduring Freedom. In total, 614 African American soldiers had fallen in these campaigns as of January 17, 2013.
- As of 2009, 24 percent of all Black armed service members served in the combat arms division. Nearly half (48 percent) of Black soldiers were enlisted in combat service support.[13]

How have military actions and policies addressed the sexuality of Black Americans?

- Black people made up 20 percent of the armed service members who were discharged under "Don't Ask, Don't Tell" (DADT).[14]
- Black military women were disproportionately affected by DADT: fewer than 1 percent of service women are Black, but 3 percent of women discharged under DADT were Black.[15]
- A study of female veterans, the majority of whom were Black women, found that 83 percent had experienced military sexual trauma (rape, sexual assault, or sexual harassment).[16]

VETERANS

Who are the living Black veterans?

- There are a total of 2.4 million Black veterans in the United States; 280,840 of them are women.[17]

- There are nearly 1.8 million Black veterans in the United States ages 18 to 64.
- There are 529,410 Black veterans in the United States age 65 and over.[18]
- 11 percent of the veteran population are Black.[19]

In which states do the largest concentrations of Black veterans reside?

- Georgia: home to 232,141 Black veterans.
- Texas: home to 220,524 Black veterans.
- Washington: home to 174,493 Black veterans.
- California: home to 173,700 Black veterans.
- Florida: home to 161,533 Black veterans.[20]

What are the employment trends for Black veterans?

- African Americans make up 12 percent of the veteran labor force.[21]
- Black veterans account for 18 percent of all veterans who are unemployed.
- The unemployment rate for Black veterans was 13 percent in 2010, more than double the 6 percent rate from 2007.
- The unemployment rate for female Black veterans is 11 percent, compared with 7 percent of female White and Latina veterans.
- At 13 percent, the unemployment rate for Black male veterans exceeds that for male White veterans (8 percent), Latino veterans (10 percent), and Asian veterans (5 percent).[22]

What are the mental and physical health trends for Black veterans?

- 43 percent of African American veterans suffer from post-traumatic stress disorder (PTSD) associated with lifetime events.[23]
- African Americans account for 10 percent of all living veterans but for 19 percent of living veterans who suffered a disabling injury while serving in the military.[24]

- 75 percent of Black veterans are served by 42 Veterans Administration (VA) hospitals (out of the 150 VA hospitals in operation across the United States).[25]
- Only 16 percent of Black veterans report feeling that they are treated with dignity when they seek medical care.[26]

How are Black veterans affected by poverty and homelessness?

- African Americans represent 11 percent of all veterans but 19 percent of all poor veterans and 35 percent of all sheltered homeless veterans in the United States.
- Nearly 40 percent of veteran families living in homeless shelters are Black.
- Poor African American veterans are more than twice as likely to be homeless as poor African American nonveterans.
- Black homeless veterans are more likely to live in cities (39 percent) than in the suburbs (27 percent).[27]

What is the financial impact of the war in Iraq on Black families?

- The total cost to date to each African American household for the war in Iraq is between $29,000 and $32,000—a figure more than three times the median value of the assets of an average African American household.
- If the debt associated with the war in Iraq is paid for by tax increases, the burden for African American households will be 14 percent lower than that of White households.[28]

Poverty and deprivation, as surely as denial of the right to vote, are erosive of human freedom and of democracy.

—A. Philip Randolph

The economic conditions of African Americans are often used as a dominant indicator of how well, as a whole, Black people are faring in the United States. Since arriving on U.S. soil as the first "stock" in the U.S. Stock Exchange, Black people have enjoyed many economic advancements and setbacks. From Oprah Winfrey to Robert Johnson, the successes of Black billionaires have been well documented. However, the highly visible success of a few African Americans can mask the widespread structural inequality plaguing many Black communities.

Research by the Economic Policy Institute has demonstrated that the consistently high rates of underemployment and unemployment among African Americans are evidence of a "permanent recession" or even a depression among Black households affected by the economic downturn.[1] Other research has shown that a crisis of low-wage jobs exists and that employment in positions that offer few opportunities for advancement can produce harmful long-term effects on the economic well-being and financial security of Black families.[2] Bias continues to play a role in the hiring process and in the workplace—an issue at the heart of some of the fiercest debates about fairness and equity. Unemployment rates remain higher for African Americans than for Americans in general or for similarly situated White Americans, forcing a disproportionate number of Black families into poverty.

This section presents statistics on the economic status of Black people nationwide—and the picture these figures paint illustrates the daunting economic challenges that remain, but it also highlights the increasing spending power and potential for upward mobility in Black America.

EMPLOYMENT

How well are Black Americans represented in the private sector, and how many are self-employed?

- 77 percent of African Americans are employed in the private sector, as compared with 79 percent of Whites and 84 percent of Latinos.[3] African American representation in the private sector by job type:
  - 3 percent of executives, senior-level officials, and managers are Black.
  - 7 percent of professionals, first and mid-level officials, and managers are Black.
  - 13 percent of technicians* and sales workers are Black.
  - 17 percent of office and clerical workers are Black.
  - 9 percent of craft workers are Black.
  - 17 percent of operatives** are Black.
  - 18 percent of laborers[†] are Black.
  - 23 percent of service workers in private industry nationwide are Black.[4]
- 4 percent of African Americans are self-employed, compared with 7 percent of Whites and 6 percent of Latinos.[5]

Are Black Americans represented in unions?

Given the nature of union employment, scholars believe that most of the reporting unionized workforce is a working population. Those who are employed in the building trades or as longshoremen may retain their union membership even when they are not currently working because their union con-

---

* "Technician" refers to a person employed to manage and operate technical equipment.

** "Operative" refers to a worker in a manufacturing industry.

† "Laborer" refers to a person employed in unskilled manual work.

sciousness tends to be stronger and their inclination to find jobs through their union affiliation greater. However, the majority of individuals employed in union jobs associated with retail or general service may not be as inclined to maintain union membership if they are unemployed.

- 13 percent of all union members are Black.
- Black people represent:
  - 14 percent of union members in the Northeast.
  - 12 percent of union members in the Midwest.
  - 24 percent of union members in the South.
  - 7 percent of union members in the West.[6]

What percentage of Black Americans work in the public and non-profit sectors?

- Approximately 12.8 percent of state and local public-sector employees are African American—a 2.3 percentage point decline since 1997.[7]
- Nearly 20 percent of all employed African Americans work for a state, local, or federal agency, compared with 14 percent of Whites and 10 percent of Latinos.[8]
- 8 percent of people on nonprofit boards of directors are African American.
- 3 percent of nonprofit CEOs are African American.[9]
- African Americans represent:
  - 4 percent of foundation CEOs and presidents.
  - 4 percent of full-time foundation executive staff.
  - 7 percent of foundation board and/or trustee members.
  - 16 percent of foundation program officers.[10]

How many Black Americans serve on private boards?

New York City is one of the world's principal financial markets. Wall Street, the city's financial district, is home to the New York Stock Exchange and other major exchanges.

- Nearly 6 percent of directors on the boards of the 25 largest employers in New York City are Black.

- As of 2010, there were a total of 697 directors on the boards of New York City's 25 largest employers; 40 of them were African Americans. This averages to fewer than two Black people per board.
- Bloomberg LLP, Goldman Sachs, Morgan Stanley, and the *New York Times* have no African Americans on their boards.[11]

What are the unemployment statistics for African Americans?

- One in four African Americans faces unemployment or underemployment.[12]
- The unemployment rate for Black high school graduates is 46 percent, more than double the rate for their White counterparts (21 percent) and significantly higher than that for their Latino counterparts (24 percent).[13]
- The unemployment rate for African Americans with a four-year college degree is 8 percent, almost double the unemployment rate for similarly educated Whites (4.5 percent).[14]
- The Black unemployment rate between May 2012 and May 2013 was virtually unchanged—resting near 13.5 percent, significantly higher than the national rate for all Americans in 2012 and 2013 (8 percent and 7.6 percent, respectively).[15]
- The average duration of unemployment for Black Americans is 24.2 weeks, compared with 17.8 weeks for White unemployed individuals and 15 weeks for unemployed Latino individuals.[16]
- Black transgender people report unemployment at a rate of 26 percent.[17]
- African Americans are underrepresented in STEM* occupations (important to the professional, scientific, and technical services industry): 6 percent of all those employed in these fields are Black.

---

*STEM is an acronym used to collectively define the fields of science, technology, engineering, and math.

Table 5. Industries Expecting the Largest Employment Growth, 2010–20

Industry	Annual average rate of change, 2010–20	Percentage of African American total employment by industry, 2011
Professional, scientific, and technical services	3%	16%
Education services	3%	8%
Health and social services	3%	6%
Construction	2%	11%

Source: U.S. Department of Labor, "The African American Labor Force in the Recovery," February 29, 2012.

- □ African Americans have a notable history in health and social assistance, an industry that the Bureau of Labor Statistics (BLS) expects to grow by 3 percent annually (on average) between 2010 and 2020, adding 5.6 million additional jobs to this sector by 2020.[18]
- □ In 2011, 43 percent of African Americans said that they plan to change jobs when the economy improves.[19]

How many Black people have felt discriminated against in the workplace?

- □ 25 percent of Black people report that they have felt discriminated against in their current job.[20]
- □ 32 percent of Black transgender people report feeling that they lost a job due to bias, compared with 26 percent of all transgender people who report having lost a job because of bias against their gender identity or expression.[21]
- □ 46 percent of Black transgender people report feeling that they were not hired for a job because of bias. This figure is comparable to the number of transgender Latinos (47 percent), and slightly higher than that for transgender Asian/Pacific Islander Americans (41 percent) who report the same.[22]

How much money do Black Americans earn?

Economist Steven Pitts at the UC Berkeley Center for Labor Research and Education wrote, "There is a two-dimensional crisis of work in the Black community," which he defined as a crisis of unemployment and a crisis of low-wage jobs, jobs earning less than $21,412 per year.[23] Though the issue gets buried by popular discourses on economic recovery, understanding the plight of low-wage workers—and 40 percent of the Black workforce is low-wage—is crucial to understanding the landscape of work in Black America.

- Nationwide, the median income for African American households is $32,229.
- The real median income* declined for Black households by 2.7 percent between 2010 and 2011.
- The current Black real median household income is 16.8 percent lower than its pre-2001 recession peak.[24]
- 10 percent of African Americans earn $100,000 or more.
- $695.6 billion: the aggregated household income of African Americans.[25]
- The gender wage gap among African Americans is smaller than that for Whites, largely because African American men earn much lower wages compared with men in other racial groups. Black men employed full-time earn on average $653 per week, 76 percent of the average salary earned by White men, and Black women earn on average $595 per week, about 85 percent of the average salary earned by White women.[26]

Research by the Brookings Institution reveals that the majority of African American children born in middle-class households grow up to have less income than their parents.[27]

---

*Real median income is defined as the income of a household after considering the effects of inflation on purchasing power.

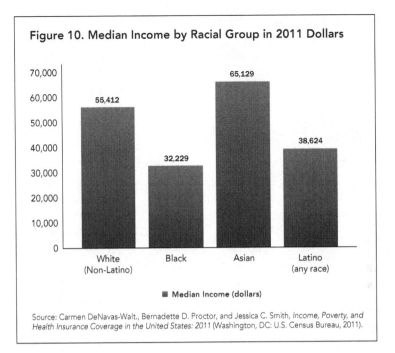

Figure 10. Median Income by Racial Group in 2011 Dollars

■ Median Income (dollars)

Source: Carmen DeNavas-Walt., Bernadette D. Proctor, and Jessica C. Smith, *Income, Poverty, and Health Insurance Coverage in the United States: 2011* (Washington, DC: U.S. Census Bureau, 2011).

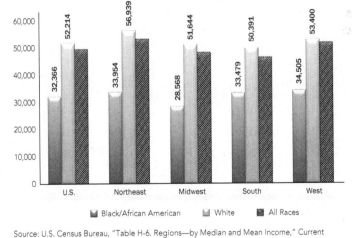

Figure 11. Median Income by Region and Racial Group in 2011 Dollars

◪ Black/African American   ◪ White   ◪ All Races

Source: U.S. Census Bureau, "Table H-6. Regions—by Median and Mean Income," Current Population Survey, 2012.

- African American households on the West Coast have the highest median income for their group: $34,505.
- African Americans in the Midwest earn the least: a median income of $28,568.[28]

POVERTY AND HOMELESSNESS

How many Black Americans live in poverty?

- According to the U.S. Census, almost 10.9 million African Americans, or 28 percent, live at or below the poverty line,* compared with 25 percent of Latinos and approximately 10 percent of White Americans.[29]
- The poverty rate for African Americans and Latinos age 65 and older is 19 percent; the rate for White Americans is 7 percent.[30]
- 23 percent of all children in the United States live in poverty, while 39 percent of Black children live in poverty.[31]
- 35 percent all female students are low-income, yet more than half of African American female students (53 percent) are low-income.[32]
- Although Black (including multiracial Black) people make up just 14 percent of the U.S. population, 37 percent of people who are homeless are Black.
- African Americans account for 50 percent of the people enrolled in programs that address chronic homelessness.[33]

What role does gender identity play in Black poverty?

- 34 percent of Black transgender people report a household income of less than $10,000 per year, twice the rate for transgender people of all races (15 percent), four times the rate for the general Black population rate (9 percent), and more than

---

*The U.S. Census Bureau uses a set of income thresholds that vary by size and composition to determine who is living in poverty. For more information, see www .census.gov/hhes/www/poverty/about/overview/ measure.html.

eight times the rate for the general U.S. population (4 percent).

- 50 percent of Black transgender people report having been compelled to sell illegal drugs or do sex work for income at some point in their lives.
- Black transgender people own homes at a rate of 14 percent, less than half the 32 percent home ownership rate of the transgender population as a whole. The home ownership rate for the general U.S. population is 67 percent.[34]
- Black (and Black multiracial) transgender people experience a particularly high rate of homelessness, 41 percent, five times the overall rate in the United States.[35]

Are Black Americans investing?

- 42 percent of Whites own an Individual Retirement Account (IRA) or Keogh Plan; 7 percent of African Americans own such accounts.
- African Americans are 23.3 percent less likely than all American families to have direct or indirect holdings of publicly traded stock.[36]
- African Americans are four times as likely as Whites to cash in their own life insurance policies early in order to cover unexpected expenses.[37]
- 62 percent of African Americans are in full-time jobs that offer an employer-sponsored retirement plan (such as a 401K), and among that group less than half (48 percent) actually participate in the program.
- One-third of African American retirees have an income in the bottom 25 percent of all incomes earned by retirees.[38]

Where do Black Americans bank and borrow money?

- 17 percent of African Americans, compared with 5 percent of Whites, turn to nontraditional sources of credit (such as loan sharks, pawnshops, and payday loans) to manage unexpected expenses.[39]
- 21 percent of Black households are "unbanked,"

meaning they do not have a checking or savings account, compared with 20 percent of Latino households, 15 percent of Native American households, 3 percent of Asian households, and 4 percent of White households.

- 34 percent of Black households are "underbanked," meaning they have an account but are underserved by their bank, compared with 30 percent of Hawaiian/Pacific Islander households, 29 percent of Latino households, 27 percent of Native American households, 17 percent of Asian households, and 16 percent of White households.

- Less than half (42 percent) of Black households are fully banked, compared with 49 percent of Latino households and 77 percent of White and Asian households.[40]

- 24 percent of Black women report facing difficulties when getting a home loan, car loan, education loan, or other type of personal credit, compared with 16 percent of White women.[41]

What is the level of debt among Black Americans?

- $5,784: the average amount of credit card debt held by African Americans, a figure that represents a 17 percent decline since 2008.

- 44 percent of African American indebted households report that their credit is "excellent" or "good," compared with 62 percent of all indebted households and 55 percent of Latino indebted households.

- More than one-third of African American households (a higher rate than their White or Latino counterparts) report having had their credit limit reduced in the past three years.[42]

- 32 percent of African American households have cited layoffs or job loss as a contributor to their current debt.

- African Americans are the most likely of all racial groups to have had negative credit experiences (calls from bill collectors, settlements with credit card companies, evictions, and foreclosures).[43]

Over half (55 percent) of African American households file Chapter 13 bankruptcy, as compared with 27 percent of mixed-race African American households that file, 29 percent of White American households, 24 percent of Asian American households, and 22 percent of Hispanic/Latino American households.[44]

- Attorneys are more likely to recommend consumer bankruptcy (Chapter 7 and Chapter 13) to African Americans (47 percent) than they are to their White counterparts (32 percent).[45]
- Since the CARD Act was signed into law in 2009, offering new transparency and accountability to consumers, 32 percent of African Americans have experienced a reduction in over-limit fees.[46]

How many Black Americans are small business owners and entrepreneurs?

- 7 percent of firms in the United States are owned by African Americans.[47]
- The number of Black-owned businesses in the United States increased by 61 percent between 2002 and 2007, reaching 1.9 million. By comparison, the overall national rate of business growth was just 18 percent during that time.
- The best states for Black businesses, based upon numbers of top-grossing Black-owned businesses, are Michigan, Virginia, Ohio, Georgia, Texas, and Pennsylvania.[48]
- 80 percent of Black CEOs report they started their businesses in order to have greater control over their own destiny.[49]

What is the status of home ownership in Black America?

- 44 percent of African Americans owned their homes at the end of 2010.
- Black Americans spend, on average, $13,503 a year on housing, $3,392 less than the average amount spent annually by all other consumers.

- The Black home ownership rate is 45.6 percent, nearly 29 percentage points lower than the rate of White home ownership. The gap between Black and White ownership has widened steadily since 1990.
- Between 1995 and 2004, the rate of home ownership among African Americans rose by 7 percent.[50]
- The foreclosure rate for African Americans is 10 percent.[51]
- African Americans are nearly twice as likely as all Americans to have been affected by the mortgage lending crisis; up to one-quarter of all African Americans who purchased a home in the years leading up to the 2008 recession may ultimately lose it.[52]
- For African Americans ages 25 to 34 and 45 to 64 (the prime periods for first-home buying and home upgrading), home ownership fell by 4 and 5 percent, respectively, in 2000 and 2010.[53]
- Between 2009 and 2012, African Americans were projected to lose $194 billion in wealth and assets during the great recession and the subsequent fallout from imbalanced recovery efforts, foreclosures, and the economic deterioration of communities deeply affected by high concentrations of loan defaults, home loss, and abandonment.[54]

What is the household wealth of Black Americans?

- The wealth gap between White and Black American families has nearly tripled since 1984, from $85,000 in that year to $236,500 in 2009.[55]
- The average household wealth (value of all assets held) of White households is $110,729, compared with $4,955 for Black households—a ratio of 22:1. The average household wealth for Latinos is $7,424.[56]
- From 2005 to 2009, median wealth fell by 53 percent among Black households* and by 16 percent among White households.

---

*Rates and averages have been adjusted for inflation.

◻ In 2005, 59 percent of Black households drew a large portion of their net worth from home equity. By 2009, 35 percent of Black households had zero or negative net worth, compared with 15 percent of White households that found themselves in the same position.[57]

Have Black Americans benefited from recession recovery efforts?

◻ In January 2007, when the recession officially began, the unemployment rate for Black workers was at 8 percent, compared with 4 percent for Whites and 6 percent for Latinos. By January 2009, the unemployment rate had climbed to 13 percent for African Americans, 10 percent for Latinos, and 7 percent for Whites. By the end of 2010, the unemployment rate for Black Americans had risen to 17 percent.[58]

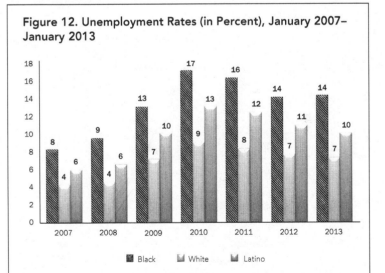

Figure 12. Unemployment Rates (in Percent), January 2007– January 2013

Source: Bureau of Labor Statistics, "The Employment Situation: January 2007," February 2, 2007; "The Employment Situation: January 2008," February 1, 2008; "The Employment Situation: January 2009," February 6, 2009; "The Employment Situation: January 2010," February 5, 2010; "The Employment Situation: January 2011," February 4, 2011; "The Employment Situation: January 2012," February 3, 2012; "The Employment Situation: January 2013," February 1, 2013.

The slower recovery for African Americans in the labor market has been partly the result of government layoffs after the official end of the 2008 recession.[59]

- Black Americans make up a disproportionate share of public sector workers, and thus have been more vulnerable to the drastic government layoffs in recent years.
- Unemployed African Americans are 60 percent more likely than unemployed non–African Americans to live in local communities with double-digit unemployment rates.[60]
- Studies have found that a spatial mismatch* may explain the relatively weak and negative employment growth in or near African American communities; this is believed to partially explain the Black-White unemployment gap.[61]
- During the most difficult part of the recent downturn, African American employment in manufacturing, financial services, education and health services, transportation and warehousing, and construction took the largest hit.[62]
- Nearly one in five African American men faced unemployment at the purported end of the recession in 2009.[63]

What is the spending power of Black Americans?

- The buying power of African Americans is expected to reach $1.1 trillion by 2015.[64]

How do advertising and media engage Black Americans?

- The total dollars spent by advertisers on African American media (Black radio, television, magazines, etc.) in 2011 was less than 2 percent of the total $120 billion spent on advertising with general market media.[65]

---

* A spatial mismatch refers to a dislocation of employment opportunities from particular residential spaces. Simply put, it is when there are limited jobs for low-income people in their home communities.

Table 6. Top 10 African American Media Advertisers

Corporation	2011	Percent Change from 2010
Procter & Gamble	$75.4 million	+3.6%
L'Oréal	$39.9 million	+4.6%
McDonald's	$34.9 million	+19.5%
Johnson & Johnson	$27.7 million	−21.2%
Verizon Communications	$26.4 million	−8.7%
National Amusements	$24 million	+15%
Hershey	$23.6 million	+49.2%
Comcast	$23.5 million	+19.4%
General Motors	$23.2 million	−30.5%
Berkshire Hathaway	$23.2 million	+7.3%
Total	$321.9 million	+2%

Source: Nielsen, "African American Consumers: Still Vital, Still Growing," 2012. Spending figures per product category have been rounded off. Nielsen notes that Hershey and Comcast were not on the Top 10 List in 2010.

Table 7. Top 10 Product Categories for Advertising to African Americans, 2012

Product category	First quarter, 2012	Percent change from first quarter, 2011
Automotive	$27.8 million	+0.6%
Quick restaurant service	$23.7 million	−3.4%
Motion picture	$22.3 million	+19.9%
Wireless telephone service	$16.2 million	+8.9%
Pharmaceutical	$16.2 million	−8.3%
Auto insurance	$14.7 million	−34.5%
Insurance	$11.2 million	+118.7%
Direct response service	$10.4 million	+15.2%
Restaurant	$9.4 million	−1.8%
Department store	$9 million	−12.8%
Total	$161 million	+0.71%

Source: Nielsen, "African American Consumers: Still Vital, Still Growing," 2012. Spending dollars per product category have been rounded off.

Where do Black Americans make purchases and what are they buying?

- 163: The number of shopping trips made by the average African American shopper in one year.
- African American shoppers spend approximately $38 during an average shopping trip.
- African Americans make more trips to convenience or gas station stores, dollar stores, and drugstores, compared with non–African American populations.
- African Americans buy hand/body lotions and other all-purpose skin creams at 54 percent and 40 percent rates, respectively, which are higher than the rates for the general population.[66]
- Black and Latino Americans spend more annually on footwear (by $107 and $149, respectively) than all other consumers.[67]

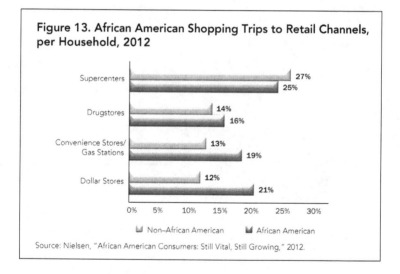

Figure 13. African American Shopping Trips to Retail Channels, per Household, 2012

Supercenters: 27% / 25%
Drugstores: 14% / 16%
Convenience Stores/Gas Stations: 13% / 19%
Dollar Stores: 12% / 21%

Legend: Non–African American / African American

Source: Nielsen, "African American Consumers: Still Vital, Still Growing," 2012.

I hold that women, as well as men, have
the right to vote. . . . I want the elective
franchise, for one, as a colored man, because
ours is a peculiar government, based upon
a peculiar idea, and that idea is universal
suffrage . . . to rule us out is to make us an
exception, to brand us with the stigma of
inferiority, and to invite to our heads the
missiles of those about us; therefore, I want
the franchise for the Black man.

—*Frederick Douglass*

Beginning with the abolitionist movement, African Americans have played a vital role in the development of American democracy through electoral politics and civic engagement. Although the road to achieving full participation in the nation's civic processes has been a stony one, the civic lives and engagement of Black Americans have improved tremendously over time. Since 1870, when the first African Americans were elected to Congress, Black people have served in the House of Representatives and the Senate. Through a series of voting battles and hard-won victories culminating in the 1965 Voting Rights Act, millions of Black people have confirmed and exercised their right to vote. The remarkable history of civil rights activism in the Black community was central to the organized political action that has made civic processes more inclusive of—and accountable to—poor people and people of color in the United States. Yet civil and human rights organizations are still needed to monitor democratic processes and protect these rights.

The following presentation of statistics on Black Americans points to general trends in electoral politics, voting, and civic engagement. These data also reveal new developments associated with the political discourse and civic practices found in Black America.

ELECTORAL POLITICS

How many Black Americans are represented among nationally elected or appointed senior officials?

◻ Barack Hussein Obama, the 44th president of the United States, is of African biracial descent and is the nation's first Black president. He was first elected to the U.S. presidency on November 4, 2008, and to a second term in 2012.[1]

◻ General Colin Powell was the first African American U.S. secretary of state. He served from 2001 to 2005.[2]

◻ Condoleezza Rice was the first female African American U.S. secretary of state. She served from 2005 to 2009.[3]

◻ Of the past three American presidents, Bill Clinton appointed the largest number of Black Americans to cabinet-level positions:
  - William Clinton: 7 Black American cabinet members.
  - George W. Bush: 4 Black American cabinet members.
  - Barack Obama: 3 Black American cabinet members.[4]

How are Black Americans situated in Congress?

◻ There are 43 African American members of the 113th Congress, including Rep. Tim Scott (R–South Carolina), who is the first African American U.S. senator from a Southern state since Reconstruction.[5]

◻ There have been a total of eight African American U.S. senators; the first was elected in 1870. They are: Hiram Revels (R-Mississippi, 1870–71); Blanche Bruce (R-Mississippi, 1875–81); Edward Brooke (R-Massachusetts, 1967–79); Carol Moseley Braun (D-Illinois, 1993–99); Barack Obama (D-Illinois, 2005–9); Roland Burris (D-Illinois, 2008–10); Tim Scott (R–South Carolina, 2013–present); and William "Mo" Cowan (D-Massachusetts, 2013–present).

◻ 2013 marks the first year that there have been two Black U.S. senators serving concurrently.[6]

Who are the Black Americans to have been appointed to the Supreme Court?

◻ There is currently one member of the U.S. Supreme Court who is African American: Justice Clarence Thomas (nominated by George H.W. Bush, confirmed in 1991).[7]

◻ Justice Thomas is the second African American ever to serve on the Supreme Court. The first was Justice Thurgood Marshall, who was nominated by Lyndon B. Johnson and served from 1967 to 1991.[8]

Which states have had Black governors?

◻ There have been four Black governors in the United States during and since Reconstruction: Pinckney Pinchback (R-Louisiana, 1872, served 35 days); Douglas Wilder (D-Virginia, 1990–94); Deval Patrick (D-Massachusetts, 2006–present); and David Paterson (D–New York, 2008–10).[9]

What representation have African Americans achieved in state legislatures?

◻ African Americans compose 8 percent of state legislators nationwide, a figure almost unchanged since 1992, when 7 percent of state legislators were Black.

◻ Georgia had the highest total number of Black state legislators in 2009: 53.

◻ At 29 percent, Mississippi has the largest proportion of Black state legislators.[10]

◻ Other states with the highest percentage of Black state senators:

- Alabama (25 percent).
- Maryland (23 percent).
- Georgia (22 percent) and South Carolina (22 percent).
- North Carolina (19 percent).
- Louisiana (18 percent) and Illinois (18 percent).[11]

◻ In 2009, there were 14 states with no Black state senators: Hawai'i, Idaho, Iowa, Massachusetts, Minnesota, Montana, New Hampshire, New Mexico,

North Dakota, South Dakota, Utah, West Virginia, Wisconsin, and Wyoming.

□ In 2009, there were 12 states with no Black state-house members: Alaska, Hawai'i, Idaho, Iowa, Maine, Montana, North Dakota, Oregon, South Dakota, Utah, Vermont, and Wisconsin.[12]

□ There are 318 Black state legislators in the South.

□ Three Black state legislators are Republican.

□ 5 percent of Black state legislators in the South were in the majority in their houses after the 2010 elections; 95 percent had minority status in Southern state legislatures.

□ Following the 2010 midterm elections, 54 percent of Black state legislators in non-Southern states attained majority status.[13]

How are Black Americans involved in the official ranks of political parties?

□ The six largest numbers of Black Republican delegates in the 2012 presidential election came from:
  - Virgin Islands (23 percent).
  - Maryland, New Jersey, and South Carolina (8 percent).
  - Michigan (7 percent).
  - Vermont (6 percent).

□ There were 18 states without a single Black Republican delegate or alternate in 2012, compared with 28 states that had no Black delegates or alternates in 2008.

□ There were 47 Black delegates at the Republican National Convention in 2012, 2 percent of the delegation as a whole.

□ According to the Joint Center for Political and Economic Studies, there are two African American members of the Republican National Committee.[14]

□ 26 percent of delegates at the 2012 Democratic National Convention were Black, nearly double the African American (including multiracial) representation in the general population.

□ There were 93 Black alternates for the 2012 Democratic National Convention.

- A greater percentage of Black Democratic delegates in 2012 were women (58 percent) than men (42 percent).
- The five states with the largest number of Black Democratic delegates in 2012:
  - Mississippi (73 percent).
  - Louisiana (72 percent).
  - Alabama (68 percent).
  - Georgia (67 percent).
  - North Carolina (50 percent).
- At the Democratic National Convention, every state had at least one Black delegate.
- African Americans represent 20 percent of the Democratic Platform Committee.[15]

What are some of the voting trends among Black Americans?

- Nearly 26 million voters report being Black or African American.[16]
- Black voters are concentrated in approximately 20 states.[17]

Among African Americans who are legally permitted to vote, 63 percent are registered.[18]

- In 2012, African Americans voted at a higher rate than other populations of color.
- Black Americans made up 12 percent of the eligible electorate but cast 13 percent of the general vote.
- In 2012, President Obama won 93 percent of the African American vote.[19]
- There was almost no gender gap among African American support for President Barack Obama, with 88 percent of Black men and 89 percent of Black women reporting a preference for the president in the 2012 election.[20]
- In 2008, young Black Americans (18- to 29-year-olds) voted at a higher rate than young White Americans (58 percent versus 52 percent, respectively).[21]

What are the major barriers to voting for Black Americans today?

The Voting Rights Act of 1965 guaranteed African Americans the right to vote. Section 5 of the act required certain jurisdictions with a history of racial discrimination to receive approval (preclearance) from the U.S. Department of Justice prior to implementing any changes to their voting rules. Several states challenged the law and in *Shelby County v. Holder* (2013), the U.S. Supreme Court determined the constitutionality of this provision. Racial justice and civil rights advocates declared that without this key provision of the Voting Rights Act, African Americans would be subject to potentially discriminatory and exclusionary tactics that could suppress their votes. In a 5–4 ruling, the Court left the preclearance provision intact, but struck down Section 4, which had established a formula for the selection of states required to receive preclearance.

How is the right to vote still being suppressed?

- 25 percent of elderly African American voters (compared with 8 percent of elderly Whites) do not possess the identification that would be required under new photo-ID laws introduced in 40 states before the 2012 election.
- Restrictions on voter registration drives profoundly affect African Americans. In Florida, 20 percent of African Americans register to vote through drives, compared with 6 percent of Whites.[22]
- Six of the nine states affected by Section 5 of the Voting Rights Act are among the highest nationwide in percentage of Black state legislators.[23]
- As of May 2013, six of the nine states previously required to get preclearance under the Voting Rights Act have moved forward with new voter ID laws; however, since the beginning of 2013, more than 82 restrictive voting bills have been introduced in 31 states—where more than 20 million Black Americans live—potentially making it more difficult for poor and elderly constituents to vote.[24]

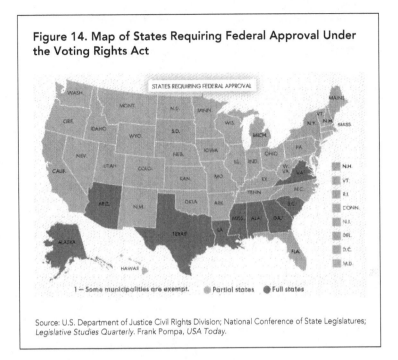

Figure 14. Map of States Requiring Federal Approval Under the Voting Rights Act

Source: U.S. Department of Justice Civil Rights Division; National Conference of State Legislatures; *Legislative Studies Quarterly*. Frank Pompa, USA Today.

FELONY DISENFRANCHISEMENT

Felony disenfranchisement is the denial of the right to vote based upon a felony conviction history. According to the Sentencing Project, felony disenfranchisement laws affect approximately 5.9 million people.

- One in every 13 African Americans of voting age is disenfranchised because of a felony conviction, a rate more than four times greater than the rate for the rest of the U.S. population.[25]
- Nearly 8 percent of the adult African American population is disenfranchised because of a felony conviction, compared with 2 percent of the rest of the population.[26]

In three states—Florida (23 percent), Kentucky (22 percent), and Virginia (20 percent)—more than one-fifth of the African American population is disenfranchised.[27]

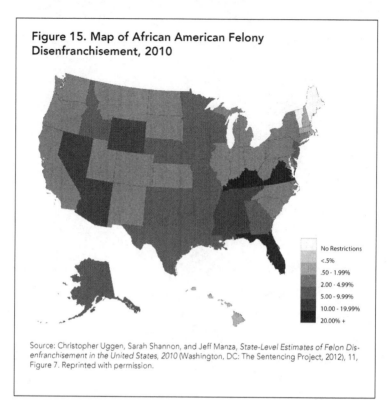

Figure 15. Map of African American Felony Disenfranchisement, 2010

Legend:
- No Restrictions
- <.5%
- .50 - 1.99%
- 2.00 - 4.99%
- 5.00 - 9.99%
- 10.00 - 19.99%
- 20.00% +

Source: Christopher Uggen, Sarah Shannon, and Jeff Manza, *State-Level Estimates of Felon Disenfranchisement in the United States, 2010* (Washington, DC: The Sentencing Project, 2012), 11, Figure 7. Reprinted with permission.

CIVIC PARTICIPATION AND COMMUNITY SERVICE

Where do Black Americans volunteer?

◻ Historically Black colleges and universities report the highest levels of student service (61 percent), compared with residential colleges (40 percent) and liberal arts colleges (38 percent).[28]

◻ Older African Americans (over age 65) have a higher rate of organizational membership than their White counterparts, especially those who are associated with a church or recreational clubs.[29]

◻ The Black church remains one of the most important venues for Black civic participation: 70 percent of Black churches operate at least one civic program, almost 60 percent operate two programs, and nearly half operate three or more civic programs.[30]

Yes, you can dance in space, and I did!

—*Dr. Mae Jemison, astronaut*

Historically, Black scientists have played a vital role in advancing the development and sustainability of our collective culture and society. From Dr. George Washington Carver's contributions to the nation's agricultural development to the work of Garrett Morgan, an inventor whose gas mask and traffic light provided the blueprint for similar devices still in use today, Black innovators have played a critical role in American science and technology.

Today, Black students in engineering degree programs face a number of special challenges. Inadequate preparation at the elementary and middle school levels and the absence of mentors, institutional investments, and social supports often prevent successful participation in science, technology, engineering, and math (STEM) fields. According to former National Society of Black Engineers board member and nuclear physicist Njema Frazier, this situation will be remedied only by "increasing the early opportunities for success in STEM-related activities for our youth. Academic summer programs, science fairs, math competitions, afterschool programs, STEM clubs, STEM conferences, role models—things of this nature are critical to early exposure, success, and efficacy for underrepresented and underserved students."

This section explores the representation of Black scientists and engineers and follows their educational paths in order to present a picture of how Black Americans are prepared to successfully enter STEM fields. This section also presents statistics on Black people and the ongoing digital divide, and a snapshot of how Black American lives have been transformed by modern tools such as cellular phones and various gaming platforms. All of these data present important insights regarding the challenges and opportunities for African Americans in science and technology.

REPRESENTATION AND EMPLOYMENT

How many Black people are employed in the science, technology, and engineering sectors?

The professional, scientific, and technical services industry has been projected to grow by 2.1 million additional jobs from 2010 to 2020.

- Black Americans represent 5 percent of all engineers in the workforce.[1]
- Black Americans represent 6 percent of the aerospace engineering workforce.[2]
- The projected annual average rate of growth in the professional, scientific, and technical services industry between 2010 and 2020 is 3 percent; Black Americans are expected to represent 16 percent of those employed in the industry during this time.[3]

Are Black Americans prepared to work in science and engineering fields?

Many STEM careers require specific training and expertise. As a set of core disciplines related to a variety of fields, STEM subject proficiency is increasingly required for participation in the global economy and workforce.

- 1.5 percent of Black computer workers live in Silicon Valley.[4]
- Nationwide, only 30 percent of Black students participate in STEM Advanced Placement coursework in high school, compared with 60 percent of Asian students and 40 percent of White students.[5]
- 37 percent of Black freshmen intend to major in a science or engineering field, compared with 38 percent of all college freshmen and 49 percent of Asian college freshmen.[6]
- Black Americans earn 5 percent of all bachelor's degrees in engineering.[7]

- Black Americans account for 7 percent of the doctorates conferred in all science and engineering fields, compared with 8 percent for Asian/Pacific Islander Americans and 6 percent for Latino Americans.[8]
- 31 percent of Black engineering, engineering technology, and computer science students leave school without a credential, compared with 10 percent of White students in the same fields.
- At a rate of 16 percent, Black engineering and computer technology students are more likely to complete associate's degrees or certificates than their Asian (2 percent), White (8 percent), or Latino (6 percent) counterparts; however, at a success rate of 31 percent, these Black students are also less likely to complete a bachelor's degree program than their Asian (73 percent), White (64 percent), or Latino (52 percent) counterparts.[9]
- The majority of Black college freshmen interested in science and engineering fields intend to major in the social sciences (13 percent), a figure attributed largely to the high percentage of Black female students (16 percent) intending to major in the social or behavioral sciences.
- 39 percent of Black male freshmen intend to major in a science or engineering field, compared with 44 percent of all male college freshmen and 55 percent of Asian male college freshmen.
- More Black female college freshmen (13 percent) than Black male freshmen (8 percent) intend to major in the biological or agricultural sciences.
- More Black male college freshmen (15 percent) than Black female freshmen (3 percent) intend to major in engineering.[10]
- The rate of doctorates conferred on Black students in science and engineering increased by nearly 8 percent between 2000 and 2009.
- The majority of Black doctoral scholars are disciplined in the social sciences (7 percent); psychology

Table 8. Percentage of Black Science and Engineering (S&E) Intended and Earned Degrees

		All S&E Majors	Biological/ Agricultural Sciences	Computer Sciences	Engineering	Math/Statistics	Physical Sciences	Social/ Behavioral Sciences
All Black students	Intended	37%	11%	3%	7%	<1%	2%	13%
	bachelor's earned	7%	4.5%	4%	2%	<1%	<1%	18%
Black female students	Intended	35%	13%	1%	3%	<1%	2%	16%
	bachelor's earned	29%	5%	2%	1%	<1%	<1%	19%
Black male students	Intended	39%	8%	5%	15%	<1%	2%	9%
	bachelor's earned	33%	4%	6%	5%	<1%	<1%	16%

Source: National Science Foundation, Women, Minorities, and Persons with Disabilities in Science and Engineering, 2013. The percentage of Black students who have earned bachelor's degrees is calculated based on the numbers of total Black graduates in all fields and Black graduates in S&E fields between 1997 and 2006.

(6 percent), agricultural sciences (5 percent), and biological sciences (4 percent) are also top disciplines.[11]

◻ Black Americans make up only 3 percent of all engineering faculty in the United States.[12]

Which schools provide the greatest support for Black engineering students?

◻ The top 10 educational institutions conferring bachelor's degrees to African Americans in science and engineering fields between 2006 and 2010 were, by number of degrees:
  - Georgia State University: 2,148
  - University of South Florida (main campus): 1,937
  - University of Maryland, College Park: 1,885

Table 9. Black Doctoral Scholars in the Sciences, 2009

Field/discipline	Percentage of Black doctoral scholars
All fields	7%
Engineering	4%
Physical sciences	3%
Earth sciences	1%
Mathematics	3%
Computer sciences	4%
Biological sciences	4%
Agricultural	5%
Social sciences	7%
Psychology	6%

Source: U.S. Census Bureau, "Table 814. Doctorates Conferred by Characteristics of Recipients: 2000 and 2009," in *Statistical Abstract of the United States: 2012*, 528.

- Howard University: 1,881
- North Carolina A&T State University: 1,863
- Florida A&M University: 1,806
- Spelman College: 1,559
- University of Florida: 1,487
- Florida State University: 1,479
- University of Phoenix (online): 1,412[13]
- Four of the institutions above are HBCUs.
- Between 2006 and 2010, 8 of the top 12 alma maters of Black students who eventually earned doctoral degrees in science and engineering fields were HBCUs:
  - 112 doctoral recipients graduated from Howard University.
  - 80 doctoral recipients graduated from Spelman College.
  - 73 doctoral recipients graduated from Florida A&M University.
  - 66 doctoral recipients graduated from Xavier University of Louisiana.

- 64 doctoral recipients graduated from Hampton University.
- 61 doctoral recipients graduated from Morehouse College and 61 from Morgan State University.
- 49 doctoral recipients graduated from North Carolina A&T State University.
- 46 doctoral recipients graduated from Southern University and A&M College and 46 from the University of Maryland, Baltimore County.
- 40 doctoral recipients graduated from Tuskegee University.
- 38 doctoral recipients graduated from University of Maryland, College Park.[14]

▫ The following institutions provided the greatest number of engineering scholarships to African American students, 2011–12:
  - Prairie View A&M University: 41
  - Louisiana State University: 36
  - Drexel University: 29
  - Georgia Institute of Technology: 29

▫ The following institutions conferred the greatest number of bachelor's degrees in engineering on African American students in 2011:
  - North Carolina A&T State University: 145
  - Georgia Institute of Technology: 111
  - Morgan State University: 71
  - Prairie View A&M University: 66[15]

In what sectors are the majority of Black scientists and engineers employed?

▫ Black scientists and engineers make up 4 percent of the total employed population in science and engineering occupations.

▫ Black scientists make up 4 percent of the total number of scientists working in science-related occupations (biological/life science, computer and information science, mathematical science, physical science, psychology, and social science).

- 61 percent of Black scientists are employed as computer and information scientists; however, Black computer and information scientists represent just 5 percent of all scientists employed in that occupation.
- 7 percent of Black scientists are employed as mathematical scientists.
- 9 percent of Black scientists are employed as social scientists; however, Black social scientists represent just 5 percent of all those employed in social science–related occupations.
- Black scientists and engineers with a master's degree make up 6 percent of the total employed population with a master's degree working in science and engineering–related occupations.
- Black scientists and engineers with a doctorate make up 4 percent of the total employed population with a doctorate working in science and engineering occupations.[16]
- Black scientists represent 9 percent of all scientists employed by the federal government.
- The rate at which the federal government hired Black scientists increased by 2.3 percent between 2006 and 2009.
- Black engineers make up approximately 6 percent of all engineers employed by the federal government.

The rate at which the federal government hired Black engineers increased by 27 percent between 2006 and 2009.[17]

What do Black doctoral recipients do with their degrees in the sciences and engineering?
- 43 percent of Black doctoral recipients go on to conduct postdoctoral study.
- 21 percent of Black doctoral recipients find academic employment.

□ 10 percent of Black doctoral recipients find employment in relevant industries.[18]

Are professional Black scientists well supported?

□ Black scientists submit 1.4 percent of the research grant proposals to the National Institutes of Health.
□ African American scientists are 13 percent less likely than White scientists to receive NIH investigator-initiated research funding.[19]

What does the digital divide look like for Black families today?

□ In 2000, only 35 percent of Black adults used the Internet. As of 2011, more than 70 percent of Black adults use the Internet. By comparison, 80 percent of White adults use the Internet.
□ Today, the majority of Black adults search online (91 percent) and use e-mail (88 percent).
□ 49 percent of Black adults access the Internet through a high-speed broadband service, compared with 66 percent of White adults and 51 percent of Latino adults.[20]
□ Black adults (74 percent) are about as likely as White adults (73 percent) to buy products online.
□ Black adults are more likely to use social networking sites (70 percent) and bank online (67 percent), compared with their White counterparts (63 percent and 62 percent, respectively).
□ Black adults are about as likely (62 percent) as their White (63 percent) and Latino (62 percent) counterparts to go online wirelessly.
□ Over twice as many Black adults (38 percent) as White adults (17 percent) access the Internet primarily using a cell phone.
□ Black adults are more likely than White adults to play a game (43 percent and 31 percent, respectively), post a photo or video online (30 percent and 18 percent), and send or receive text messages (76 percent and 70 percent).[21]

BLACK AMERICANS, GAMING, AND TECHNOLOGICAL INNOVATION

What are some trends among African Americans in the world of video games?

- 2 percent of game developers in the United States are Black.[22]
- Black youth have a longer exposure—approximately 30 more minutes each day—to video games across all platforms than their White counterparts.[23]
- Approximately 10 percent of characters in the virtual gaming domain are identifiably Black; the majority of these characters are gangsters, street people, and images of real-life athletes.[24]

African American characters are underrepresented in video games by approximately 13 percent.[25]

What are some trends among Black youth in cell phone and new media use?

- Black youth spend an hour and 28 minutes per day using their phones for music, games, and videos more than their White and Latino counterparts.
- A greater proportion of Black youth (59 percent) spend some part of their day using a cell phone to listen to music, play games, or watch television than their White (33 percent) or Latino (53 percent) counterparts.
- Black youth spend more time—over 50 additional minutes per day—texting than their White and Latino counterparts.[26]
- According to a Harvard University study of names and Internet searches, online searches for names ethnically associated with Black Americans are more likely to bring up advertisements related to criminal activity—a circumstance that arguably exposes unconscious societal biases.

- A typical Black American name* entered in an online search is 25 percent more likely than a typical White American name to produce results that prompt the user to search for a criminal conviction history associated with that name.[27]

Are African Americans involved in the field of robotics?

Robotics is an emerging field that showcases talent for innovation and applied physics. As they are in other areas of science and technology, African Americans are underrepresented in robotics. However, significant investments have been made to increase their participation and that of other people of color in the field.

- $18.5 million: The amount of a grant to Spelman College and Morehouse College to develop robotic devices that "interface with the human nervous system."[28]
- 15: the number of educational institutions, including seven research institutions and eight HBCUs, that are collaborating to encourage African Americans to pursue robotics research.[29]
- According to NASA, there are 65 universities that offer large robotics programs nationwide. Of these programs, only one—Florida A&M University's—is an HBCU.[30]

How diverse are the companies that drive technology in the United States?

- According to the *San Jose Mercury News*, the combined workforce of 10 of Silicon Valley's largest companies grew by 16 percent between 1999 and 2005; however, during that period, the small population of Black workers at these companies dropped by 16 percent.[31]

---

*The Harvard scholars conducting the study used names racially and ethnically identifiable as African American, such as "Trevon Jones," "DeShawn," "Latanya," or "Latisha." They also tested names typically perceived as White American, such as Kristen, Jill, or Dustin (Latanya Sweeney, "Discrimination in Online Ad Delivery," *Queue* 11, no. 3 [2013]).

□ An examination of diversity at five large technology companies in Silicon Valley revealed an underrepresentation of Black Americans:

Table 10. Percent of Black Americans in Silicon Valley Tech Companies

	Cisco	Dell	eBay	Ingram Micro	Intel
Officer/manager	2%	2%	4%	0%	0%
Mid-level officer/manager	2%	6%	2%	6%	2%
Professional	3%	6%	2%	4%	3%
Technician	8.5%	11%	5%	12%	7%
Sales worker	3%	8%	10%	4%	2%
Administration/other	6%	25%	9%	17%	4%

Source: "How Diverse Is Silicon Valley?" CNN Money, 2013, money.cnn.com/interactive/technology/tech-diversity-data/?iid=EL.

CODA

African Americans by Gender

B lack female identity has been historically constructed by myths and stereotypes—from the
hypersexual "Jezebel" to the vindictive "Sapphire" caricature on *Amos and Andy*. These caricatures of Black
femininity allow for the construction of public memes
that are sometimes inconsistent with data. Below is a
collection of data on dominant public perceptions that
describe or influence the construction of Black female
identity.

*Black women are uncomfortable in their own skin;
that's why they spend so much on hair weaves and
other products that give them a less African appearance. After all, one woman writing on the* **Huffington
Post** *"confessed" to having spent more than $25,000
on hair weaves and extensions because of her racial
identity crisis.*[1]

What do the numbers say?

- Estimates on the total dollars spent by Black
  women on hair care exceed $500 billion.[2]
- Black households spend more than $600 mil-
  lion on hair care products, including more than
  $200 million on wigs and hairpieces (there was
  a 20 percent decline in Black spending on wigs
  between 2010 and 2011).[3]
- The number of natural hair shows for African
  Americans is increasing. For nearly two decades, natural stylist and entrepreneur Taliah
  Waajid has sponsored a Natural Hair Health and
  Beauty Show; as the largest natural hair show in
  the country, it has attracted as many as 35,000
  attendees.[4]
- One 2011 study found that 36 percent of Black
  women *do not* use chemical straightening products to alter the texture of their hair—an increase from 26 percent in 2010. This study also

found that sales of chemical relaxer kits dropped by 17 percent between 2006 and 2011.[5]

☐ Black teenage girls show high levels of self-esteem and display a higher satisfaction with their physical appearance than do their Latina and White counterparts. A recent national study suggested that Black girls were "protected" against low self-esteem by their resistance to external factors such as others' disapproval and competition from peers.[6]

Is the popular perception of Black female discomfort on point?

No. Black females—for the most part—love themselves, weave or no weave. However, the politics associated with the texture and styling of Black women's hair are alive and well. It is true that Black women on average spend a disproportionately high share of their income on hair care products, and there is a lingering concern about whether wearing natural hair might be seen as a political statement and affect advancement in the workplace. However, Black women's disproportionate spending on hair products has historically been informed by everything from the Europeanized standards of beauty in America to the absence of appropriate products for the many different types and textures of "Black" hair, which makes it necessary for women to test multiple products in order to find what works best on their own—an expensive process.

Black women have children to exploit welfare benefits. It may no longer be politically correct (if it ever was) to use the Ronald Reagan–coined term "welfare queen," but the sentiment lingers in conservative public discourses—for example, in the notorious label right-wingers gave President Obama, "food stamp president," and the governmental response (or lack thereof) to poverty among Black women and other women of color. According to legal scholar Kaaryn Gustafson, "This image of the lazy African-American woman who refuses to get a job and keeps having kids is pretty enduring. It's always been a good way to distract the pub-

lic from any meaningful conversations about poverty and inequality."[7]

What do the numbers say?

- ❑ Most recipients of public assistance are not Black; however, African Americans, who now account for less than one-third of Temporary Assistance for Needy Families (TANF) recipients, are still overrepresented among those receiving such assistance. The percentage of Black households receiving TANF declined from 39 to 33 percent between 2000 and 2009.[8]
- ❑ The unemployment rate for African American women jumped from 7 percent in February 2007 to 13 percent in February 2010.
- ❑ The unemployment rate for African American female heads of household was 15 percent in 2010. These women bore the sole or primary financial responsibility for their families.[9]
- ❑ 46 percent of Black women report feeling that they have all of the education and skills they need in order to be competitive in the current job market, compared with 55 percent of White women.
- ❑ 46 percent of Black women think that the economic system is stacked against Black people, compared with 27 percent of White women who agree the system is stacked against Black people.[10]

Is the popular perception on point?

No. In 2012, it was publicly revealed that Reagan's "welfare queen" label was worse than pejorative, it was a fabrication.[11] Not only was this mythical woman a figment of his political imagination, but "her" story was a grotesque exploitation of public fears about entitlements and loss. Receiving public assistance is about poverty, not about laziness. There are certainly instances of individuals who abuse the public assistance system, but the stigma associated with being Black, female, and receiving public assistance has reinforced what sociologist Daniel Patrick Moynihan imagined in 1965 as a "tangle of pathology"[12] that has since unfairly stigmatized those Black women and their families who live in poverty.

Black girls are fine! It's the Black boys who need our attention in schools, the economy, and the criminal justice system.

What do the numbers say?

- The suspension rate for Black girls is 11 percent, compared with 6 percent of Native American girls, 4 percent of Latinas, and 3 percent of White girls.[13]
- Between the fourth quarter of 2007 and the fourth quarter of 2012, the unemployment rate for Black girls ages 16 to 19 increased dramatically—from 27 percent to 40 percent.[14]
- Overall, between 2000 and 2010, the rate of youth cases involving detention has declined by about one-third for cases of ungovernability, runaways, and curfew violations, offenses that are often associated with girls. However, racial disparities have remained constant. Between 1999 and 2010, the proportion of Black girls in residential placement has remained relatively unchanged—between 35 percent and 36 percent of girls in residential custody are Black.[15]
- Among female youth, Black girls have the highest case rate of offenses against persons (assault, robbery, rape, etc.), 18.9—14 times the rate for Asian females (1.3), more than twice the rate for Native American females (8.2), and more than triple the rate for White females (5.2).[16]
- Black girls are assigned by the justice system to residential placement at a rate of 214 per 100,000 (21.4 percent), compared with a rate of 8.3 percent and 6.8 percent for Latina and White girls, respectively.[17]

Is the popular perception on point?

No. Black girls are more likely to experience negative school, economic, and criminal justice outcomes—when they are compared with other girls. The boys-versus-girls framework obscures the situation of girls because overall they have a lower delinquency rate than their male counterparts. The racial disparities associated with the rate of growth among suspension cases is greater among girls than among boys, meaning that the zero tolerance policies that push out students through suspension and expulsion disproportionately affects Black girls. The comparison between Black girls and Black boys is an inappropriate one and serves only to distract us from what should be our true goal—addressing the racial disparities that affect them both.

Many Black women are fat because they want to be. Black women are overweight or obese because they are politically and aesthetically motivated to be obese, even though they thereby increase their risk of preventable chronic diseases.[18]

What do the numbers say?

- Four out of five Black women are overweight or obese.
- African American women are 70 percent more likely to be obese than White women.[19]
- 30 percent of African American women ages 18 and over are overweight but not obese, compared with 27 percent of White women.[20]
- 20 percent of Black high school girls are overweight, compared with 14 percent of White high school girls.[21]
- A study by Wake Forest University found that approximately one-third of Black women avoid exercise because of complications associated with hair care (for example, they are reluctant to overwash fragile, chemically processed hair or "sweat out" the process

that has altered the natural, curly, or coarse texture of their hair).[22]

Is the popular perception on point?

No. Who wants to be overweight or, worse, obese and have to deal with disorders that accompany such conditions? Yes, there are different standards of beauty in the Black community that does not embrace an ultra-thin ideal; however, Black women and girls are overweight for a host of reasons, including a negative relationship with food (for example, binge eating, especially of "comfort" foods); unequal access to high-quality foods (which are often more expensive than nonfattening foods); environmental factors (residing in a food desert); as well as a cultural appreciation for a curvier body. The preponderance of fast food restaurants in low-income communities also plays a role. As policy scholar Maya Rockeymoore noted, "Many African-American communities are oversaturated with fast food restaurants selling cheap foods and beverages that are high in calories and fat but of low nutritional value."[23] These reasons have little to do with a conscious decision to be overweight or obese.

Black women are fine with being single parents. They "hold it down" for the household when their male partner is not available.

What do the numbers say?

- ◻ 67 percent of Black women report that being married is important, compared with 77 percent of White women.[24]
- ◻ 28 percent of Black women are married, compared with 54 percent of White women.[25]
- ◻ 29 percent of Black females are heads of household, meaning that they are unmarried but can claim a dependent, and 21 percent of Black females live in single households with no children.[26]

- 79 percent of Black women report that having children is important, compared with 87 percent of White women.
- Only 34 percent of Black women report believing that having a child without being married is acceptable, compared with 65 percent of Black men and 60 percent of White women who report believing the same.[27]

Is the popular perception on point?

No. Although Black women will perform their duties as primary caregivers for children, they are less likely than either Black men or White women to think that it is okay to be a single parent.

OTHER FACTS ABOUT BLACK WOMEN AND GIRLS

Demographics

- 91 percent of Black females living in the United States were born in the United States.[28]
- 40 percent of foreign-born Black females in the United States entered the country in 2000 or later.[29]
- 27 percent of Black females are under the age of 18.
- 69 percent of Black females are age 21 or older.
- 10 percent of Black females are age 65 or older.[30]

Geography/Location

- 56 percent of Black females live in the South.
- 18 percent of Black females live in the Northeast.
- 17 percent of Black females live in the Midwest.
- 9 percent of Black females live in the West.[31]

Household and Marital Status

- 33 percent of families headed by Black women live in a home they own, compared with 60 percent of families headed by White women.[32]
- 46 percent of Black women have never been married, compared with 23 percent of White women.

- 13 percent of Black women are divorced, compared with just under 12 percent of White women.
- Nearly 5 percent of Black women are separated from their husbands or partners.[33]

Family and Relationships

- 76 percent of Black women say that being in a good romantic relationship is important.
- 98 percent of Black women say that being close with their family is important.
- 36 percent of Black women report that they have helped a friend or family member with child care on a regular basis, compared with 24 percent of White women who report the same.
- 49 percent of Black women report that they have helped an elderly relative or family member on a regular basis.[34]

Race and Relationships

- 76 percent of Black women report that all, most, or some of their friends are of a different race than they are; 77 percent of White women report the same.
- Black women (50 percent) are more likely to report having dated someone of a different race than are White women (40 percent) but less likely than Black men (68 percent).[35]

Opinions on LGBT Relationships

- 34 percent of Black women say that a romantic relationship between two women is acceptable.
- 30 percent of Black women say that a romantic relationships between two men is acceptable.
- 33 percent of Black women say that marriage between two people of the same sex is acceptable.
- 57 percent of Black women report having a family member or close friend who is gay or lesbian.[36]

Opinions on Black life

- 51 percent of Black women report being satisfied

with their life as a whole; a similar proportion of White women (50 percent) report the same.

- 10 percent of Black women report that the single most important problem they face is their career, compared with 4 percent of White women who report the same.
- 95 percent of Black women report that being respected by others is important, compared with 98 percent of White women who report the same.[37]

73 percent of Black women feel that, all things considered, it is a good time to be a Black woman in America, as compared with 69 percent of Black men and 71 percent of White men who feel it is a good time to be a Black woman in America.[38]

- A slightly greater proportion of Black women (25 percent) than White women (20 percent) report feeling that they are often treated with less respect than other people.
- 21 percent of Black women report that they receive poorer service than other people at restaurants or stores, compared with 12 percent of White women who report the same.
- 21 percent of Black women report that people often ignore or overlook them. Among those who report being ignored or overlooked, 39 percent think that it is mainly because of their race and 7 percent believe that it is because of both their race and gender.
- 86 percent of Black women believe that racism is a problem in today's society, compared with 77 percent of White women who believe the same.
- 80 percent of Black women believe that sexism is a problem in today's society, as do 78 percent of White women.[39]

Education

- There are two Black colleges with an exclusively

female student population: Spelman College and Bennett College.[40]

85 percent of Black women today have earned a high school diploma or a higher degree, compared with just 33 percent in 1970.[41]

- 21 percent of Black women today have earned a bachelor's or higher degree, compared with just 5 percent in 1970.[42]

Jobs, business, and money

- Black women make 62 cents for every dollar earned by their White male counterparts.[43]
- 1 percent of female executives/senior-level officials and managers in the private sector are Black.
- 3 percent of female first/mid-level officials and managers in the private sector are Black.
- 5 percent of female professionals in the private sector are Black.
- 8 percent of female sales workers in the private sector are Black.
- 13 percent of female office and clerical workers in the private sector are Black.
- 6 percent of female laborers in the private sector are Black.
- 14 percent of female service workers in the private sector are Black.[44]
- Black women have started businesses at three to five times the rate of other Americans who start businesses. The number of businesses owned by African American women grew by nearly 67 percent between 2002 and 2007, despite the financial obstacles.[45]
- An equal proportion of Black and White women (33 percent) report that money is the most important problem in their life.

- 60 percent of Black women feel that being wealthy is important, as compared with 46 percent of White women.
- 39 percent of Black women worry about losing their job.
- 73 percent of Black women worry about not having enough money to pay their bills.
- 23 percent of Black women report being laid off themselves or having another family member in their household who has been laid off.
- 60 percent of Black women report having loaned or given money to family or friends to help with expenses.
- 34 percent of Black women report having borrowed or received money from family or friends to help with expenses.
- Black women (27 percent) are more than twice as likely to report having trouble paying their rent or mortgage than are White women (12 percent).
- 20 percent of Black women reported an increase in their credit debt in 2011, compared with 23 percent of White women.[46]

Health

- Black women are 1.4 times more likely to die from liver and intrahepatic bile duct (IBD) cancer than are White women.[47]
- Black women's death rate from heart disease: 195.4 per 100,000.[48]
- Between 2007 and 2010, 44 percent of Black women ages 20 and over were reported to have high blood pressure, compared with 28 percent of White women.[49]
- Between 2007 and 2010, the proportion of African American women reported with high cholesterol (26 percent) was slightly lower than that of White women (27 percent).[50]
- The rate of abortions among Black women ages

15 to 44 has declined significantly over recent decades—from 64 percent in 1990 to 48 percent in 2007. Black women are still more likely than their White counterparts to have an abortion.[51]

Justice

- Black women make up approximately 3 percent of full-time, sworn personnel in local police departments nationwide.[52]
- 45 percent of women who report worrying about being the victim of a violent crime are Black.[53]
- Between 1985 and 2009, the case rate for public order offenses (graffiti, disorderly conduct, etc.) for Black females increased by 250 percent, the largest relative increase among all female offenders in this category.[54]
- Black females ages 21 to 25 account for 14 percent of all individuals sentenced in U.S. district courts under the U.S. Sentencing Commission guidelines, compared with 13 percent for White females and 17 percent for Latina females in this age category.
- Black females ages 26 to 30 account for 20 percent of all individuals sentenced in U.S. district courts under the U.S. Sentencing Commission guidelines, compared with 15 percent for White females and 19 percent for Latina females in this age category.[55]
- Black girls represent the fastest-growing segment of the juvenile justice population in secure confinement.[56]

Black females are imprisoned at a rate almost three times that of their white counterparts.[57]

- 15 percent of Black female state prisoners report inmate-on-inmate sexual victimization, compared with 13.7 percent of all female inmates and 5 percent of the total population of inmates.

- 4 percent of Black female state prisoners report staff sexual misconduct, comparable to the reports of all inmates and slightly lower than the proportion of male inmates who experience this type of misconduct (5 percent).[58]
- Between 2000 and 2009, the rate of incarceration for all Black women declined by 31 percent.[59]

The war on drugs

- Between 1996 and 2006, the majority of the women sentenced for drug offenses involving crack cocaine were Black.
- Between 1986 and 1991, the incarceration rate for Black women increased by 828 percent. Between 1990 and 1996, the rate of increase for Black women was 72 percent.[60]
- Between 1997 and 2009, there was a 27 percent decline in drug offense case rates for Black female youth, compared with a 23 percent increase for White and Native American girls.[61]

Media, scholarship, and public consciousness have distorted the Black male identity for centuries. Mythologized and stereotyped, Black men have always had to confront and seek to modify their image in the public sphere. Below is a collection of the dominant public perceptions that describe or influence the construction of Black male identity.

There are more Black men in prison than in college.

What do the numbers say?

- There are 600,000 more Black men in college than there are in prison.
- There was a 109 percent increase in Black male college enrollment between 2001 and 2011.[1]
- There are more than 550,000 inmates in state and federal prison, making Black men 36 percent of all males incarcerated in federal and state prisons. More than 3 percent of all Black males and nearly 7 percent of Black males ages 25 to 39 were incarcerated in 2011.[2]
- More than 1 million Black males were enrolled in college in 2009, and over 1.3 million Black (including Black multiracial) males ages 18 and over earned a bachelor's degree in 2010.[3]

Is the popular perception on point?

According to education scholar Ivory Toldson, it may never have been on point. Though Black male endangerment was (and remains) a popular theme in the public discourse on academic underperformance and violence victimization, statistics make clear that there are not more Black men in prison than there are in college. Although Black males do experience an incredibly disproportionate, unjust incarceration rate—more than nine times the rate of White males—it is time for our narrative to better reflect the data.

Black men can't find employment, especially after the recession—and if they have a criminal conviction history, forget it.

What do the numbers say?

- Nationwide, the unemployment rate for all Black males over the age of 16 was 5 percent in 2007—a figure that doubled in 2009 and now stands at nearly 14 percent.[4]
- 7 percent of Black men report that the single most important problem they face is their career.
- 42 percent: the proportion of Black men who think that the economic system is stacked against Black people, compared with 22 percent of White men who report feeling the same.
- 35 percent of Black men report being laid off themselves or having another family member in their household who has been laid off, compared with 17 percent of White men who report the same situation.
- More Black women (42 percent) than Black men (28 percent) think it's a bad time to be a Black man in America.[5]
- One study found that White male job applicants *with* a criminal conviction history received more favorable treatment from potential employers (17 percent) than Black male job applicants *without* a criminal conviction history (14 percent).[6]

Is the popular perception on point?

It is true that Black men are facing a difficult recovery from the recession that began in 2007. It is an oversimplification of the problem to suggest that they cannot find work, but in general Black men are experiencing disproportionate unemployment. The data on criminal conviction history and employment suggest that Black men (and women) have a tougher time finding employment if they have a criminal record.

*Most Black males want to be ballplayers and hip-hop artists. Even Michelle Obama has said that Black youth are preoccupied with being "ballers and rappers."**

What do the numbers say?

- 83 percent of Black youth say that they aspire to go to college.[7]
- 53 percent of Black high school males say they hope for a career in sports or entertainment, compared with 28 percent of White high school males.[8]
- 90 percent of Black males in community colleges report that their primary goals are being financially well off and helping others.[9]

Is the popular perception on point?

Black males are significantly more likely to report an interest in a sports or entertainment career than are their White counterparts; however, this limited scope of aspiration is often attributed to exposure. For some Black males, the desire to attend college is coupled with their desire to play professional sports. An exploratory study in Los Angeles found that youth from urban, low-income environments showed interest in careers that are associated with high levels of compensation, but that their career interests were also influenced by their work history.[10] Educational history and performance may also prevent Black males from realizing their plans to attend college. Ultimately, there is nothing wrong with dreaming of a life free of financial worry; however, more work must be done to educate Black males, and others, about the diversity of

---

*In 2013, Michelle Obama's commencement speech at Bowie State University included a segment in which she claimed that too many Black youth were distracted by the fantasy of being entertainers or professional ballplayers. In the speech, she stated, "Today, instead of walking miles every day to school, they're sitting on couches for hours, playing video games, watching TV. Instead of dreaming of being a teacher or a lawyer or a business leader, they're fantasizing about being a baller or a rapper" ("Michelle Obama Says Too Many Black Kids Are Trying to Be 'Ballers' and Rappers," Your Black World, May 2013, www.yourblackworld.net/2013/05/black-news/michelle-obama-says-too-many-black-kids-are-trying-to-be-ballers-and-rappers/).

professions that can provide a foundation for a higher quality of life.

OTHER FACTS ABOUT BLACK MEN AND BOYS

Demographics

- 91 percent of Black males living in the United States were born in the United States.[11]
- 44 percent of foreign-born Black males in the United States entered the country in 2000 or later.[12]
- 31 percent of Black males are under the age of 18.
- 64 percent of Black males are age 21 or older.
- 7 percent of Black males are age 65 or older.[13]

Geography/location

- 56 percent of Black males live in the South.
- 17 percent of Black males live in the Northeast.
- 17 percent of Black males live in the Midwest.
- 10 percent of Black males live in the West.[14]

Household and marital status

- 74 percent of Black men say that being married is important, compared with 79 percent of White men.[15]
- 35 percent of Black adult men are married, compared with 56 percent of White men.
- 49 percent of Black men have never been married, compared with 30 percent of White men.
- 10 percent of Black men are divorced, the same percentage as White men.[16]
- 6 percent of Black males are heads of household.
- 17 percent of Black males live in single households without children.[17]
- 44 percent of families headed by Black men live in homes they own, compared with 69 percent of White families headed by White men.
- 56 percent of families headed by Black men live in homes they rent, compared with only 31 percent of White families headed by White men.[18]

Family and relationships

- 82 percent of Black men say that having children is important.
- 89 percent of Black men say that being in a good romantic relationship is important.
- 97 percent of Black men say that being close to their family is important.
- 40 percent of Black men report that they have helped a friend or family member with child care on a regular basis, compared with 17 percent of White men who report the same.
- 48 percent of Black men report that they have helped an elderly relative or family member on a regular basis, compared with 38 percent of White men who report the same.
- 84 percent of Black men report that all, most, or some of their friends are of a different race than they are, compared with 78 percent of White men who report the same.[19]
- Black men (68 percent) are more likely to report having dated someone of a different race than are White men (51 percent) or Black women (50 percent).

Opinion on LGBT relationships

- 44 percent of Black men say that a romantic relationship between two women is acceptable.
- 34 percent of Black men say that a romantic relationship between two men is acceptable.
- 48 percent of Black men report having a family member or close friend who is gay or lesbian.[20]

Opinion on Black life

- 46 percent of Black men report being satisfied with their life as a whole, compared with 48 percent of White men who report the same.[21]

69 percent of Black men think it's a good time to be a Black man in America.[22]

- 61 percent of Black men report that having enough free time to do the things they want to do is important.
- 93 percent of Black and White men report that being respected by others is important.
- A greater proportion of Black men (26 percent) than White men (15 percent) report feeling that they are often treated with less respect than other people.
- Black men (32 percent) are more than twice as likely as White men (13 percent) to report that people often ignore or overlook them. Among those Black men who report being ignored or overlooked, 47 percent think that it is mainly because of their race and 7 percent believe that it is because of both their race and gender.
- 88 percent of Black men believe that racism is a problem in today's society.
- 78 percent of Black men believe that sexism is a problem in today's society, compared with just over half (58 percent) of White men who believe the same.[23]

Education

- Each decade, the number and percentage of Black men who earn a college degree increases. In 2010, 15.8 percent of Black males over age 25 completed college, an increase from 13.2 percent in 2000. In 1990, the proportion of Black males over age 25 who had completed college was just 11 percent.[24]
- Black males make up less than 2 percent of students taking the Graduate Record Examination, a requirement for admission to most graduate schools, and those who do take the test score significantly lower than White students on the exam. The mean verbal score for Black males is 404, compared with 516 for White males, and the mean quantitative score for Black males is 456, compared with 609 for White males.[25]

Education and money

- 16 percent of Black men believe that coming from money and knowing the right people matters more than education for getting ahead in life today, compared with 27 percent of White men who believe the same.

◻ Black men (55 percent) are less likely than White men (66 percent) to report feeling that they have all of the education and skills they need in order to be competitive in the current job market.[26]

Jobs, business, and money

◻ About 2 percent of male executives/senior-level officials and managers in the private sector are Black.

◻ Nearly 4 percent of male first/mid-level officials and managers in the private sector are Black.

◻ 2 percent of male professionals in the private sector are Black.

◻ 5 percent of male technicians and sales workers in the private sector are Black.

◻ 4 percent of male office and clerical workers in the private sector are Black.

◻ 8 percent of male craft workers in the private sector are Black.

◻ 12 percent of male operatives and laborers in the private sector are Black.

◻ 9 percent of male service workers in the private sector are Black.[27]

◻ Black men make up 3 percent of the scientists and engineers working in science or engineering occupations.[28]

◻ 30 percent of Black men report that money is the most important problem in their lives.

◻ 60 percent of Black men feel that being wealthy is important.[29]

40 percent of Black men worry about losing their job.[30]

◻ 66 percent of Black men worry about not having enough money to pay their bills.

◻ 64 percent of Black men report having loaned

or given money to family or friends to help with expenses.

- 32 percent of Black men report having borrowed or been given money from family or friends to help with expenses.
- Black men (33 percent) are three times more likely to report having trouble paying their rent or mortgage than White men (11 percent).
- Twice as many Black men (32 percent) as White men (16 percent) report facing difficulty when getting a home loan, car loan, education loan, or other type of personal credit.
- 20 percent of Black men reported an increase in their credit debt in 2011.[31]

Health

- 70 percent of Black men ages 20 and over are overweight or obese.[32]
- 37 percent of African American males age 18 and over are overweight but not obese, compared with 41 percent of White males.[33]
- Between 2007 and 2010, 23 percent of Black boys ages 6 to 11 were overweight, compared with 19 percent of White boys.[34]
- 13 percent of Black high school boys are overweight, compared with 15 percent of White high school boys.
- 18 percent of Black high school boys are obese, compared with 15 percent of White high school boys.[35]
- Black men are 70 percent more likely to have liver and intrahepatic bile duct (IBD) cancer than are White men.[36]
- About 41 percent of Black men ages 20 and over have high blood pressure, compared with 31 percent of White men.[37]
- A smaller percentage of African American men (25 percent) have high cholesterol than White men (28 percent).[38]

Justice

- Black men make up 9 percent of full-time, sworn personnel in local police departments nationwide.[39]
- Between 1985 and 2009, Black male youth showed higher rates of delinquency than all other racial groups.
- Between 1985 and 2009, Black male youth were charged with person offenses (assault, robbery, rape, etc.) at a rate two to four times higher than that for White and Native American males and seven to ten times higher than that for Asian males.[40]
- Between 1985 and 2009, the case rate for public order offenses (graffiti, littering, disorderly conduct, etc.) for Black males increased by 154 percent, the largest relative increase among all male youth in this category.[41]
- Black males ages 21 to 25 account for 16 percent of all individuals sentenced in U.S. district courts under the U.S. Sentencing Commission guidelines, compared with 10 percent for White males and nearly 16 percent for Latino males in this age category.
- Black males ages 26 to 30 account for 22 percent of all individuals sentenced in U.S. district courts under the U.S. Sentencing Commission guidelines, compared with 14 percent for White males and 21 percent for Latino males in this age category.[42]
- The drug offense case rate for Black males increased in the 1990s, peaked in 1996, and then declined by 42 percent through 2009.[43]

One in 12 Black males ages 18 to 64 is incarcerated, compared with one in every 87 White males and one in 36 Latino males.[44]

- In 2010, more young (20- to 34-year-old) African American men without a high school diploma or GED were behind bars (37 percent) than were employed (26 percent).[45]
- 63 percent of Black males in state and federal prison

are age 39 or younger, compared with 52 percent of White male state and federal prisoners.[46]

- 3 percent of all Black males are in state or federal prison, compared with 1 percent of Latino males and 0.5 percent of White males.
- Black males are imprisoned at more than nine times the rate of White males.
- Black and Latino males age 65 or older are imprisoned at rates between three and five times those of White males in that age category.
- Excluding the oldest and youngest groups, Black males are imprisoned at a rate that ranges between five and seven times the rate for White males.[47]
- 3 percent of Black and Latino male prisoners report inmate-on-inmate sexual victimization, compared with 6 percent of White male prisoners.
- Approximately 7 percent of Black male inmates report staff sexual misconduct in prison, higher than that for both White (4.5 percent) and Latino (4 percent) male inmates.[48]

My hope is that the statistics in this book inspire further investigations and explorations into the lives and experiences of Black Americans. It is important to remember that data presented in this fashion—however helpful—are limited by the questions *that have already been asked*. In other words, what we know from this collection of statistics is directly related to the questions researchers have posed—what they wanted to know and how they felt it was best to construct the inquiry and their findings. But this collection might also prompt us to ponder: What has not been asked? What else do we want to know about these and other aspects of the Black experience?

Although I carefully considered the inclusion of the particular statistics contained in this book, there are a number of limitations associated with interpreting them. First, many data sources present information for people of color as a whole, rather than by racial and ethnic subdivisions, drawing comparisons only in relation to their White counterparts. There are also many surveys and other data sets that include the participation of only Black and White populations, limiting the extent to which we might be able to examine trends specific to Black Americans in relation to other non-White populations. Second, the data presented in this book include statistics from sources that asked individuals to self-identify as Black Americans. These data are subject to the common limitations associated with using self-reported data in association with race and ethnicity, where the data presented are only as reliable as the source's own knowledge of his or her heritage. These data were collected from a variety of sources and may be subject to sampling variability, variant methodology and data collection methods, and other possible causes of error.

Finally, although quantitative data are powerful tools for analysis, I would caution against interpreting the condition of African Americans solely through a quantitative lens. The reader should combine this book with other documents, media, and studies exploring the lived experiences of Black Americans in order to understand the dynamic nature and fuller narrative of African American lives. Qualitative and other participatory research methods play a critical role in the telling of these stories, in the formation of responses to racial inequality, and in the election of promising approaches to achieve racial justice and a more equitable society.

African American Policy Forum
   aapf.org

A. Philip Randolph Institute
   www.apri.org

Association of Black Psychologists
   www.abpsi.org

Black Aids Institute
   www.blackaids.org

Black Worker Center, Center for Labor Research and
   Education, University of California at Berkeley
   laborcenter.berkeley.edu/blackworkers/resources
   .shtml

Center for Social Inclusion
   www.centerforsocialinclusion.org

Economic Policy Institute
   www.epi.org

Equal Justice Society
   www.equaljusticesociety.org

Green for All
   greenforall.org

Joint Center for Political and Economic Studies
   www.jointcenter.org

The Institute for Diversity and Ethics in Sport
   www.tidesport.org

NAACP (National Association for the Advancement of
   Colored People)
   www.naacp.org

National Association of Black Social Workers
   www.nabsw.org

National Black Women's Justice Institute
   blackwomensjustice.org

National Coalition on Black Civic Participation
   ncbcp.org

National Council of Negro Women
www.ncnw.org

National Council on Crime and Delinquency
www.nccdglobal.org

National Equity Project
nationalequityproject.org

National Urban League
nul.iamempowered.com

National Society of Black Engineers
www.nsbe.org

The Praxis Project
www.thepraxisproject.org

Schomburg Center for Research in Black Culture
www.nypl.org/locations/schomburg

The Sentencing Project
www.sentencingproject.org

Unity Fellowship Church Movement
www.unityfellowshipchurch.org

W. Haywood Burns Institute
www.burnsinstitute.org

PREFACE

1. Ian Haney Lopez, "The Social Construction of Race," *Harvard Law Review* 29, no. 1 (1994), faculty.oxy.edu/ron/msi/05/texts/Haney Lopez-SocialConstructionOfRace.pdf.

2. W.E.B. Du Bois, *The Souls of Black Folk* (1903; New York: Dover, 1994).

INTRODUCTION: Numbers Never Speak for Themselves by Khalil Gibran Muhammad

1. The reference to Big Data is to an earlier period when demographics (population statistics) exploded during the second industrial revolution, just as there is now an explosion of quantitative information driven by information technology as explained in Victor Mayer Schonberger and Kenneth Cukier, *Big Data: A Revolution That Will Transform How We Live, Work, and Think* (Boston, MA: Houghton Mifflin Harcourt, 2013).

2. W.E.B. Du Bois, *Dusk of Dawn: An Essay Towards an Autobiography of Race Concept* (New York: Harcourt, Brace & World, 1940), 58.

3. Marcus Anthony Hunter, *Black Citymakers: How the Philadelphia Negro Changed Urban America* (New York: Oxford University Press, 2013).

4. "Civil rights" refers to the Reconstruction amendments (Thirteenth, Fourteenth, and Fifteenth), abolishing slavery, establishing citizenship and equal protection rights, and establishing the right to vote for Black men.

5. "Review of *The Philadelphia Negro*, by W.E.B. Du Bois," *American Historical Review* 6, no. 1 (1900): 162–64.

6. "Book Notes," *Political Science Quarterly* 17, no. 3 (1902): 547.

7. Carl Kelsey, "Review of *The Souls of Black Folk*, by W.E.B. Du Bois," *Annals of the American Academy of Political and Social Science* 22 (July 1903): 230–32.

8. Khalil Gibran Muhammad, *The Condemnation of Blackness: Race, Crime, and the Making of Modern Urban America* (Cambridge, MA: Harvard University Press, 2010).

THE BASICS: The Demographics of Black America

1. U.S. Census Bureau, "United States—Race and Hispanic Origin: 1790 to 1990," 2002, www.census.gov/population/www /documentation/twps0056/tab01.pdf.

2. Barrett A. Lee, John Iceland, and Gregory Sharp, *Racial and Ethnic Diversity Goes Local: Charting Change in American Communities Over Three Decades* (Providence, RI: U.S. 2010 Project, 2012), www.s4.brown.edu/us2010/Data/Report/report08292012.pdf.

3. Sonya Rastogi, Tallese D. Johnson, Elizabeth M. Hoeffel, and Malcolm P. Drewery, *The Black Population, 2010* (Washington, DC: U.S. Census Bureau, 2011), www.census.gov/prod/cen2010/briefs /c2010br-06.pdf.

4. Ibid.; Lindsay Hixson, Bradford B. Hepler, and Myoung Ouk

Kim, "The White Population, 2010," 2010 Census Brief, September 2011, www.census.gov/prod/cen2010/briefs/c2010br-05.pdf.

5. Rastogi et al., *The Black Population, 2010*.

6. Ibid.

7. U.S. Census Bureau, "Table 4. Nativity and Citizenship Status by Sex, for Black Alone and White Alone, Not Hispanic: 2011," Black Alone Population in the United States: 2011, www.census.gov/population/race /data/ppl-ba11.html.

8. U.S. Census Bureau, "Table 5. Year of Entry of the Foreign-Born Population by Sex, for Black Alone and White Alone, Not Hispanic: 2011," Black Alone Population in the United States: 2011.

9. U.S. Census Bureau, "Table 1. Population by Sex and Age, for Black Alone and White Alone, Not Hispanic, 2011," Black Alone Population in the United States: 2011.

EDUCATION

1. *San Antonio Independent School District v. Rodriguez*, 411, U.S. 1 (1973).

2. U.S. Census Bureau, "Educational Attainment by Race and Hispanic Origin, 2010," *Statistical Abstract of the United States: 2012*, www.census .gov/compendia/statab/2012/tables/12s0229.pdf.

3. U.S. Census Bureau, "Educational Attainment in the United States: 2009," 2012, www.census.gov/prod/2012pubs/p20-566.pdf.

4. National Center for Education Statistics, "Fast Facts: Degrees Conferred by Sex and Race," Institute of Education Sciences, U.S. Department of Education, 2012, nces.ed.gov/fastfacts/display.asp?id =72.

5. U.S. Census Bureau, "Table 300: Degrees Earned by Level and Race/Ethnicity: 1990 and 2009," *Statistical Abstract of the United States: 2012*, www.census.gov/compendia/statab/2012/tables/12s0299.pdf.

6. National Center for Education Statistics, "Fast Facts: Degrees Conferred by Sex and Race."

7. Michele Foster, *Black Teachers on Teaching* (New York: The New Press, 1997).

8. Jan Hughes and Oi-man Kwok, "Influence of Student–Teacher and Parent–Teacher Relationships on Lower Achieving Readers' Engagement and Achievement in the Primary Grades," *Journal of Educational Psychology* 99, no 1 (2007): 39–51.

9. Ibid.

10. Schools and Staffing Survey, "Number and Percentage of Teachers by School Type, Race/Ethnicity, and Sex, 2007–08," National Center for Education Statistics, Institute of Education Sciences, U.S. Department of Education, nces.ed.gov/surveys/sass/tables/sass0708_029_t12n.asp.

11. National Center for Education Statistics, "Table 75: Percentage of Public School Teachers of Grades 9 Through 12, by Field of Main Teaching Assignment and Selected Demographic and Educational Characteristics: 2007–08," *Digest of Education Statistics*, October 2009, nces.ed.gov /programs/digest/d11/tables/dt11_075.asp.

12. Ulrich Boser, *Teacher Diversity Matters: A State-by-State Analysis of Teachers of Color* (Washington, DC: Center for American Progress,

2011), www.americanprogress.org/issues/2011/11/pdf/teacher_diversity .pdf.

13. Jackie Zubrzycki, "Race and the Principal Pipeline," *District Dossier* blog, *Education Week*, November 12, 2012, blogs.edweek.org/edweek /District_Dossier/2012/11/race_and_the_principal_pipelin.html.

14. "The University of Phoenix Is a Pillar of African American Higher Education," *Journal of Blacks in Higher Education*, February 9, 2012, www.jbhe.com/2012/02/the-university-of-phoenix-is-a-pillar-of-african -american-higher-education/.

15. American Council on Education, "Leading Demographic Portrait of College Presidents Reveals Ongoing Challenges in Diversity, Aging," press release, March 12, 2012, www.acenet.edu/news-room/Pages/ACPS -Release-2012.aspx.

16. "University of Phoenix Is a Pillar of African American Higher Education."

17. American Council on Education, "Leading Demographic Portrait of College Presidents Reveals Ongoing Challenges in Diversity, Aging."

18. American Bar Association, "Law School Staff by Gender and Ethnicity," 2012, www.americanbar.org/content/dam/aba/administrative /legal_education_and_admissions_to_the_bar/statistics/ls_staff_gender _ethn.authcheckdam.pdf.

19. Boser, *Teacher Diversity Matters*.

20. Thomas D. Snyder and Sally A. Dilow, *Digest of Education Statistics 2011*, NCES 2012-001 (Washington, DC: National Center for Education Statistics, 2012).

21. Ibid.

22. College Board Advocacy and Policy Center, "The College Completion Agenda," November 13, 2012, completionagenda.college board.org/percentage-3-and-4-year-olds-enrolled-preschool-programs -or-kindergarten-programs.

23. Snyder and Dilow, *Digest of Education Statistics 2011*.

24. Susan Aud, Sidney Wilkinson-Flicker, Paul Kristapovich, et al., *The Condition of Education 2013*, NCES 2013-037 (Washington, DC: National Center for Education Statistics, 2011), nces.ed.gov/pubs2013/2013037.pdf; National Association of Independent Schools, "NAIS Facts at a Glance," 2013, www.nais.org/Articles/Documents/NAISFactsAtAGlance201213.pdf.

25. Stephen P. Broughman and Nancy L. Swaim, "Table 9: Percentage Distribution of Private School Students, by Racial/Ethnic Background and Selected School Characteristics: United States, 2011–12," in *Characteristics of Private Schools in the United States: Results from the 2011–12 Private School Universe Survey: First Look* (Washington, DC: National Center for Education Statistics, 2013), nces.ed.gov/pubs2013/2013316.pdf.

26. National Association of Independent Schools, "NAIS Facts at a Glance."

27. Aud et al., *Condition of Education 2013*.

28. National Center for Education Statistics, "Fast Facts: Public School Choice Programs," Institute of Education Sciences, U.S. Department of Education, nces.ed.gov/fastfacts/display.asp?id=6.

29. District of Columbia Public Schools, "Facts and Statistics: General Data About DCPS: Schools, Demographics and Performance," dc.gov /DCPS/About+DCPS/Who+We+Are/Facts+and+Statistics.

30. Terris Ross, Grace Kena, Amy Rathbun, et al., *Higher Education: Gaps*

in *Access and Persistence Study*, NCES 2012-046 (Washington, DC: National Center for Education Statistics, 2012), nces.ed.gov/pubs2012/2012046.pdf.

31. Gary Orfield, *Reviving the Goal of an Integrated Society: A 21st Century Challenge* (Los Angeles, CA: Civil Rights Project/Proyecto Derechos Civiles at UCLA, 2009), civilrightsproject.ucla.edu/research/k-12 -education/integration-and-diversity/reviving-the-goal-of-an-integrated -society-a-21st-century-challenge/orfield-reviving-the-goal-mlk-2009.pdf.

32. See Beth Harry and Janette Klingner, *Why Are So Many Minority Children in Special Education?: Understanding Race and Disability in Schools* (New York: Teachers College Press, 2005).

33. Aud et al., *Condition of Education 2011.*

34. Ibid.

35. Ibid.

36. Alliance for Excellent Education, "Prioritizing the Nation's Lowest-Performing High Schools," issue brief, April 2010, www.all4ed.org/files /PrioritizingLowestPerformingSchools.pdf.

37. Susan Aud, William Hussar, Frank Johnson, et al., "Table A-4-1. Number and Percentage Distribution of Public Charter Schools and Students, by Selected Student and School Characteristics: Selected School years, 1999–2000 Through 2009–10," in *The Condition of Education 2012*, NCES 2012-045 (Washington, DC: National Center for Education Statistics, 2012), 132, nces.ed.gov/pubs2012/2012045.pdf.

38. National Alliance for Public Charter School, "Details from the Dashboard: Charter School Race/Ethnicity Demographics," n.d., www .publiccharters.org/data/files/Publication_docs/NAPCS%202010-2011 %20Race_Ethnicity%20Details%20from%20the%20Dashboard_20120516 T152831.pdf.

39. National Center for Education Statistics, "Fast Facts: Home-schooling," Institute of Education Sciences, U.S. Department of Education, nces.ed.gov/fastfacts/display.asp?id=91.

40. Ross et al., *Higher Education.*

41. Aud et al., "Indicator 13: Concentration of Students Eligible for Free- or Reduced-Price Lunch," *Condition of Education 2012*, 42, nces.ed .gov/pubs2012/2012045.pdf.

42. Susan Aud, Angela KewalRamani, and Lauren Frohlich, "Table 35. Average Hours Spent on Homework Per Week and Percentage of 9th-Through 12th-Grade Students Who Did Homework Outside of School and Whose Parents Checked That Homework Was Done, by Frequency of Doing Homework and Race/Ethnicity: 2007," in *America's Youth: Transitions to Adulthood*, NCES 2012-026 (Washington, DC: National Center for Education Statistics, 2011), nces.ed.gov/pubs2012/2012026 /tables/table_35.asp.

43. Ross et al., *Higher Education.*

44. Aud et al., *Condition of Education 2011.*

45. Office of Civil Rights, "Discipline," in "The Transformed Civil Rights Data Collection (CRDC)," U.S. Department of Education, March 2012, www2.ed.gov/about/offices/list/ocr/docs/crdc-2012-data-summary.pdf.

46. Daniel J. Losen and Jonathan Gillespie, *Opportunities Suspended: The Disparate Impact of Disciplinary Exclusion from School* (Los Angeles, CA: Civil Rights Project/Proyecto Derechos Civiles at UCLA, 2012).

47. Office of Civil Rights, "Discipline."

48. Ibid.

49. National Center for Education Statistics, "Status Dropout Rates of 16- Through 24-Year-Olds in the Civilian, Noninstitutionalized Population, by Race/Ethnicity: Selected Years, 1990–2010," 2012, Institute of Education Sciences, U.S. Department of Education, nces.ed.gov/fastfacts/display.asp ?id=16.

50. William J. Hussar and Tabitha M. Bailey, *Projections of Education Statistics by 2019*, 38th ed., NCES 2011-017 (Washington, DC: National Center for Education Statistics, 2011), 9.

51. U.S. Census Bureau, "Table 274. Employment Status of High School Graduates and Dropouts Not Enrolled in School by Sex and Race: 1980 to 2010," in *Statistical Abstract of the United States: 2012*, www.census.gov /compendia/statab/2012/tables/12s0272.pdf.

52. Bureau of Labor Statistics, "Table 5. Duration of Employment Relationship with a Single Employer for All Jobs from Age 18 to Age 25 in 1998–2010 by Educational Attainment, Sex, Race, and Hispanic or Latino Ethnicity," March 27, 2013, economic news release, U.S. Department of Labor, www.bls.gov/news.release/nlsyth.t05.htm.

53. *The SAT© Report on College & Career Readiness: 2012* (New York: College Board, 2012), media.collegeboard.com/homeOrg/content/pdf /sat-report-college-career-readiness-2012.pdf.

54. Office of Civil Rights, "Discipline."

55. Khadijah Rentas, "Study: Achievement Gap Narrows Between Black, White Students," CNN, July 16, 2009, www.cnn.com/2009/US/07/16 /education.gaps/index.html.

56. Ross et al., *Higher Education*.

57. Ibid.

58. Ibid.

59. Ibid.

60. Ibid.

61. Office of Civil Rights, "Discipline."

62. *The 9th Annual AP© Report to the Nation* (New York: College Board, 2013), media.collegeboard.com/digitalServices/pdf/ap/rtn/9th-annual/9th -annual-ap-report-single-page.pdf.

63. *SAT© Report on College & Career Readiness: 2012*.

64. Ibid.

65. Scott Jaschik, "SAT Scores Drop Again." *Inside Higher Ed*, September 25, 2012, www.insidehighered.com/news/2012/09/25/sat-scores-are -down-and-racial-gaps-remain.

66. National Center for Education Statistics, "SAT Mean Scores of College-Bound Seniors, by Race/Ethnicity: Selected Years, 1986–87 Through 2010–11," Institute of Education Sciences, U.S. Department of Education, 2012, nces.ed.gov/fastfacts/display.asp?id=171.

67. Ross et al., *Higher Education*.

68. Ibid.

69. Ibid.

70. U.S. Census Bureau, "Educational Attainment in the United States: 2009—Detailed Tables," www.census.gov/hhes/socdemo/education/data /cps/2009/tables.html; Ross et al., *Higher Education*. Note that 54 percent

of Black male ninth graders expect to complete college or obtain a graduate or professional degree, as compared with 56 percent of White male ninth graders. Sixty-one (61) percent of Black female ninth graders and 63 percent of White female ninth graders expect to complete their college, graduate, or professional degree.

71. National Center for Education Statistics, "Table 237. Total Fall Enrollment in Degree-Granting Institutions, by Level of Student, Sex, Attendance Status, and Race/Ethnicity: Selected Years, 1976 Through 2010," *Digest of Education Statistics*, November 2011, nces.ed.gov/pro grams/digest/d11/tables/dt11_237.asp. Note that there were 3,038,800 Black students enrolled in degree-granting institutions in the fall of 2010.

72. National Center for Education Statistics, "Fast Facts: Back to School Statistics," Institute of Education Sciences, U.S. Department of Education, 2012, nces.ed.gov/fastfacts/display.asp?id=372.

73. National Center for Education Statistics, "Table 213. Enrollment Rates of 18- to 24-Year-Olds in Degree-Granting Institutions, by Level of Institution and Sex and Race/Ethnicity of Student: 1967 Through 2010," *Digest of Education Statistics*, August 2011, nces.ed.gov/programs/digest /d11/tables/dt11_213.asp. Note that NCES counts all individuals enrolled in college as "high school completers" whether or not a student who is enrolled in college actually reported high school completion.

74. "University of Phoenix Is a Pillar of African American Higher Education."

75. Center for Community College Student Engagement, "CCSSE National Student Characteristics," 2012, www.ccsse.org/survey/national2 .cfm.

76. "University of Phoenix Is a Pillar of African American Higher Education."

77. Association of American Medical Schools, "First-Time Enrollees to U.S. Medical Schools, 2005–2012," 2012, www.aamc.org/download /310122/data/2012applicantandenrollmentdatacharts.pdf.

78. Laura Castillo-Page, *Diversity in Medical Education: Facts & Figures 2012* (Washington, DC: Association of American Medical Colleges, 2012), members.aamc.org/eweb/upload/Diversity%20in%20Medical%20 Education%20Facts%20and%20Figures%202012.pdf.

79. American Bar Association, "Total Minority J.D. Enrollment, 1987–2011," 2012, www.americanbar.org/content/dam/aba/administrative/legal _education_and_admissions_to_the_bar/statistics/jd_enrollment_minority .authcheckdam.pdf.

80. Brenda Bautsch, "Reforming Remedial Education," National Conference of State Legislatures, January 2011, www.ncsl.org/documents/educ /ReformingRemedialEd.pdf.

81. National Center for Education Statistics, "Fast Facts: Degrees Conferred by Sex and Race," Institute of Education Sciences, U.S. Department of Education, nces.ed.gov/fastfacts/display.asp?id=72.

82. University of Phoenix, *2011 Academic Annual Report* (Tempe, AZ: University of Phoenix, 2012), cdn.assets-phoenix.net/content/dam/alt cloud/doc/about_uopx/academic-annual-report-2011.pdf.

83. White House Initiative on Historically Black Colleges and Universities, "HBCUs and 2020 Goal," n.d., www.ed.gov/edblogs/whhbcu/.

84. Bureau of Labor Statistics, "Table 1. Labor Force Status of 2012 High School Graduates and 2011–12 High School Dropouts 16 to 24 Years Old by School Enrollment, Educational Attainment, Sex, Race, and Hispanic or Latino Ethnicity, October 2012," U.S. Department of Labor, April 17, 2013, www.bls.gov/news.release/hsgec.t01.htm.

ENVIRONMENT

1. Bureau of Labor Statistics, "The BLS Green Jobs Definition," U.S. Department of Labor, January 25, 2013, www.bls.gov/green/overview .htm#Definition.

2. Office of the Vice President, *Staff Report: Green Jobs: A Pathway to a Strong Middle Class* (Washington, DC: Middle Class Task Force, 2009), www.whitehouse.gov/assets/documents/mctf_one_staff_report_final.pdf.

3. Algernon Austin, "Infrastructure Investments and Latino and African American Job Creation," issue brief #352, Economic Policy Institute, March 14, 2013, www.epi.org/publication/infrastructure-investments-latino -african/.

4. J. Andrew Hoerner and Nia Robinson, *A Climate of Change: African Americans, Global Warming, and a Just Climate Policy in the U.S.* (Oakland, CA: Environmental Justice and Climate Change Initiative and Redefining Progress, 2008).

5. Redefining Progress, *Energy, Economics, and the Environment: Effects on African Americans* (Washington, DC: American Association of Blacks in Energy, 2004), www.aabe.org/docs/whitepapers/docs/1-State-of -Energy-in-Black-America-Report.pdf.

6. Ibid.

7. Hoerner and Robinson, *Climate of Change*; Redefining Progress, *Energy, Economics, and the Environment*.

8. U.S. Census Bureau, "Table 5. Summary Statistics for Black- or African American–Owned Firms by State and Kind of Business: 2007," 2007 Survey of Business Owners, February 8, 2011, www2.census.gov /econ/sbo/07/final/tables/black_table5.pdf.

9. Algernon Austin, "Are Green Jobs 'Good Jobs' for African Americans?," presentation at "Not Just 'Getting By': Achieving Economic Security Among African Americans," Congressional Black Caucus Foundation, Annual Legislative Conference, September 25, 2009.

10. Hoerner and Robinson, *Climate of Change*.

11. Ibid.

12. Thomas W. Sanchez, Rich Stolz, and Jacinta S. Ma, *Moving to Equity: Addressing Inequitable Effects on Transportation Policies on Minorities* (Cambridge, MA: Civil Rights Project, Harvard University, 2003).

13. Redefining Progress, *African Americans and Climate Change: An Unequal Burden* (Washington, DC: Congressional Black Caucus Foundation, 2004).

14. Redefining Progress, *Energy, Economics, and the Environment*.

15. Susan A. Perlin, David Wong, and Ken Sexton, "Residential Proximity to Industrial Sources of Air Pollution: Interrelationships Among Race, Poverty, and Age," *Journal of the Air & Waste Management Association* 51, no. 3 (2011): 406–21.

16. Robert Bullard, "Talking Clean, Acting Dirty: How Energy Apartheid

Hurts African Americans," OpEdNews.com, February 21, 2011, www.oped news.com/articles/Talking-Clean-Acting-Dirt-by-Robert-Bullard-110218 -353.html.

17. Redefining Progress, *Energy, Economics, and the Environment*.

18. Ibid. See also "Coal Power-Plant Pollution Effects on African Americans," Appropedia, www.appropedia.org/Coal_power-plant_pollution _effects_on_African_Americans.

19. Marie Lynn Miranda, Sharon E. Edwards, Martha H. Keating, and Christopher J. Paul, "Making the Environmental Justice Grade: The Relative Burden of Air Pollution Exposure in the United States," *International Journal of Environmental Research and Public Health* 8, no. 6 (2011): 1755–771, doi:10.3390/ijerph8061755.

20. Robert D. Bullard, "Blacks and Latinos on the Frontline for Environmental Justice: Strengthening Alliances to Build Healthy and Sustainable Communities," working paper, National Black Latino Summit, n.d.

21. Benjamin J. Apelberg, Timothy J. Buckley, and Ronald H. White, "Socioeconomic and Racial Disparities in Cancer Risk from Air Toxins in Maryland," *Environmental Health Perspectives* 113, no. 6 (2005): 750–56.

22. M.C. White, R.A. Etzel, W.D. Wilcox, and C. Lloyd, "Exacerbations of Childhood Asthma and Ozone Pollution in Atlanta," *Environmental Research* 65, no. 1 (1994): 56–68.

23. Office of Minority Health, U.S. Department of Health and Human Services, "Asthma and African Americans," updated August 8, 2013. minorityhealth.hhs.gov/templates/content.aspx?ID=6170.

24. "Reducing Asthma Disparities," National Heart, Lung, and Blood Institute, n.d., www.nhlbi.nih.gov/health/prof/lung/asthma/naci/discover /disparities.htm.

25. Mark Baldassare, Dean Bonner, Sonja Petek, and Jui Shrestha, *PPIC Statewide Survey: Californians and the Environment* (San Francisco, CA: Public Policy Institute of California, 2012).

26. Melonie Heron, Donna L. Hoyert, Sherry L. Murphy, et al., "Deaths: Final Data for 2006," *National Vital Statistics Reports* 57, no. 14 (2009).

27. Madeline U. Shalowitz, Laura M. Sadowski, Rajesh Kumar, et al., "Asthma Burden in a Citywide, Diverse Sample of Elementary Schoolchildren in Chicago," *Ambulatory Pediatrics* 7, no. 4 (2007): 271–77.

28. Mo Mayrides and Richard Levy, *Ethnic Disparities in the Burden and Treatment of Asthma* (Reston, VA: Asthma and Allergy Foundation of America/National Pharmaceutical Council), aafa.org/pdfs/Disparities.PDF.

29. Baldassare et al., *Californians and the Environment*.

30. Redefining Progress, *Energy, Economics, and the Environment*.

31. Bullard, "Blacks and Latinos on the Frontline for Environmental Justice."

32. Hoerner and Robinson, *Climate of Change*.

33. Ibid.; L. Kalkstein, "Impacts of Global Warming on Human Health: Heat Stress-Related Mortality," in *Global Climate Change: Implications, Challenges, and Mitigation Measures*, ed. S. Majumdar, L. Kalkstein, B. Yarnal, et al. (Easton, PA: Pennsylvania Academy of Science, 1992).

34. U.S. Census Bureau, *Current Population Survey, 2004*, cited in Hoerner and Robinson, *Climate of Change*, 11.

35. Marie S. O'Neill, Antonella Zanobetti, and Joel Schwartz, "Disparities

by Race in Heat-Related Mentality in Four US Cities: The Role of Air Conditioning Prevalence," *Journal of Urban Health* 82, no. 2 (2005): 191–97.

36. Hoerner and Robinson, *Climate of Change.*

37. Bill Quigley, "Half New Orleans Poor Permanently Displaced: Failure or Success?," Share the World's Resources, March 5, 2008, www.stwr.org /united-states-of-america/half-new-orleans-poor-permanently-displaced -failure-or-success.html.

38. Hoerner and Robinson, *Climate of Change.*

39. Joan Brunkard, Gonza Namulanda, and Raoult Ratard, "Hurricane Katrina Deaths, Louisiana, 2005," *Disaster Medicine and Public Health Preparedness* 2, no. 4 (2008): 215–23, new.dhh.louisiana.gov/assets/docs /katrina/deceasedreports/KatrinaDeaths_082008.pdf.

40. Donna L. Brazile, "New Orleans: Next Steps on the Road to Recovery," 233–37 in *The State of Black America 2006* (Washington, DC: National Urban League, 2006).

41. Elizabeth Fussell, Narayan Sastry, and Mark VanLandingham, "Race, Socioeconomic Status, and Return Migration to New Orleans after Hurricane Katrina," *Population and Environment* 31, no. 1–3 (2010): 20–42.

42. Allison Suppan Helmuth and Jane M. Henrici, "Women in New Orleans: Race, Poverty, and Hurricane Katrina," fact sheet, Institute for Women's Policy Research, August 2010, www.iwpr.org/initiatives/katrina -the-gulf-coast.

43. Office of the Press Secretary, "Remarks by the President to the Nation on the BP Oil Spill," Oval Office, White House, June 15, 2010, www .whitehouse.gov/the-press-office/remarks-president-nation-bp-oil-spill.

44. Brentin Mock, "BP Recognizes Health Concerns in Settlement," Institute for Southern Studies, March 5, 2012, www.southernstudies.org /2012/03/bp-recognizes-health-concerns-in-settlement.html.

45. Brentin Mock, "Black Gulf Fishers Face a Murky Future," *The Root*, May 25, 2010, www.theroot.com/views/invisible-fishermen-oil-spill. According to Byron Encalade, president of the Louisiana Oystermen Association, Black oystermen began owning their own boats in the 1960s and 1970s, but they were limited by government policies regulating where they could fish and harvest. In 2010, Encalade was quoted in The Root saying, "Through the years, due to unfair policies from both the state and federal governments, we've lost about 90% of our oyster farms, and probably the same amount of boats. . . . There are probably just a few black families left with oyster boats that support the rest of what's left of the small black fisherman community here."

46. Women and Their Children (WATCH) study cited in Mark Schleifstein, "BP Deepwater Horizon Spill: Scientists Say Seafood Safe, but Health Effects Being Measured," *The Times-Picayune*, January 22, 2013, www.nola.com/news/gulf-oil-spill/index.ssf/2013/01/bp_deepwater _horizon_spill_sci.html; Jennifer Tobin-Gurley, Lori Peek, and Jennifer Loomis, "Displaced Single Mothers in the Aftermath of Hurricane Katrina: Resource Needs and Resource Allocation," *International Journal of Mass Emergencies and Disasters* 28, no. 2 (2010): 170–206, wsnet.colostate .edu/CWIS584/Lori_Peek/Data/Sites/1/1-research/publicationpdfs/tobin -gurley,peek,loomis2010.pdf.

ENTERTAINMENT AND SPORTS

1. National Association of Broadcasters, "Broadcast Television and Radio in African-American Communities," April 2013, www.nab.org/mpres /BroadcastTVandRadio-AACommunities_NAB.pdf.

2. Nielsen, "African-American Consumers: Still Vital, Still Growing," 2013, www.nielsen.com/africanamerican.

3. Dorothy Pomerantz, "Oprah Winfrey," in "The Highest-Paid TV Personalities," Forbes, August 8, 2013, www.forbes.com/pictures/mfl45eghjh /oprah-winfrey-26/.

4. National Association of Broadcasters, "Broadcast Television and Radio in African-American Communities."

5. Box Office Mojo, "People Index: By Gross," n.d., boxofficemojo .com/people/?view=Actor&sort=sumgross&p=.htm.

6. Ruthie Hawkins, "Black Millionaire: The 15 Richest Black Actors," Rolling Out, February 13, 2013, rollingout.com/entertainment/the-15 -richest-black-actors-of-all-time/.

7. "DGA Report Assesses Director Diversity in Hiring Practices for Episodic Television," press release, Directors Guild of America, September 27, 2012, www.dga.org/News/PressReleases/2012/092712-DGA-Report -Assesses-Director-Diversity-in-Hiring-Practices.aspx.

8. Screen Actors Guild, "2007 & 2008 Casting Data Reports," n.d., www .sagaftra.org/files/sag/documents/2007-2008_CastingDataReports.pdf.

9. Ibid.

10. Darnell Hunt, "WGAW 2013 TV Staffing Brief," Writers Guild of America, West, 2013, www.wga.org/uploadedFiles/who_we_are/tvstaffing brief2013.pdf.

11. Steve Pond, "Cheryl Boone Isaacs Elected Academy's First African-American President," MSN Entertainment, July 30, 2013, movies.msn.com /movies/article.aspx?news=820697.

12. John Horn, Nicole Sperling, and Doug Smith, "Oscar Voters Overwhelmingly White, Male," Los Angeles Times, February 19, 2012, www.latimes.com/entertainment/news/movies/academy/la-et-unmasking -oscar-academy-project-html,0,7473284.htmlstory.

13. Bill Goodykoontz, "Despite Oscar Notice, Black Actors Still Hit Limits in Film," USA Today, February 24, 2012, usatoday30.usatoday.com /life/movies/movieawards/oscars/story/2012-02-24/race-in-hollywood /53238028/1.

14. "List of Black Academy Award Winners and Nominees," Wikipedia, en.wikipedia.org/wiki/List_of_black_Academy_Award_winners_and _nominees.

15. Horn et al., "Oscar Voters Overwhelmingly White, Male."

16. Nielsen, "African-American Consumers."

17. Kelli Goff, "Finding Diversity Behind the Scenes on the Great White Way Is an Issue Even in the Age of Obama," The Root, April 27, 2013, www .theroot.com/views/black-producers-still-rare-broadway.

18. "The Great Black Way? Black Tony Award Winners," The Root, n.d., www.theroot.com/multimedia/tony-award-winnners-gallery.

19. Marissa Lee, "Asian American Actors Are Missing on Broadway Stages," Racebending.com, February 17, 2012, www.racebending.com/v4 /blog/coalition-nyc-asian-americans-missing-broadway-stages/.

20. Goff, "Finding Diversity."

21. "The Great Black Way?"

22. Nielsen Holdings, "The Nielsen Company & Billboard's 2012 Music Industry Report," press release, Business Wire, January 4, 2013, www .businesswire.com/news/home/20130104005149/en/Nielsen-Company -Billboard's-2012-Music-Industry-Report.

23. "Artists of the Decade," Best of the 2000s, *Billboard*, n.d., www.bill board.com/articles/news/266420/artists-of-the-decade.

24. Edna Gunderson, "Prince Shows Off a Different Side for '21 Nights,'" *USA Today*, September 27, 2008, usatoday30.usatoday.com/life /books/news/2008-09-25-prince-21-nights_N.htm.

25. Recording Industry Association of America, "RIAA Awards Eagles' 'Their Greatest Hits 1971–1975' at 25 Million: The Top Selling Group Once Again Ties Michael Jackson's 'Thriller' as RIAA's Highest Certified Album of All Time," news release, September 2013, www.riaa.com/newsitem.php ?news_year_filter=&resultpage=126&id=0B391377-DEA6-2540-878F -A62C9A23A1B7.

26. Kevin Williams and David Keen, *2008 Survey of Public Participation in the Arts*, Research Report #49 (Washington, DC: National Endowment for the Arts, 2008), arts.gov/research/2008-SPPA.pdf.

27. Ibid.

28. "Study Shows Black Youth Are Politically Involved, Critical of Rap Music and Skeptical of a Post-Racial Society," UChicago News, October 19, 2010, news.uchicago.edu/article/2010/10/19/study-shows-black-youth-are-politically-involved-critical-rap-music-and-skeptical.

29. Joan Anderman, "Hip-Hop Setting the Beat in First, Black Artists Hold Billboard's Top 10," *Boston Globe*, October 4, 2003.

30. Vanna Le, "No. 6: Kevin Hart," in "The Top-Earning Comedians of 2013," *Forbes*, July 11, 2013, www.forbes.com/pictures/eimi451dg/no-6 -kevin-hart/.

31. Williams and Keen, *2008 Survey of Public Participation in the Arts*.

32. Nielsen, "African-American Consumers."

33. Richard Lapchick with Philip Costa, Tamara Sherrod, and Rahman Anjorin, *The 2012 Racial and Gender Report Card: National Football League* (Orlando, FL: Institute for Diversity and Ethics in Sport, 2012), www.tidesport.org/RGRC/2012/2012_NFL_RGRC.pdf.

34. Richard Lapchick with Orlando Gunn, Aaron Trigg, et al., *The 2012 Racial and Gender Report Card: Major League Soccer* (Orlando, FL: Institute for Diversity and Ethics in Sport, 2012), www.tidesport.org/RGRC /2012/2012_MLS_RGRC.pdf.

35. Richard Lapchick with Andrew Hippert, Stephanie Rivera, et al., *The 2013 Racial and Gender Report Card: National Basketball Association* (Orlando, FL: Institute for Diversity and Ethics in Sport, 2013), www.tide sport.org/RGRC/2013/2013_NBA_RGRC.pdf.

36. Richard Lapchick, Michelle Milkovich, and Stacie O'Keefe, *The 2012 Racial and Gender Report Card: Women's National Basketball Association* (Orlando, FL: Institute for Diversity and Ethics in Sport, 2012), www.tide sport.org/RGRC/2012/2012_WNBA_RGRC.pdf.

37. Richard Lapchick with Cory Bernstine, Giomar Nunes, et al., *The*

2013 Racial and Gender Report Card: Major League Baseball (Orlando, FL: Institute for Diversity and Ethics in Sport, 2013), www.tidesport.org /RGRC/2013/2013_MLB_RGRC_Final_Correction.pdf.

38. Walter E. Williams, "Are We Equal?," New American, March 7, 2013, www.thenewamerican.com/reviews/opinion/item/14924-are-we-equal.

39. Lapchick et al., 2012 Racial and Gender Report Card: Major League Soccer.

40. Gregg Rosenthal, "No African-American NFL Head Coaches Hired in 2013," NFL.com, January 17, 2013, www.nfl.com/news/story/0ap1000 000127869/article/no-africanamerican-nfl-head-coaches-hired-in-2013.

41. Lapchick et al., 2012 Racial and Gender Report Card: National Football League.

42. Lapchick et al., 2013 Racial and Gender Report Card: National Basketball Association.

43. Lapchick et al., 2012 Racial and Gender Report Card: Women's National Basketball Association.

44. Lapchick et al., 2013 Racial and Gender Report Card: Major League Baseball.

45. Lapchick et al., 2012 Racial and Gender Report Card: Major League Soccer.

46. Lapchick et al., 2012 Racial and Gender Report Card: National Football League.

47. Lapchick et al., 2013 Racial and Gender Report Card: National Basketball Association.

48. Lapchick et al., The 2012 Racial and Gender Report Card: Women's National Basketball Association.

49. Lapchick et al., 2013 Racial and Gender Report Card: Major League Baseball.

50. Lapchick et al., 2012 Racial and Gender Report Card: National Football League.

51. Lapchick et al., 2012 Racial and Gender Report Card: Major League Soccer.

52. Lapchick et al., 2013 Racial and Gender Report Card: National Basketball Association.

53. Lapchick et al., The 2012 Racial and Gender Report Card: Women's National Basketball Association.

54. Lapchick et al., 2013 Racial and Gender Report Card: Major League Baseball.

55. Lapchick et al., 2012 Racial and Gender Report Card: National Football League.

56. Lapchick et al., 2013 Racial and Gender Report Card: National Basketball Association.

57. Lapchick et al., The 2012 Racial and Gender Report Card: Women's National Basketball Association.

58. Lapchick et al., 2013 Racial and Gender Report Card: Major League Baseball.

59. Richard Lapchick, Claire Burnett, Reggie Gossett, et al., The 2012 Associated Press Sports Editors Racial and Gender Report Card (Orlando, FL: Institute for Diversity and Ethics in Sport, 2013), www.tidesport.org /RGRC/2012/2012_APSE_RGRC.pdf.

60. Erika V. Hall and Robert W. Livingston, "The Hubris Penalty: Biased Responses to 'Celebration' Displays of Black Football Players," *Journal of Experimental Social Psychology* 48, no. 4 (2012): 899–904.

HEALTH

1. Lyrics to Memphis Minnie's "Jitis Blues," www.lyricsmania.com/jitis _blues_lyrics_memphis_minnie.html.

2. Amy Jeter, "Tour's Mission in Hampton: More Black Doctors . . . Stat," *The Virginian-Pilot*, February 12, 2012, hamptonroads.com/2012/02 /more-black-doctors-needed-stat.

3. Department for Professional Employees, "Nursing: A Profile of the Profession," fact sheet, AFL-CIO, 2012, peaflcio.org/wp-content/uploads /Nursing-A-Profile-of-the-Profession-2012.pdf.

4. Bureau of Labor Statistics, "11. Employed Persons by Detailed Occupation, Sex, Race, and Hispanic or Latino Ethnicity, 2011," Current Population Survey, 2012, www.bls.gov/cps/cpsaat11.pdf.

5. Thomas Morgan, "The Education and Medical Practice of Dr. James McCune Smith (1813–1865), First Black American to Hold a Medical Degree," *Journal of the National Medical Association* 95, no. 7 (July 2003): 603–14, www.ncbi.nlm.nih.gov/pmc/articles/PMC2594637/pdf/jnma00311-0106.pdf.

6. Association of American Medical Colleges, "Medical School Enrollment Continues to Climb with New Diversity Gains: New Residency Positions Needed for M.D.s to Complete Training," press release, October 23, 2012, www.aamc.org/newsroom/newsreleases/310002/121 023.html.

7. "The Top Feeder Schools for Black Applicants to U.S. Medical Schools," *Journal of Blacks in Higher Education*, July 6, 2012, www.jbhe.com/2012/07 /the-top-feeder-schools-for-black-applicants-to-u-s-medical-schools/.

8. "A Check-Up of Blacks in U.S. Medical Schools," *Journal of Blacks in Higher Education*, April 12, 2012, www.jbhe.com/2012/04/a-check-up-of -blacks-in-u-s-medical-schools/.

9. Laura Castillo-Page, *Diversity in Medical Education: Facts and Figures 2012* (Washington, DC: Association of American Medical Colleges, 2012), members.aamc.org/eweb/upload/Diversity%20in%20Medical%20 Education%20Facts%20and%20Figures%202012.pdf.

10. Carmen DeNavas-Walt, Bernadette D. Proctor, and Jessica C. Smith, *Income, Poverty, and Health Insurance Coverage in the United States: 2011*, Current Population Reports P60-243 (Washington, DC: U.S. Census Bureau, 2012), www.census.gov/prod/2012pubs/p60-243.pdf.

11. *Kids Count Data Book 2012* (Baltimore, MD: Annie E. Casey Foundation, 2012), datacenter.kidscount.org/DataBook/2012/OnlineBooks/KIDS COUNT2012DataBookFullReport.pdf.

12. National Gay and Lesbian Task Force, National Black Justice Coalition, and the National Center for Transgender Equality, "Injustice at Every Turn: A Look at Black Respondents in the National Transgender Discrimination Survey," September 25, 2011.

13. Joyce A. Martin, Brady E. Hamilton, Stephanie J. Ventura, et al., "Births: Final Data for 2010," *National Vital Statistics Report* 61, no. 1 (2012), www.cdc.gov/nchs/data/nvsr/nvsr61/nvsr61_01.pdf.

14. "Personal Factors That Influence Contraceptive Use," in *Breaking the Contraceptive Barrier: Techniques for Effective Contraceptive Consultations* (Washington, DC: Association of Reproductive Health Professionals, 2008), www.arhp.org/Publications-and-Resources/Clinical -Proceedings/Breaking-the-Contraceptive-Barrier/Personal-Factors.

15. Martha Waggoner, "No Money for Forced Sterilization Victims in North Carolina," Huffington Post, June 20, 2012, www.huffingtonpost .com/2012/06/27/no-money-for-forced-steri_n_1630417.html; Lutz Kaelber, "Eugenics: Compulsory Sterilization in 50 American States," presentation at the 37th annual meeting of the Social Science History Association, November 1–4, 2012, www.uvm.edu/~lkaelber/eugenics/.

16. Martin et al., "Births: Final Data for 2010."

17. Ibid.

18. Ibid.

19. *Health, United States, 2011, with Special Feature on Socioeconomic Status and Health* (Hyattsville, MD: National Center for Health Statistics, 2012), 10, www.cdc.gov/nchs/data/hus/hus11.pdf.

20. National Alliance on Mental Illness, "African American Community Mental Health Fact Sheet," n.d., www.nami.org/Template.cfm?Section =Fact_Sheets1&Template=/ContentManagement/ContentDisplay.cfm &ContentID=53812.

21. Office of Minority Health, "Mental Health and African Americans," U.S. Department of Health and Human Services, December 5, 2012, minorityhealth.hhs.gov/templates/content.aspx?ID=6474.

22. *Health, United States, 2011.*

23. Jeannine S. Schiller, Jacqueline W. Lucas, Brian W. Ward, and Jennifer A. Peregoy, "Table 14. Age-Adjusted Percentages of Feelings of Sadness, Hopelessness, Worthlessness, or That Everything Is an Effort Among Persons Aged 18 Years and Over, by Selected Characteristics: United States, 2010," in "Summary Health Statistics for U.S. Adults: National Health Interview Survey, 2010," *Vital and Health Statistics* 10, no. 252 (2012): 55–57.

24. "Major Depressive Episode Among Full-Time College Students and Other Young Adults, Aged 18 to 22," *NSDUH Report*, May 3, 2012, www .samhsa.gov/data/2k12/NSDUH060/SR060CollegeStudentsMDE2012 .htm.

25. Office of Minority Health, "Mental Health and African Americans."

26. National Gay and Lesbian Task Force et al., "Injustice at Every Turn."

27. Kenneth D. Kochanek, Jiaquan Xu, Sherry L. Murphy, et al., "Table 17. Age-Adjusted Death Rates for 113 Selected Causes, Enterocolitis Due to *Clostridium Difficile*, Drug-Induced Causes, Alcohol-Induced Causes, and Injury by Firearms, by Hispanic Origin, Race for Non-Hispanic Population, and Sex: United States, 2009," in "Deaths: Final Data for 2009," *National Vital Statistics Reports* 60, no. 3 (2011): 75–80 www.cdc.gov/nchs/data/nvsr /nvsr60/nvsr60_03.pdf.

28. "Table 39. Death Rates for Suicide, by Sex, Race, Hispanic Origin, and Age: United States, Selected Years 1950–2008," in *Health United States, 2011.*

29. Centers for Disease Control and Prevention, "1991–2011 High School Youth Risk Behavior Survey Data," apps.nccd.cdc.gov/youthonline.

30. Agency for Healthcare Research and Quality, "Table 17_3_1-2b: Adults Who Received Mental Health Treatment or Counseling in the Last 12 Months, by Ethnicity, 2008," in *2010 National Healthcare Quality and Disparities Report*, February 2011, www.ahrq.gov/research/findings /nhqrdr/nhqrdr10/17_utilization/T17_3_1-2b.html.

31. Injury Prevention & Control: Data and Statistics (WISQARSTM), National Center for Injury Prevention and Control, Centers for Disease Control and Prevention, www.cdc.gov/injury/wisqars/index.html.

32. "Table 17_3_1-2b," *2010 National Healthcare Quality and Disparities Report*.

33. Marc Mauer, *The Changing Racial Dynamics of the War on Drugs* (Washington, DC: The Sentencing Project, 2009), 7.

34. Substance Abuse and Mental Health Services Administration, "Race/Ethnicity," in *Results from the 2011 National Survey on Drug Use and Health: Summary of National Findings* (Rockville, MD: Substance Abuse and Mental Health Services Administration, 2012), www.samhsa .gov/data/nsduh/2k11results/nsduhresults2011.htm#7.1.4.

35. Danice K. Eeton, Laura Kann, Steven Kinchen, et al., "Youth Risk Behavior Surveillance—United States, 2009," *CDC Surveillance Summaries* 59, no. SS-5 (2010): 1–142.

36. Substance Abuse and Mental Health Services Administration, "Non-Hispanic Black Substance Abuse Treatment Admissions for Cocaine Decreased from 2000 to 2010," Treatment Episode Data Set, February 19, 2013, www.samhsa.gov/data/spotlight/Spot109-Cocaine-Trends.pdf.

37. Substance Abuse and Mental Health Services Administration, "Table 1.33A—Cocaine Use in Lifetime, Past Year, and Past Month Among Persons Aged 18 or Older, by Demographic Characteristics: Numbers in Thousands, 2010 and 2011" and "Table 1.34A—Crack Use in Lifetime, Past Year, and Past Month Among Persons Aged 12 or Older, by Demographic Characteristics: Numbers in Thousands, 2010 and 2011," in *Results from the 2011 National Survey on Drug Use and Health: Detailed Tables*, www .samhsa.gov/data/NSDUH/2011SummNatFindDetTables/NSDUH-DetTabs PDFWHTML2011/2k11DetailedTabs/Web/HTML/NSDUH-DetTabsSect1pe Tabs1to46-2011.htm.

38. "Table 3.97.2012. Respondents Reporting Whether They Drink More Than They Should," *Sourcebook of Criminal Justice Statistics*, 2012, www .albany.edu/sourcebook/pdf/t3972012.pdf.

39. Eaton et al., "Youth Risk Behavior Surveillance—United States, 2009."

40. "Table 3.100.2011. Respondents Reporting Whether Drinking Has Ever Been a Source of Family Trouble," *Sourcebook of Criminal Justice Statistics*, 2011, www.albany.edu/sourcebook/pdf/t31002011.pdf.

41. "Table 3.96.2012. Reported Alcohol Use," *Sourcebook of Criminal Justice Statistics*, 2012, www.albany.edu/sourcebook/pdf/t3962012.pdf.

42. Eaton et al., "Youth Risk Behavior Surveillance—United States, 2009," 62–65, 73–90. See also "Table 3.56.2009. High School Students Reporting Involvement in Delinquent and Risk-Related Behaviors, by Sex, Race, Ethnicity, and Grade Level, United States," *Sourcebook of Criminal Justice Statistics*, 2009, www.albany.edu/sourcebook/pdf/t3562009.pdf.

43. "Table 62. Current Cigarette Smoking Among Adults, by Sex, Race, Hispanic Origin, Age, and Education Level: United States, Average Annual,

Selected Years 1990–1992 Through 2008–2010," in *Health, United States, 2011.*

44. "Gay Urbanites More Aware of Their HIV Status, but Prevalence Holds Steady," AIDSmeds, March 14, 2013, www.aidsmeds.com/articles/1667_23637.shtml.

45. H. Irene Hall, Ruiguang Song, Philip Rhodes, et al., "Estimation of HIV Incidence in the United States," *JAMA*, 300, no. 5 (2008): 520–29.

46. Centers for Disease Control and Prevention, "HIV Among African Americans," February 2013, www.cdc.gov/hiv/topics/aa/pdf/HIV_among _African_Americans_final.pdf.

47. Bernard M. Branson, H. Hunter Handsfield, Margaret A. Lampe, et al., "Revised Recommendations for HIV Testing of Adults, Adolescents, and Pregnant Women in Health-Care Settings," *MMWR Recommendations and Reports* 55, no. R-14 (2006): 1–17; see also Kelly A. Gebo, John A. Fleishman, Richard Conviser, "Racial and Gender Disparities in Receipt of Highly Active Antiretroviral Therapy Persist in a Multistate Sample of HIV Patients in 2001," *Journal of Acquired Immune Deficiency Syndrome* 38, no. 1 (2005): 96–103; "Vital Signs: HIV Testing and Diagnosis Among Adults—United States, 2001–2009," *Morbidity and Mortality Weekly Report* 59, no. 47 (2010): 1550–55.

48. Centers for Disease Control and Prevention, "HIV Among African Americans."

49. National Gay and Lesbian Task Force et al., "Injustice at Every Turn."

50. Centers for Disease Control and Prevention, "HIV Among African Americans."

51. Ibid.

52. Helena A. Kwakwa, Patrick Doggett, Regina Ubaldi-Rosen, et al., "African-Born Men in the United States Are Diagnosed with HIV Later than African-Born Women," *Journal of the National Medical Association* 104, no. 1–2 (2012): 14–19.

53. Fox Chase Cancer Center, "African Americans and Cancer," Temple University, n.d., www.fccc.edu/cancer/minorities.

54. Ibid. See also Wexner Medical Center, "Prostate Cancer in African-American Men," Ohio State University, n.d., medicalcenter.osu.edu/patient care/healthcare_services/prostate_health/prostate_cancer/prostate _cancer_african_americans/Pages/index.aspx.

55. Fox Chase Cancer Center, "African Americans and Cancer."

56. Office of Minority Health, "Diabetes and African Americans," U.S. Department of Health and Human Services, August 28, 2012, minority health.hhs.gov/templates/content.aspx?lvl=2&lvlID=51&ID=3017.

57. Fox Chase Cancer Center, "African Americans and Cancer."

58. "Fatal Injury Data," Injury Prevention & Control: Data and Statistics (WISQARSTM), December 1, 2011, www.cdc.gov/injury/wisqars/fatal .html.

59. Schiller et al., "Table 8. Age-Adjusted Percentages of Selected Diseases and Conditions Among Persons Aged 18 Years and Over, by Selected Characteristics: United States, 2010," in "Summary Health Statistics for U.S. Adults: National Health Interview Survey, 2010," 37–39.

60. Ibid.

61. Office of Minority Health, "Diabetes and African Americans."

62. Division of Diabetes Translation, "Age-Adjusted Percentage of Adults Aged 18 Years or Older with Diagnosed Diabetes Reporting Visual Impairment, by Race/Ethnicity, United States, 1997–2011," National Center for Chronic Disease Prevention and Health Promotion, Centers for Disease Control and Prevention, September 21, 2012,www.cdc.gov/diabetes/statistics/visual/fig5.htm.

63. Centers for Disease Control, "Age-Adjusted Hospital Discharge Rates for Nontraumatic Lower Extremity Amputation per 1,000 Diabetic Population, by Race, United States, 1988–2009," Data and Trends, March 9, 2012, www.cdc.gov/diabetes/statistics/lea/fig6.htm.

64. Office of Minority Health, "Diabetes and African Americans."

65. Schiller et al., "Table 31. Age-Adjusted Percent Distributions of Body Mass Index Among Persons Aged 18 Years and Over, by Selected Characteristics: United States, 2010," in "Summary Health Statistics for U.S. Adults: National Health Interview Survey, 2010," 106–8.

66. Health, United States, 2011.

67. Federal Interagency Forum on Child and Family Statistics, "HEALTH7 Obesity: Percentage of Children Ages 6–17 Who Are Obese by Age, Race and Hispanic Origin, and Gender, Selected Years 1976–2010," in America's Children: Key National Indicators of Well-Being, 2012, www.childstats.gov/americaschildren/tables/health7.asp. Figures reflect measures from 2009–2010.

68. Danice K. Eaton, Laura Kann, Steven Kinchen, et al., "Table 101. Percentage of High School Students Who Were Obese and Who Were Overweight, by Sex, Race/Ethnicity, and Grade—United States," in "Youth Risk Behavior Surveillance—United States, 2011," Morbidity and Mortality Weekly Report 61, no. 4 (2012), www.cdc.gov/mmwr/pdf/ss/ss6104.pdf.

69. U.S. Census Bureau, "Table 686. Average Annual Expenditures of All Consumer Units by Race, Hispanic Origin, and Age of Householder: 2009," Statistical Abstract of the United States: 2012, www.census.gov/compendia/statab/2012/tables/12s0686.pdf.

70. John A. Romley, Deborah Cohen, Jeanne Ringel, and Roland Sturm, "Alcohol and Environmental Justice: The Density of Liquor Stores and Bars in Urban Neighborhoods in the United States," Journal of Studies on Alcohol and Drugs 68, no. 1 (2007): 48–55; Thomas A. LaVeist and John M. Wallace Jr., "Health Risk and Inequitable Distribution of Liquor Stores in African American Neighborhoods," Social Science and Medicine 51, no. 4 (2000): 613–17.

71. "Density of Neighborhood Liquor Stores Is Especially Risky for African-Americans Who Drink, Study Finds," Science Daily, February 15, 2011, www.sciencedaily.com/releases/2011/02/110215164256.htm.

72. "America's Worst 9 Food Deserts," NewsOne, September 22, 2011, newsone.com/1540235/americas-worst-9-urban-food-deserts/; U.S. Census Bureau, "State & County QuickFacts," n.d., quickfacts.census.gov/qfd/index.html.

73. Paula Dutko, Michele Ver Ploeg, and Tracey Farrigan, "Characteristics and Influential Factors of Food Deserts," Economic Research Report No. 140, U.S. Department of Agriculture, August 2012, www.ers.usda.gov/media/883903/err140.pdf.

74. Cheryl D. Fryar and R. Bethene Ervin, "Caloric Intake from Fast

Food Among Adults: United States, 2007–2010," NCHS data brief, no. 114, February 2013, www.cdc.gov/nchs/data/databriefs/db114.pdf

75. Schiller et al., "Table 2. Age-Adjusted Percentages of Selected Circulatory Diseases Among Persons Aged 18 Years and Over, by Selected Characteristics: United States, 2010," in "Summary Health Statistics for U.S. Adults: National Health Interview Survey, 2010," 19–21.

76. Office of Minority Health, "Heart Disease and African Americans," U.S. Department of Health and Human Services, minorityhealth.hhs.gov /templates/content.aspx?lvl=3&lvlID=6&ID=3018.

77. Kochanek et al., "Table 17. Age-Adjusted Death Rates," in "Deaths: Final Data for 2009."

78. Schiller et al., "Table 2. Age-Adjusted Percentages."

JUSTICE

1. W.E.B. Du Bois, "The Spawn of Slavery," *Missionary Review of the World* 14 (October 1901): 737–45.

2. Michelle Alexander, *The New Jim Crow: Mass Incarceration in the Age of Colorblindness* (New York: The New Press, 2010), 15.

3. Brian A. Reaves, "Local Police Departments, 2007," NCJ 231174, Bureau of Justice Statistics, December 2010, 14, www.bjs.gov/content /pub/pdf/lpd07.pdf.

4. Matthew J. Hickman and Brian A. Reaves, "Police Departments in Large Cities, 1990–2000," NCJ 175703, Bureau of Justice Statistics, May 5, 2002, www.bjs.gov/content/pub/pdf/pdlc00.pdf.

5. Matthew J. Hickman and Brian A. Reaves, "Law Enforcement Management and Administrative Statistics, 2000: Data for Individual State and Local Agencies with 100 or More Officers," NCJ 203350, Bureau of Justice Statistics, March 2004, 243, www.bjs.gov/index.cfm?ty=pbdetail&iid=1052.

6. Federal Bureau of Investigation, "Law Enforcement Officers Feloniously Killed, Race and Sex of Victim Officer, 2002–2011," *Crime in the United States 2011*, www.fbi.gov/about-us/cjis/ucr/leoka/2011/tables /table-11; "Table 3.160.2010. Persons Identified in the Felonious Killing of Law Enforcement Officers, by Demographic Characteristics and Prior Record, United States," *Sourcebook of Criminal Justice Statistics*, 2011, www.albany.edu/sourcebook/pdf/t31602010.pdf.

7. Pew Research Center for the People & the Press, "Views of Law Enforcement, Racial Progress and News Coverage of Race," March 30, 2012, www.people-press.org/2012/03/30/blacks-view-of-law-enforcement -racial-progress-and-news-coverage-of-race/.

8. National Opinion Research Center, *General Social Surveys, 1972– 2002* (Storrs, CT: Roper Center for Public Opinion Research, University of Connecticut); see also *Sourcebook of Criminal Justice Statistics*, 2003, NCJ 208756 (Washington, DC: Bureau of Justice Statistics, 2005), 122–23.

9. National Opinion Research Center, *General Social Surveys, 1972–2002*.

10. "Table 2.73. High School Seniors Reporting Positive Attitudes Toward the Performance of the Police and Other Law Enforcement Agencies, by Sex, Race, Region, College Plans, and Illicit Drug Use, United States 1991–2003," *Sourcebook of Criminal Justice Statistics*, 2003, 164, www.albany.edu/sourcebook/pdf/t273.pdf.

11. Darren K. Carlson, "Racial Profiling Seen as Pervasive, Unjust," Gallup, July 20, 2004, www.gallup.com/poll/12406/racial-profiling-seen-pervasive-unjust.aspx.

12. "Table 2.0002.2005. Respondents' Perceptions of Police Brutality in Their Area," *Sourcebook of Criminal Justice Statistics*, 2011, www.albany.edu/sourcebook/pdf/t200022005.pdf.

13. "Table 2.21.2011. Respondents' Ratings of the Honesty and Ethical Standards of Police, by Demographic Characteristics, United States," *Sourcebook of Criminal Justice Statistics*, 2011, www.albany.edu/source book/pdf/t2212011.pdf.

14. "Table 2.12.2012. Reported Confidence in the Police, by Demographic Characteristics, United States," *Sourcebook of Criminal Justice Statistics*, 2011, www.albany.edu/sourcebook/pdf/t2122012.pdf.

15. Federal Bureau of Investigation, "Persons Arrested," *Crime in the United States 2011*, www.fbi.gov/about-us/cjis/ucr/crime-in-the-u.s/2011/crime-in-the-u.s.-2011/persons-arrested/persons-arrested.

16. Bureau of Justice Statistics, "Traffic Stops," www.bjs.gov/index.cfm?ty=tp&tid=702; Christine Eith and Matthew R. Durose, "Contacts Between Police and Public, 2008," NCJ 234599, Bureau of Justice Statistics, October 2011, /bjs.gov/content/pub/pdf/cpp08.pdf.

17. William H. Frey, "Melting Pot Cities and Suburbs: Racial and Ethnic Change in Metro America in the 2000s," Brookings Institution, May 4, 2011, www.brookings.edu/research/papers/2011/05/04-census-ethnicity-frey; Federal Bureau of Investigation, "Table 49: Arrests: Cities by Race, 2011," *Crime in the United States 2011*, www.fbi.gov/about-us/cjis/ucr/crime-in-the-u.s/2011/crime-in-the-u.s.-2011/tables/table-49.

18. Federal Bureau of Investigation, "Table 67: Arrests: Suburban Areas by Race, 2011," *Crime in the United States 2011*, www.fbi.gov/about-us/cjis/ucr/crime-in-the-u.s/2011/crime-in-the-u.s.-2011/tables/table-67; Frey, "Melting Pot Cities and Suburbs."

19. Janice C. Probst, Michael E. Samuels, Kristen P. Jespersen, et al., "Minorities in Rural America: An Overview of Population Characteristics," Norman J. Arnold School of Public Health, University of South Carolina, 2002, rhr.sph.sc.edu/report/minoritiesInRuralAmerica.pdf; Federal Bureau of Investigation, "Table 61A: Arrests: Nonmetropolitan Areas by Race, 2011," *Crime in the United States 2011*, www.fbi.gov/about-us/cjis/ucr/crime-in-the-u.s/2011/crime-in-the-u.s.-2011/tables/table-61.

20. E. Franklin Frazier, "Rebellious Youth," in *The Negro Family in the United States* (Chicago: University of Chicago Press, 1939).

21. Federal Bureau of Investigation, "Table 43B: Arrests by Race, 2011," *Crime in the United States, 2011*, www.fbi.gov/about-us/cjis/ucr/crime-in-the-u.s/2011/crime-in-the-u.s.-2011/tables/table-43.

22. Ibid.

23. Office of Civil Rights, "Discipline," in "The Transformed Civil Rights Data Collection (CRDC)," U.S. Department of Education, March 2012, www2.ed.gov/about/offices/list/ocr/docs/crdc-2012-data-summary.pdf.

24. "Table 4.10.2010. Arrests, by Offense Charged, Age Group, and Race, United States," *Sourcebook of Criminal Justice Statistics*, 2011, www.albany.edu/sourcebook/pdf/t4122010.pdf.

25. Federal Bureau of Investigation, "Table 49: Arrests: Cities by Race, 2011."

26. Federal Bureau of Investigation, "Table 67: Arrests: Suburban Areas by Race, 2011."

27. Federal Bureau of Investigation, "Table 61: Arrests: Nonmetropolitan Areas by Race, 2011."

28. Durose and Eith, "Contacts Between the Police and the Public, 2008."

29. Ronald Weitzer and Steven A. Tuch, "Race and Perceptions of Police Misconduct," *Social Problems* 51, no. 3 (2004): 305–25, web.missouri.edu /~jlfm89/Race%20Perceptions%20of%20Police%20Misconduct.pdf.

30. Ibid.

31. National Gay and Lesbian Task Force, National Black Justice Coalition, and the National Center for Transgender Equality, "Injustice at Every Turn: A Look at Black Respondents in the National Transgender Discrimination Survey," September 25, 2011.

32. "Table 2.38. Respondents Reporting Whether They Feel Afraid to Walk Alone at Night in Their Own Neighborhood, by Demographic Characteristics, United States, Selected Years 1973–2002," *Sourcebook of Criminal Justice Statistics*, 2003, www.albany.edu/sourcebook/pdf/t238 .pdf.

33. Shannon Catalano, "Intimate Partner Violence, 1993–2010," NCJ 239203, Bureau of Justice Statistics, November 2012, bjs.gov/content/pub /pdf/ipv9310.pdf.

34. "Table 2.40.2007. Respondents Reporting Whether They Engaged in Selected Behaviors Because of Concern over Crime, by Sex and Race, United States," *Sourcebook of Criminal Justice Statistics*, 2011, www.albany .edu/sourcebook/pdf/t2402007.pdf.

35. Tracey Kyckelhahn, Allen J. Beck, and Thomas H. Cohen, "Characteristics of Suspected Human Trafficking Incidents, 2007–08," NCJ 224526, Bureau of Justice Statistics, January 2009, 5, bjs.ojp.usdoj.gov /content/pub/pdf/cshti08.pdf.

36. Jayne E. Robinson, "Table 9. Personal Crimes, 2008: Victimization Rates for Persons Age 12 or Older, by Race and Age of Victims and Type of Crime," in *Criminal Victimization in the United States, 2008 Statistical Tables*, NCJ 227669 (Washington, DC: Bureau of Justice Statistics, 2010), bjs.ojp.usdoj.gov/content/pub/pdf/cvus08.pdf.

37. Federal Bureau of Investigation, *Crime in the United States 2010*; see also "Table 3.124.2010. Murders and Nonnegligent Manslaughters Known to Police, by Sex, Race, and Age of Victim, United States," *Sourcebook of Criminal Justice Statistics*, 2011, www.albany.edu/sourcebook/pdf /t31242010.pdf; U.S. Census Bureau, "Table 311. Murder Victims by Age, Sex, and Race: 2008," *Statistical Abstract of the United States: 2012*, www .census.gov/compendia/statab/2012/tables/12s0311.pdf.

38. Jennifer L. Truman and Michael Planty, "Table 5. Rate and Percent Change of Violent Victimization, by Demographic Characteristics of Victim, 2002, 2010, and 2011," in "Criminal Victimization, 2011," NCJ 239437, Bureau of Justice Statistics, 5, www.bjs.gov/content/pub/pdf/cv11.pdf.

39. "Table 3.0007.2011. Respondents Reporting Incidents of Identity Theft, by Demographic Characteristics, United States, 2011," *Sourcebook of Criminal Justice Statistics*, 2011, www.albany.edu/sourcebook/pdf /t300072011.pdf.

40. Robinson, "Table 9. Personal Crimes, 2008: Victimization Rates."

41. "Table 2.71. High School Seniors Reporting That They Worry About Crime and Violence, by Sex, Race, Region, College Plans, and Illicit Drug Use, United States, 1991–2003," *Sourcebook of Criminal Justice Statistics*, 2003, www.albany.edu/sourcebook/pdf/t271.pdf.

42. Danice K. Eeaton, Laura Kann, Steven Kinchen, et al., "Youth Risk Behavior Surveillance–United States, 2009," *CDC Surveillance Summaries* 59, no. SS-5 (2010): 62–65, 73–90. See also "Table 3.56.2009. High School Students Reporting Involvement in Delinquent and Risk-Related Behaviors, by Sex, Race, Ethnicity, and Grade Level, United States," *Sourcebook of Criminal Justice Statistics*, 2009, www.albany.edu/sourcebook/pdf/t356 2009.pdf.

43. "Table 3.42. High School Seniors Reporting Victimization Experiences at School in Last 12 Months, by Type of Victimization and Race, United States, 1991–2003," *Sourcebook of Criminal Justice Statistics*, 2003, www.albany.edu/sourcebook/pdf/t342.pdf.

44. "Table 3.61.2007. Students Age 12 to 18 Reporting Victimization, Bullying, Hate-Related Behavior, and Gangs at School, by Student Characteristics, United States, 2007," *Sourcebook of Criminal Justice Statistics*, 2011, www.albany.edu/sourcebook/pdf/t3612007.pdf.

45. Vinti Singh, "Kid Bullied to Leave School Because He Wasn't 'Black Enough,'" *Connecticut Post*, January 3, 2012, www.ctpost.com/local /article/Kid-bullied-to-leave-school-because-he-wasn-t-2866806.php.

46. American University, "Study Reveals Youth Attitudes About Guns," news release, Newswise, January 14, 2013, www.newswise.com/articles /study-reveals-youth-attitudes-about-guns.

47. Eaton et al., "Youth Risk Behavior Surveillance—United States, 2009."

48. "Table 2.11.2012. Reported Confidence in the Criminal Justice System, by Demographic Characteristics, United States," *Sourcebook of Criminal Justice Statistics*, 2011, www.albany.edu/sourcebook/pdf/t211 2012.pdf.

49. "Table 2.0013.2010. Attitudes Toward Approaches to Lowering the Crime Rate in the United States, by Demographic Characteristics, United States," *Sourcebook of Criminal Justice Statistics*, 2011, www.albany.edu /sourcebook/pdf/t200132010.pdf.

50. "Table 2.39.2011. Respondents Reporting Concern About Crime Victimization, by Sex and Race, United States," *Sourcebook of Criminal Justice Statistics*, 2011, www.albany.edu/sourcebook/pdf/t2392011.pdf.

51. Federal Bureau of Investigation, "Table 5.1. Murder Victims of 9/11/2001 Terrorist Attacks by Race, Sex, and Location," in *Crime in the United States, 2001* (Washington, DC: U.S. Department of Justice, 2002).

52. Ibid.

53. Ibid.

54. American Bar Association, "Lawyer Demographics," 2012, www .americanbar.org/content/dam/aba/migrated/marketresearch/Public Documents/lawyer_demographics_2012_revised.authcheckdam.pdf.

55. ABA Center for Racial and Ethnic Diversity, *2010–2011 Annual Report* (Chicago, IL: American Bar Association, 2012), www.american bar.org/content/dam/aba/administrative/diversity/diversitycenter_annual report_201011_final.authcheckdam.pdf.

56. Bureau of Labor Statistics, "Employed Persons by Detailed Occupation, Sex, Race, and Hispanic or Latino Ethnicity, 2011," Current Population Survey, 2012, www.bls.gov/cps/cpsaat11.pdf.

57. Federal Judicial Center, "Diversity on the Bench." www.fjc.gov/serv let/nDsearch?race=African+American (accessed January 13, 2013).

58. Sheldon Goldman, "Reagan's Judicial Legacy: Completing the Puzzle and Summing Up," *Judicature* 72, no. 6 (1989): 324–25; and Sheldon Goldman, Elliot Slotnick, and Sara Schiavoni, "Obama's Judiciary at Midterm," *Judicature* 94, no. 6 (2011): 297. See also "Table 1.81.2010. Characteristics of Presidential Appointees to U.S. Courts of Appeals Judgeships, by Presidential Administration, 1963–2010," *Sourcebook of Criminal Justice Statistics*, 2011, www.albany.edu/sourcebook/pdf/t1812010.pdf.

59. Supreme Judicial Court, "E. Inclusion of Minorities and Women," in "The Massachusetts Jury System," 2007, www.mass.gov/courts/sjc/jury -system-e.html.

60. *Batson v. Kentucky*, 476 U.S. 79, 106 S. Ct. 1712, 90 L. Ed. 2d 69 (1986).

61. Equal Justice Initiative, *Illegal Racial Discrimination in Jury Selection: A Continuing Legacy* (Montgomery, AL: Equal Justice Initiative, 2010).

62. Shamena Anwar, Patrick Bayer, and Randi Hjalmarsson, "The Impact of Jury Race in Criminal Trials," *Quarterly Journal of Economics* 127, no. 2 (2012): 16, doi:10.1093/qje/qjs014.

63. Equal Justice Initiative, *Illegal Racial Discrimination in Jury Selection*, 14.

64. U.S. Census Bureau, "Tuscalaloosa, Alabama," in "State & County QuickFacts," 2013, quickfacts.census.gov/qfd/states/01/01125.html; Equal Justice Initiative, *Illegal Racial Discrimination in Jury Selection*.

65. Ibid., 39.

66. "Table 2.47. Attitudes Toward Severity of Courts in Own Area, by Demographic Characteristics, United States, Selected Years 1985–2002," *Sourcebook of Criminal Justice Statistics*, 2003, www.albany.edu/source book/pdf/t247.pdf.

67. "Table 2.14.2012. Reported Confidence in the U.S. Supreme Court, by Demographic Characteristics, United States," *Sourcebook of Criminal Justice Statistics*, 2012, www.albany.edu/sourcebook/pdf/t2142012.pdf.

68. "Table 2.19.2011. Respondents' Ratings of the Honesty and Ethical Standards of Lawyers, by Demographic Characteristics, United States," *Sourcebook of Criminal Justice Statistics*, 2011, www.albany.edu/source book/pdf/t2192011.pdf.

69. U.S. Sentencing Commission, "Table 4. Race of Offenders in Each Primary Offense Category," in *2011 Sourcebook of Federal Sentencing Statistics*, www.ussc.gov/Research_and_Statistics/Annual_Reports_and _Sourcebooks/2011/Table04.pdf.

70. E. Ann Carson and William J. Sabol, "Prisoners in 2011," NCJ 239808, Bureau of Justice Statistics, December 2012, 9, www.bjs.gov/content/pub /pdf/p11.pdf.

71. Equal Justice Initiative, *Illegal Racial Discrimination in Jury Selection*, 14.

72. Tushar Kansal, "Racial Disparity in Sentencing: A Review of the Literature," The Sentencing Project, January 2005, 11, www.sentencing project.org/doc/publications/rd_sentencing_review.pdf.

73. Charles Puzzanchera, Benjamin Adams, and Sarah Hockenberry, *Juvenile Court Statistics 2009* (Pittsburgh, PA: National Center for Juvenile Justice, 2012), 20, staging.ncjj.org/pdf/jcsreports/jcs2009.pdf.

74. Ibid.

75. National Center for Juvenile Justice, *Easy Access to Juvenile Court Statistics: 1985–2010*, Office of Juvenile Justice and Delinquency Programs, www.ojjdp.gov/ojstatbb/ezajcs/. See also "Table 5.61.2008. Characteristics of Juvenile Offenders in Cases Disposed by Juvenile Courts, by Type of Offense, United States," *Sourcebook of Criminal Justice Statistics*, 2011, www.albany.edu/sourcebook/pdf/t5612008.pdf.

76. Puzzanchera et al., *Juvenile Court Statistics 2009*, 20.

77. Christopher Hartney and Fabiana Silva, *And Justice for Some: Differential Treatment of Youth of Color in the Justice System* (Oakland, CA: National Council on Crime and Delinquency, 2007), www.nccdglobal.org/sites/default/files/publication_pdf/justice-for-some.pdf.

78. "Table 2.48. Attitudes Toward the Treatment of Juveniles Who Commit Violent Crimes, by Demographic Characteristics, United States, 2003," *Sourcebook of Criminal Justice Statistics*, 2003, www.albany.edu/sourcebook/pdf/t248.pdf.

79. Note that 21 percent of the staff is Black. "Table 1.107. Characteristics of Federal Bureau of Prisons Staff, by Race and Ethnicity, January 2004," *Sourcebook of Criminal Justice Statistics*, 2003, 99, www.albany.edu/sourcebook/pdf/t1107.pdf.

80. "Table 1.101. Jail Staff and Correctional Officers, by Race, Hispanic Origin, Region, and Jurisdiction, June 30, 1999," *Sourcebook of Criminal Justice Statistics*, 2003, 94, www.albany.edu/sourcebook/pdf/t1101.pdf.

81. Carson and Sabol, "Prisoners in 2011."

82. Todd D. Minton, "Jail Inmates at Midyear 2011—Statistical Tables," NCJ 237961, Bureau of Justice Statistics, April 2012, 7, www.bjs.gov/content/pub/pdf/jim11st.pdf. See also U.S. Census Bureau, "Table 349. Jail Inmates by Sex, Race, and Hispanic Origin: 1990 to 2009," *Statistical Abstract of the United States: 2012*, 218.

83. Carson and Sabol, "Prisoners in 2011." Note that 63 percent of Black and Latino male prisoners are under the age of 40, compared with 52 percent of White male prisoners. Sixty (60) percent of Black and White female prisoners are under the age of 40, compared with 67 percent of Latina prisoners.

84. Federal Bureau of Prisons, "State of the Bureau 2010," www.bop.gov/news/PDFs/sob10.pdf.

85. Note that this figure refers to time served until the first release and does not include additional time served if the individual recidivates. Thomas P. Bonczar, "Table 11. First Releases from State Prison, 2009: Sentence Length and Time Served in Prison, by Offense and Race," Bureau of Justice Statistics, Office of Justice Programs, U.S. Department of Justice, May 5, 2011.

86. Christopher J. Mumola, "Veterans in Prison or Jail," NCJ 178888, Bureau of Justice Statistics, January 2000, 4, 12, Table 15; and Margaret E. Noonan and Christopher J. Mumola, "Veterans in State and Federal Prison, 2004," NCJ 217199, Bureau of Justice Statistics, May 2007, pp. 1, 9, Appendix Table 1, p. 10. See also "Table 6.0007.2004. Veterans and

Nonveterans in State and Federal Prisons, by Selected Characteristics, United States, 1997 and 2004," *Sourcebook of Criminal Justice Statistics,* 2004, www.albany.edu/sourcebook/pdf/t600072004.pdf.

87. Christopher J. Mumola and Margaret E. Noonan, "Table 1. Number of State Prisoner Deaths, by Cause of Death, 2001–2006" and "Table 4. Number of State Prisoner Deaths, by Selected Characteristics, 2001–2006," in *Deaths in Custody Statistical Tables* (Washington, DC: Bureau of Justice Statistics, 2008), bjs.gov/content/dcrp/dcst.pdf; see also "Table 6.0010.2006. Deaths of Prisoners in State Correctional Facilities, by Cause of Death and Selected Prisoner Characteristics, 2001–2006," *Sourcebook of Criminal Justice Statistics,* www.albany.edu/sourcebook/pdf/t600102006.pdf.

88. Hartney and Silva, *And Justice for Some.*

89. National Center for Juvenile Justice, *Easy Access to the Census of Juveniles in Residential Placement: 1997–2010,* www.ojjdp.gov/ojstatbb/ezacjrp/.

90. Ibid. Note that, in California, nearly 3,000 Black youth were placed in private and public residential correctional facilities in 2010, with 2,568 and 2,463 Black youth in residential placement, respectively.

91. Puzzanchera et al., *Juvenile Court Statistics 2009.*

92. Allen J. Beck and Candace Johnson, "Sexual Victimization Reported by Former State Prisoners, 2008," NCJ 237363, Bureau of Justice Statistics, May 2012, bjs.ojp.usdoj.gov/content/pub/pdf/svrfsp08.pdf.

93. National Gay and Lesbian Task Force, "Injustice at Every Turn."

94. Mumola and Noonan, "Table 1," and "Table 3. Mortality Rate Per 100,000 Local Jail Inmates, by Cause of Death, 2000–2006," in *Deaths in Custody Statistical Tables.* See also "Table 6.0014.2005. Deaths of Youths in State Juvenile Correctional Facilities, by Cause of Death and Selected Characteristics, 2002–2005," *Sourcebook of Criminal Justice Statistics,* www.albany.edu/sourcebook/pdf/t600142005.pdf.

95. Margaret E. Noonan, "Mortality in Local Jails and State Prisons, 2000–2010—Statistical Tables," NCJ 239911, Bureau of Justice Statistics, www.bjs.gov/content/pub/pdf/mljsp0010st.pdf.

96. Ashley Nellis, *The Lives of Juvenile Lifers: Findings from a National Survey* (Washington, DC: The Sentencing Project, 2012), 16, sentencingproject.org/doc/publications/jj_The_Lives_of_Juvenile_Lifers.pdf.

97. Deborah Fins, *Death Row U.S.A.: Spring 2012* (New York: NAACP Legal Defense and Educational Fund, 2012), 1–38, www.naacpldf.org/files/publications/DRUSA_Spring_2012.pdf.

98. Tracy L. Snell, "Capital Punishment, 2010—Statistical Tables," NCJ 236510, Bureau of Justice Statistics, December 2011, bjs.ojp.usdoj.gov/index.cfm?ty=tp&tid=18.

99. Death Penalty Information Center, "Death Sentences in 2012," www.deathpenaltyinfo.org/2012-sentencing.

100. "Table 2.52.2011. Attitudes Toward the Death Penalty for Persons Convicted of Murder, by Demographic Characteristics, United States," *Sourcebook of Criminal Justice Statistics,* 2011, www.albany.edu/sourcebook/pdf/t2522011.pdf.

101. "Table 2.58.2011. Respondents Reporting Whether They Believe the Death Penalty Acts as a Deterrent to Murder, by Demographic

Characteristics, United States," *Sourcebook of Criminal Justice Statistics*, 2011, www.albany.edu/sourcebook/pdf/t2582011.pdf.

102. "Table 2.54.2011. Attitudes Toward Fairness of the Application of the Death Penalty, by Demographic Characteristics, United States," *Sourcebook of Criminal Justice Statistics*, 2011, www.albany.edu/source book/pdf/t2542011.pdf.

103. Hartney and Silva, *And Justice for Some*.

104. Christopher J. Lyons and Becky Pettit, "Compounded Disadvantage: Race, Incarceration, and Wage Growth," *Social Problems* 58, no. 2 (2011): 257–80.

105. Note that the *total* number of drug offenders in state and federal prisons increased between 1999 and 2005. See Marc Mauer, *The Changing Racial Dynamics of the War on Drugs* (Washington, DC: The Sentencing Project, 2009).

106. U.S. Sentencing Commission, *Report to the Congress: Cocaine and Federal Sentencing Policy* (Washington, DC: U.S. Sentencing Commission, 2007).

107. Substance Abuse and Mental Health Services Administration, "Figure 2.11. Past Month Illicit Drug Use Among Persons Aged 12 or Older, by Race/Ethnicity: 2002–2011," in *Results from the 2011 National Survey on Drug Use and Health: Summary of National Findings*, NSDUH Series H-44, HHS Publication No. (SMA) 12-4713 (Rockville, MD: Substance Abuse and Mental Health Services Administration, 2012), www.samhsa .gov/data/nsduh/2k11results/nsduhresults2011.htm#2.7; Federal Bureau of Investigation, "Table 43: Arrests by Race, 2011."

108. Federal Bureau of Investigation, "Table 49: Arrests: Cities by Race"; Federal Bureau of Investigation, "Table 55. Arrests: Metropolitan Counties by Race, 2011," *Crime in the United States 2011*, www.fbi.gov/about-us/cjis /ucr/crime-in-the-u.s/2011/crime-in-the-u.s.-2011/tables/table-55; "Table 61. Arrests: Suburban Areas by Race, 2011."

109. Ezekiel Edwards, Will Bunting, and Lynda Garcia, *The War on Marijuana in Black and White: Billions of Dollars Wasted on Racially Biased Arrests* (New York; American Civil Liberties Union, 2013), www.aclu.org /files/assets/aclu-thewaronmarijuana-rel2.pdf.

110. Mauer, *Changing Racial Dynamics of the War on Drugs*.

111. U.S. Sentencing Commission, "Chapter 8: Mandatory Minimum Penalties for Drug Offenses," in *Report to the Congress: Mandatory Minimum Penalties in the Federal Criminal Justice System* (Washington, DC: U.S. Sentencing Commission, 2011), www.ussc.gov/Legislative_and _Public_Affairs/Congressional_Testimony_and_Reports/Mandatory _Minimum_Penalties/20111031_RtC_PDF/Chapter_08.pdf.

112. Mauer, *Changing Racial Dynamics of the War on Drugs*, 10.

113. Ibid., 6. Note that in 1999 African Americans were 43 percent (N=31,097) of those in federal prison for drug offenses, and by 2005 they still represented 43 percent (N=40,812) of those in federal prisons for drug offenses.

114. Mauer, *Changing Racial Dynamics of the War on Drugs*, 4–6. Note that in 1999 African Americans were 58 percent (N=144,700) of those in state prisons for drug offenses, and by 2005 they represented 45 percent (N=113,500) of those in state prison for drug offenses. Authors of the study

producing these figures note that the decline could be a signal of "shifted location of imprisonment."

115. "Table 2.0021.2011. Attitudes Toward Legalization of the Use of Marijuana, by Demographic Characteristics, United States," *Sourcebook of Criminal Justice Statistics*, 2011, www.albany.edu/sourcebook/pdf /t200212011.pdf.

116. "Table 2.43. Attitudes Toward the Level of Spending to Deal with Drug Addiction, by Demographic Characteristics, United States, Selected Years 1985–2002," *Sourcebook of Criminal Justice Statistics* 2003, 136–37, www.albany.edu/sourcebook/pdf/t243.pdf.

117. "Table 2.97. Attitudes Toward Laws Regulating the Distribution of Pornography, by Demographic Characteristics, United States, Selected Years, 1987–2002," *Sourcebook of Criminal Justice Statistics*, 2003, 182–83, www.albany.edu/sourcebook/pdf/t297.pdf.

118. "Table 2.101.2011. Attitudes Toward the Legality of Abortion, by Demographic Characteristics, United States," *Sourcebook of Criminal Justice Statistics*, 2011, www.albany.edu/sourcebook/pdf/t21012011.pdf.

119. Pew Research Center for the People & the Press, "Few Say Religion Shapes Immigration, Environment Views: Religion and the Issues," September 17, 2010, www.people-press.org/2010/09/17/few-say-religion -shapes-immigration-environment-views.

120. Mark Motivans, "Immigration Offenders in the Federal Justice System, 2010," NCJ 238581, Bureau of Justice Statistics, July 2012, bjs.gov /content/pub/pdf/iofjs10.pdf.

121. "Zimmerman Verdict: Poll Finds Chasm Between Black and White Reactions," Washington Post–ABC News poll, July 24, 2013.

122. "Table 2.60.2011. Respondents Reporting Having a Gun in Their Home, by Demographic Characteristics, United States," *Sourcebook of Criminal Justice Statistics*, 2011, www.albany.edu/sourcebook/pdf/t260 2011.pdf.

123. "Table 2.64.2011. Attitudes Toward Laws Covering the Sale of Firearms, by Demographic Characteristics, United States," *Sourcebook of Criminal Justice Statistics*, 2011, www.albany.edu/sourcebook/pdf/t2642011.pdf.

124. "Table 2.0040.2010. Respondents Reporting Whether They Think Gun Control or the Right to Own a Gun Is More Important, by Demographic Characteristics, United States 2010," *Sourcebook of Criminal Justice Statistics*, 2011, www.albany.edu/sourcebook/pdf/t200402010.pdf.

125. John Roman, "Race, Justifiable Homicide, and Stand Your Ground Laws: Analysis of FBI Supplementary Homicide Report Data," Urban Institute, July 2013, www.urban.org/UploadedPDF/412873-stand-your -ground.pdf.

LIFESTYLE AND IDENTITY

1. Washington Post–Kaiser Family Foundation Poll, October 6–November 2, 2011, www.washingtonpost.com/wp-srv/politics/polls/post kaiserpoll_110211.html.

2. Media Behavior Institute, USA TouchPoints Study, 2012.

3. Ibid.

4. Sonya Rastogi, Tallese D. Johnson, Elizabeth M. Hoeffel, and Malcolm P. Drewery, "The Black Population, 2010," 2010 Census Briefs,

U.S. Census Bureau, September 2011, www.census.gov/prod/cen2010 /briefs/c2010br-06.pdf.

5. U.S. Census Bureau, "Table 16. Regional Distribution of the Population by Sex, for Black Alone and White Alone, Not Hispanic: 2011," Black Alone Population in the United States: 2011, www.census.gov/population /race/data/ppl-ba11.html.

6. Rastogi et al., "Black Population, 2010."

7. U.S. Census Bureau, "Table 16. Regional Distribution of the Population."

8. William H. Frey, "The New Great Migration: Black Americans' Return to the South, 1965–2000," Brookings Institution, May 2004, www.brookings .edu/research/reports/2004/05/demographics-frey.

9. Rastogi et al., "Black Population, 2010."

10. Craig Gurian, "Mapping and Analysis of New Data Documents Still-Segregated America," Remapping Debate, January 18, 2011, www .remappingdebate.org/map-data-tool/mapping-and-analysis-new-data -documents-still-segregated-america.

11. Daniel Denvir, "Ten Most Segregated Urban Areas in America," Salon, March 29, 2011, www.salon.com/2011/03/29/most_segregated _cities/. See also "Black-White Segregation Indices for Metro Areas," William Frey's analysis of 1990, 2000, and 2010 censuses, www.psc.isr .umich.edu/dis/census/segregation2010.html.

12. John R. Logan and Wenquan Zhang, "Global Neighborhoods: New Evidence from Census 2010," US2010 Project, November 2011, www.s4 .brown.edu/us2010/Data/Report/globalfinal2.pdf.

13. U.S. Census Bureau, "Table 2. Marital Status of the Population 15 Years and Over by Sex, for Black Alone and White Alone, Not Hispanic, 2011," Black Alone Population in the United States: 2011.

14. Jeffrey S. Passel, Wendy Wang, and Paul Taylor, Marrying Out: One-in-Seven New U.S. Marriages Is Interracial or Interethnic (Washington, DC: Pew Research Center, 2012), www.pewsocialtrends.org/files/2010/10/755 -marrying-out.pdf.

15. Wendy Wang, The Rise of Intermarriage: Rate, Characteristics Vary by Race and Gender (Washington, DC: Pew Research Center, 2012), www .pewsocialtrends.org/files/2012/02/SDT-Intermarriage-II.pdf.

16. Jeffrey M. Jones, "Record-High 86% Approve of Black-White Marriages," Gallup, September 12, 2011, www.gallup.com/poll/149390/Record -High-Approve-Black-White-Marriages.aspx.

17. U.S. Census, "Households and Families: 2010," 2010 Census Briefs, April 2012, www.census.gov/prod/cen2010/briefs/c2010br-14.pdf.

18. Linda Jacobson, Mark Mather, and Genevieve DuPuis, "Household Change in the United States," Population Bulletin 67, no. 1 (September 2012).

19. U.S. Census Bureau, "Table 14. Housing Tenure by Household Type, for Black Alone and White Alone, Not Hispanic Households: 2011," Black Alone Population in the United States: 2011.

20. U.S. Census Bureau, "Table 15. Housing Tenure by Family Type, for Black Alone and White Alone, Not Hispanic Families: 2011," Black Alone Population in the United States: 2011.

21. U.S. Census Bureau, "Table C9. Children by Presence and Type of Parent(s), Race, and Hispanic Origin: 2012: Black Alone or in Combination with

One or More Other Races," America's Families and Living Arrangements: 2012, www.census.gov/hhes/families/data/cps2012.html.

22. Gary J. Gates and Frank Newport, "Special Report: 3.4% of U.S. Adults Identify as LGBT," Gallup, October 12, 2012, www.gallup.com/poll /158066/special-report-adults-identify-lgbt.aspx.

23. U.S. Census Bureau, "Grandparents Living with Own Grandchildren Under 18 Years by Responsibility for Own Grandchildren and Age of Grandparent (Black or African American Alone)," 2011 American Community Survey 1-Year Estimates, factfinder2.census.gov/faces/tableservices /jsf/pages/productview.xhtml?src=bkmk. See also Gretchen Livingston and Kim Parker, "Since the Start of the Great Recession, More Children Raised by Grandparents," Pew Research on Social & Demographic Trends, September 9, 2010, www.pewsocialtrends.org/2010/09/09/since-the-start-of -the-great-recession-more-children-raised-by-grandparents/.

24. Washington Post–Kaiser Family Foundation Poll, October 6– November 2, 2011.

25. Gary J. Gates, "Family Formation and Raising Children Among Same-Sex Couples," Family Focus on . . . LGBT Families, no. FF51, National Council on Family Relations, williamsinstitute.law.ucla.edu/wp-content /uploads/Gates-Badgett-NCFR-LGBT-Families-December-2011.pdf.

26. Michelle Y. Green, "Minorities as Majority: Disproportionality in Child Welfare and Juvenile Justice," Children's Voice, November– December 2001, 8–13.

27. U.S. Government Accountability Office, African American Children in Foster Care: Additional HHS Assistance Needed to Help States Reduce the Proportion in Care, Report to the Chairman, Committee on Ways and Means, U.S. House of Representatives, July 2007, GAO-07-816, www.gao .gov/new.items/d07816.pdf.

28. Kids Count Data Center, "Children in Foster Care by Race or Hispanic Origin," Annie E. Casey Foundation, 2011, datacenter.kidscount.org /data/acrossstates/Rankings.aspx?ind=6246; Child Welfare Information Gateway, "Foster Care Statistics 2011," Children's Bureau, January 2013, www.childwelfare.gov/pubs/factsheets/foster.pdf.

29. Kids Count Data Center, "Children in Foster Care by Race or Hispanic Origin."

30. Children's Bureau, AFCARS Report, No. 19, July 2012, www.acf.hhs .gov/sites/default/files/cb/afcarsreport19.pdf.

31. U.S. Government Accountability Office, African American Children in Foster Care.

32. Maia Szalavitz, "Why Are So Many Foster Care Children Taking Antispychotics?," Time, November 29, 2011, healthland.time.com/2011/11 /29/why-are-so-many-foster-care-children-taking-antipsychotics/.

33. U.S. Government Accountability Office, African American Children in Foster Care.

34. Children's Bureau, AFCARS Report.

35. "Adoption Statistics," Statistic Brain, April 19, 2013, www.statistic brain.com/adoption-statistics/.

36. Child Welfare Information Gateway, "Foster Care Statistics, 2011."

37. Pew Forum on Religion and Public Life, U.S. Religious Landscape Survey, 2007, religions.pewforum.org/reports.

38. Neha Sahgal and Greg Smith, "A Religious Portrait of African Americans," Pew Forum on Religion and Public Life, January 30, 2009, www.pewforum.org/A-Religious-Portrait-of-African-Americans.aspx.

39. Pew Forum on Religion and Public Life, U.S. Religious Landscape Survey.

40. Sahgal and Smith, "Religious Portrait of African Americans."

41. Muslim West Facts Project, *Muslim Americans: A National Portrait* (Washington, DC: Gallup/Coexist Foundation), www.gallup.com/strategic consulting/153572/REPORT-Muslim-Americans-National-Portrait.aspx; Sahgal and Smith, "Religious Portrait of African Americans."

42. Gates and Newport, "Special Report: 3.4% of U.S. Adults Identify as LGBT."

43. Aisha C. Moodie-Mills, *Jumping Beyond the Broom: Why Black Gay and Transgender Americans Need More than Marriage Equality* (Washington, DC: Center for American Progress, 2012), www.american progress.org/wp-content/uploads/issues/2012/01/pdf/black_lgbt.pdf.

44. Pew Research Center for the People & the Press, "Growing Support for Gay Marriage: Changed Minds and Changing Demographics," March 20, 2013, www.people-press.org/files/legacy-pdf/3-20-13%20Gay%20Marriage%20Release%20UPDATE.pdf.

45. "Table 2.99.2012. Attitudes Toward the Legality of Homosexual (Gay or Lesbian) Relations, by Demographic Characteristics, United States," *Sourcebook of Criminal Justice Statistics*, 2012, www.albany.edu/source book/pdf/t2992012.pdf.

46. Pew Research Center for the People & the Press, "Half Say View of Obama Not Affected by Gay Marriage Decision," press release, May 14, 2012, www.people-press.org/files/legacy-pdf/05-14-2012%20gay%20mar riage-obama%20final.pdf.

MILITARY SERVICE

1. U.S. Department of Defense, "Organization of the Department of Defense (DOD)," Directorate for Organizational and Management Planning, n.d., odam.defense.gov/omp/Functions/Organizational_Portfo lios/Organization_and_Functions_Guidebook.html.

2. U.S. Census Bureau, "Table 514: Ready Reserve Personnel by Race, Hispanic Origin, and Sex: 1990 to 2010," *Statistical Abstract of the United States: 2012*, www.census.gov/compendia/statab/2012/tables/12s0514 .pdf.

3. Lolita C. Baldor, "Black Military Officers Rare 60 Years After Military Desegregated: AP," *Huffington Post*, July 23, 2008, www.huffingtonpost. com/2008/07/23/black-military-officers-r_n_114474.html

4. Department of Army Demographics, *Blacks in the U.S. Army: Then and Now* (Washington, DC: U.S. Army, 2010), www.armyg1.army.mil/hr/ docs/demographics/MRA_booklet_10-ARMY.pdf.

5. Erik Holmes, "General: Racism Still Deserves Dialogue," *Air Force Times*, February 21, 2009.

6. Air Force Personnel Center, "Air Force Military Demographics," 2013, www.afpc.af.mil/library/airforcepersonneldemographics.asp.

7. U.S. Census Bureau, "Table 514: Ready Reserve Personnel."

8. Kelly Kennedy, "West Point, ROTC Struggle to Recruit African

Americans," *Army Times*, September 26, 2006, www.kellykennedy.net/west pointminority.pdf.

9. Department of Army Demographics, *Blacks in the U.S. Army*.

10. Baldor, "Black Military Officers Rare 60 Years After Military Desegregated."

11. Holmes, "General: Racism Still Deserves Dialogue."

12. Department of Army Demographics, *Blacks in the U.S. Army*.

13. Ibid.

14. Brittany L. Stalsburg, "Lesbian, Gay, Bisexual and Transgender (LGBT) Women in the Military," fact sheet, Service Women's Action Network, March 2010, servicewomen.org/wp-content/uploads/2012/10/Final-DADT-Fact-Sheet-10.4.12.pdf.

15. Jorge Rivas, "ACLU Wins Full Severance Pay for Troops Discharged Under 'Don't Ask, Don't Tell,'" Colorlines.com, January 9, 2013, colorlines.com/archives/2013/01/aclu_wins_full_severance_pay_for_troops_discharged_under_dont_ask_dont_tell.html. See also Stalsburg, "Lesbian, Gay, Bisexual and Transgender (LGBT) Women in the Military."

16. Ursula A. Kelly, Kelly Skelton, Meghna Patel, and Bekh Bradley, "More Than Military Sexual Trauma: Interpersonal Violence, PTSD, and Mental Health in Women Veterans," *Research in Nursing & Health* 34, no. 6 (2011): 457–67, www.ncdsv.org/images/RNH_MoreThanMilitarySexualTrauma_7-27-11.pdf.

17. U.S. Census Bureau, "How Do We Know?: A Snapshot of Our Nation's Veterans," www.census.gov/how/infographics/veterans.html. See also "Table 522. Veterans Status by Sex, Race, and Hispanic Origin: 2009," *Statistical Abstract of the United States: 2012*, www.census.gov/compendia/statab/2012/tables/12s0522.pdf.

18. "Table 522. Veterans Status by Sex, Race, and Hispanic Origin: 2009."

19. National Center for Veterans Analysis and Statistics, "Minority Veterans: 2011," U.S. Department of Veterans Affairs, May 2013, www.va.gov/vetdata/docs/SpecialReports/Minority_Veterans_2011.pdf.

20. National Center for Veteran Analysis and Statistics, "Table 8L. Living Veterans by State, Race/Ethnicity, Gender, 2010–2040," U.S. Department of Veterans Affairs, www.va.gov/VETDATA/docs/Demographics/New_Vetpop_Model/8lVetPop11_Race_State.xlsx.

21. Naeesa Aziz, "Black Veterans Suffer High Unemployment," BET.com, November 7, 2011, www.bet.com/news/national/2011/11/04/black-veterans-suffer-high-unemployment.html.

22. U.S. Department of Labor, "The Veteran Labor Force in the Recovery," November 3, 2011, www.dol.gov/_sec/media/reports/VeteransLaborForce/VeteransLaborForce.pdf.

23. Chalsa M. Loo, "PTSD Among Ethnic Minority Veterans," National Center for PTSD, January 1, 2007 (updated April 4, 2012), www.ptsd.va.gov/professional/pages/ptsd-minority-vets.asp.

24. Rich Morin, "For Many Injured Veterans, a Lifetime of Consequences," Pew Research on Social & Demographic Trends, November 8, 2011, www.pewsocialtrends.org/files/2011/11/Wounded-Warriors.pdf.

25. Aishish K. Jha, Roslyn Stone, Judith Lave, et al., "The Concentration of Hospital Care for Black Veterans in Veterans Affairs Hospitals: Implications

for Clinical Outcomes," *Journal for Healthcare Quality* 32, no. 6 (2010): 52–61, doi:10.1111/j.1945-1474.2010.00085.x.

26. Nathaniel M. Rickles, Silvia Domínguez, and Hortensia Amaro, "Perceptions of Healthcare, Health Status, and Discrimination Among African-American Veterans," *Journal of Health Disparities Research and Practice* 4, no. 2 (2010): 50–68, hdl.handle.net/2047/d20000982.

27. U.S. Department of Veterans Affairs National Center on Homelessness Among Veterans, *Veteran Homelessness: A Supplemental Report to the 2010 Annual Homeless Assessment Report to Congress* (Washington, DC: U.S. Department of Veterans Affairs, 2011), www.va.gov/HOMELESS /docs/2010AHARVeteransReport.pdf.

28. J. Andrew Hoerner and Nia Robinson, *A Climate of Change: African Americans, Global Warming, and a Just Climate Policy in the U.S.* (Oakland, CA: Environmental Justice and Climate Change Initiative and Redefining Progress, 2008).

MONEY AND JOBS

1. Algernon Austin, "What a Recession Means for Black America," Economic Policy Institute, January 18, 2008, www.epi.org/publication /ib241/.

2. Steven C. Pitts, *Black Workers in the Bay Area: Employment Trends and Job Quality: 1970–2000* (Berkeley: Center for Labor Research and Education, 2008).

3. U.S. Department of Labor, "The African American Labor Force in the Recovery," February 29, 2012, www.dol.gov/_sec/media/reports/Black LaborForce/BlackLaborForce.pdf.

4. U.S. Equal Employment and Opportunity Commission, "2011 Job Patterns for Minorities and Women in Private Industry (EEO-1)," 2012, www1.eeoc.gov/eeoc/statistics/employment/jobpat-eeo1/2011/index.cfm.

5. U.S. Department of Labor, "African American Labor Force in the Recovery."

6. Steven C. Pitts, "Data Brief: Blacks in Unions: 2012," Center for Labor Research and Education, laborcenter.berkeley.edu/blackworkers /blacks_in_unions12.pdf.

7. David Cooper, Mary Gable, and Algernon Austin, "The Public Sector Jobs Crisis," Economic Policy Institute, May 2, 2012, www.epi.org /publication/bp339-public-sector-jobs-crisis/.

8. U.S. Department of Labor, "African American Labor Force in the Recovery."

9. BoardSource, *Nonprofit Governance Index 2012: Data Report 1: CEO Survey of BoardSource Members* (Washington, DC: BoardSource, 2012), 10, static.squarespace.com/static/50c7bd57e4b0455b1700d7e5/t /5187d7b1e4b07f4d551eafac/1367857073598/BoardSrc%20NPO%202012 %20Governance%20Index%20Report%20.pdf.

10. D5, *State of the Work: The Road to Greater Diversity, Equity, and Inclusion in Philanthropy* (Chicago: D5 Coalition, 2012), www.d5coalition .org/wp-content/uploads/2012/05/D5_State_of_the_Work_2012.pdf.

11. John Morning, "Marking Time: Black Board Participation in New York City, 2.0," Dēmos, April 10, 2012, www.demos.org/sites/default/files /publications/MarkingTime_Demos.pdf.

12. Joint Economic Committee, "Understanding the Economy: Long-Term Unemployment in the African American Community," U.S. Senate, March 2010, www.jec.senate.gov/public/index.cfm?a=Files.Serve&File_id =f7a324ea-4998-4a96-aeea-0265a3a68aae.

13. Bureau of Labor Statistics, "Table 1. Labor Force Status of 2012 High School Graduates and 2011–12 High School Dropouts 16 to 24 Years Old by School Enrollment, Educational Attainment, Sex, Race, and Hispanic or Latino Ethnicity, October 2012," economic news release, www.bls.gov /news.release/hsgec.t01.htm.

14. Joint Economic Committee, "Understanding the Economy."

15. Bureau of Labor Statistics, "The Employment Situation—June 2013," news release, July 5, 2013, www.bls.gov/news.release/pdf/empsit.pdf.

16. Bureau of Labor Statistics, "A-36. Unemployed Persons by Age, Sex, Race, Hispanic or Latino Ethnicity, Marital Status, and Duration of Unemployment," Current Population Survey, 2013, www.bls.gov/web /empsit/cpseea36.pdf.

17. National Gay and Lesbian Task Force, National Black Justice Coalition, and the National Center for Transgender Equality, "Injustice at Every Turn: A Look at Black Respondents in the National Transgender Discrimination Survey," September 25, 2011.

18. U.S. Department of Labor, "African American Labor Force in the Recovery."

19. CareerBuilder, "2011 Diversity in the Workplace: A CareerBuilder Study," 2011, img.icbdr.com/images/jp/pdf/BRO-0053_DiversityReport _2011.pdf.

20. Ibid.

21. National Gay and Lesbian Task Force et al., "Injustice at Every Turn"; National Center for Transgender Equality, "ENDA by the Numbers," 2010, transequality.org/Resources/enda_by_the_numbers.pdf.

22. National Gay and Lesbian Task Force et al., "Injustice at Every Turn."

23. Pitts, Black Workers in the Bay Area, 2.

24. Carmen DeNavas-Walt., Bernadette D. Proctor, and Jessica C. Smith, Income, Poverty, and Health Insurance Coverage in the United States: 2011 (Washington, DC: U.S. Census Bureau, 2011), www.census.gov /prod/2012pubs/p60-243.pdf.

25. Nielsen, "African American Consumers: Still Vital, Still Growing," 2013, www.nielsen.com/africanamerican.

26. U.S. Department of Labor, "African American Labor Force in the Recovery."

27. U.S. Census Bureau, "Table H6. Regions—by Median and Mean Income," Current Population Survey, 2012, www.census.gov/hhes/www /income/data/historical/household/.

28. Julia B. Isaacs, "Economic Mobility of Black and White Families," Brookings Institution, November 2007,www.brookings.edu/papers/2007 /11_blackwhite_isaacs.aspx.

29. DeNavas-Walt et al., Income, Poverty, and Health Insurance Coverage in the United States: 2011.

30. Nari Rhee, "Black and Latino Retirement (In)security," research brief, Center for Labor Research and Education, February 2012, laborcenter .berkeley.edu/research/retirement_in_security2012.pdf.

31. Kids Count Data Center, "Children in Poverty by Race and Ethnicity," 2011, datacenter.kidscount.org/data/tables/44-children-in-poverty-by-race-and-ethnicity?loc=1&loct=2#detailed/1/any/false/867,133,38,35,18/10,11,9,12,1,185,13/324,323.

32. Sophia Kerby, "The State of Women of Color in the United States," Center for American Progress, July 17, 2012, www.americanprogress.org/wp-content/uploads/issues/2012/07/pdf/women_of_color_brief.pdf.

33. Substance Abuse and Mental Health Services Administration, "Current Statistics on the Prevalence and Characteristics of People Experiencing Homelessness in the United States," July 2011, homeless.samhsa.gov/ResourceFiles/hrc_factsheet.pdf.

34. National Gay and Lesbian Task Force et al., "Injustice at Every Turn."

35. Ibid.

36. Insight Center for Community Economic Development, "The Racial Gap in Savings and Investments," fact sheet, spring 2009, www.insightcced.org/uploads/CRWG/Racial%20Gap%20in%20Savings%20and%20Investments%20Spring%202009.pdf.

37. Amy Traub and Catherine Ruetschlin, *The Plastic Safety-Net: Findings from the 2012 National Survey on Credit Card Debt of Low- and Middle-Income Households* (New York: Demos, 2012), www.demos.org/publication/plastic-safety-net.

38. Rhee, "Black and Latino Retirement (In)security."

39. Traub and Ruetschlin, *Plastic Safety-Net*.

40. Federal Deposit Insurance Corporation, *2011 FDIC National Survey of Unbanked and Underbanked Households* (Washington, DC: Federal Deposit Insurance Corporation, 2012), www.fdic.gov/householdsurvey/2012_unbankedreport.pdf.

41. Washington Post–Kaiser Family Foundation Poll, October 6–November 2, 2011, www.washingtonpost.com/wp-srv/politics/polls/postkaiserpoll_110211.html.

42. Ibid.

43. Traub and Ruetschlin, *Plastic Safety-Net*.

44. Jean Braucher, Dov Cohen, and Robert M. Lawless, "Race, Attorney Influence, and Bankruptcy Chapter Choice," *Journal of Empirical Legal Studies* 9, no. 3 (2012): 393–429, doi: 10.1111/j.1740-1461.2012.01264.x.

45. Ibid.

46. Traub and Ruetschlin, *Plastic Safety-Net*.

47. U.S. Census Bureau, "State and County Quickfacts," 2013, quickfacts.census.gov/qfd/states/00000.html.

48. Patrice Peck, "The Best States for Black Business Owners," *Huffington Post*, July 25, 2012, www.huffingtonpost.com/2012/07/23/best-states-black-owners_n_1696402.html.

49, Thomas D. Boston, "The Role of Black-Owned Businesses in Black Community Development," in *Jobs and Economic Development in Minority Communities*, ed. Paul Ong and Anastasia Loukaitou-Sideris (Philadelphia, PA: Temple University Press, 2006), 162.

50. Rolf Pendall, Lesley Freiman, Dowell Myers, and Selma Hepp, *Demographic Challenges and Opportunities for U.S. Housing Markets* (Washington, DC: Bipartisan Policy Center, 2012), bipartisanpolicy.org/sites/default/files/BPC%20Housing%20Demography.pdf.

51. Debbie Gruenstein Bocian, Wei Li, Carolina Reid, and Roberto G. Quercia, *Lost Ground 2011: Disparities in Mortgage Lending and Foreclosures* (Durham, NC: Center for Responsible Lending, 2011), www.responsiblelending.org/mortgage-lending/research-analysis/Lost-Ground-2011.pdf.

52. Ibid.

53. Pendall et al., *Demographic Challenges and Opportunities for U.S. Housing Markets*.

54. Bocian et al., *Lost Ground 2011*.

55. Thomas Shapiro, Tatjana Meschede, and Sam Osoro, "The Roots of the Widening Racial Wealth Gap: Explaining the Black-White Economic Divide," Institute on Assets and Social Policy, Brandeis University, February 2013, iasp.brandeis.edu/pdfs/Author/shapiro-thomas-m/racialwealthgapbrief.pdf.

56. Tami Luhby, "Worsening Wealth Inequality by Race," CNNMoney, June 21, 2012, money.cnn.com/2012/06/21/news/economy/wealth-gap-race/index.htm.

57. Kochhar et al., *Twenty to One*.

58. U.S. Department of Labor, "African American Labor Force in the Recovery"; Bureau of Labor Statistics, "Unemployment in December 2010," January 11, 2011, www.bls.gov/opub/ted/2011/ted_20110111.htm.

59. U.S. Department of Labor, "African American Labor Force in the Recovery."

60. Ibid.

61. Steven Raphael, "The Spatial Mismatch Hypothesis and Black Youth Joblessness," *Journal of Urban Economics* 43, no. 1 (1998): 79–111; and Harry J. Holzer, "The Spatial Mismatch Hypothesis: What Has the Evidence Shown?" *Urban Studies* 28, no. 1 (1991): 105–22. See also U.S. Department of Labor, "African American Labor Force in the Recovery."

62. U.S. Department of Labor, "African American Labor Force in the Recovery."

63. Joint Economic Committee, "Understanding the Economy."

64. Nielsen, "African-American Consumers."

65. Ibid.

66. Ibid.

67. U.S. Census Bureau, "Table 686. Average Annual Expenditures of All Consumer Units by Race, Hispanic Origin, and Age of Householder: 2009," *Statistical Abstract of the United States: 2012*, www.census.gov/compendia/statab/2012/tables/12s0686.pdf.

POLITICS, VOTING, AND CIVIC ENGAGEMENT

1. White House, "President Barack Obama," www.whitehouse.gov/administration/president-obama.

2. Office of the Historian, "Biographies of the Secretaries of State: Colin L. Powell," U.S. Department of the State, history.state.gov/departmenthistory/people/powell-colin-luther.

3. "Condoleezza Rice," Bio.com, www.biography.com/people/condoleezza-rice-9456857.

4. Lauren Victoria Burke, "Bush, Clinton Still Lead President Obama in Black Cabinet Picks," Politic365, March 6, 2013, politic365.com/2013/03/06/bush-clinton-still-lead-president-obama-in-black-cabinet-picks/.

5. Morgan Whitaker, "113th Congress: Most Diverse, Most Like the Rest of America," MSNBC, January 3, 2013, tv.msnbc.com/2013/01/03/113th -congress-most-diverse-most-like-the-rest-of-america/.

6. U.S. Senate, "Breaking New Ground—African American Senators," n.d., www.senate.gov/pagelayout/history/h_multi_sections_and_teasers /Photo_Exhibit_African_American_Senators.htm.

7. "Clarence Thomas," Bio.com, www.biography.com/people/clarence -thomas-9505658.

8. Ibid.; Thurgood Marshall College, "About Us," n.d., marshall.ucsd .edu/about/index.html.

9. Reuters, "FactBox: Black U.S. Senators and Governors," June 29, 2008, www.reuters.com/article/2008/06/30/us-usa-politics-black-idUSN 2044253720080630.

10. National Conference of State Legislatures, "Number of African American Legislators, 2009," www.ncsl.org/legislatures-elections/legis data/african-american-legislators-1992-to-2009.aspx.

11. Ibid.; Richard Wolf, "Voting Rights Act: A Political Twist for the South," USA Today, February 23, 2013, www.usatoday.com/story/news /politics/2013/02/23/voting-rights-act-southern-legislatures-race-politics /1939353/.

12. National Conference of State Legislatures, "Number of African American Legislators, 2009."

13. David A. Bositis, "Resegregation in Southern Politics?," Research Brief, Joint Center for Political and Economic Studies, November 2011, www.jointcenter.org/research/resegregation-in-southern-politics.

14. Ibid.

15. David A. Bositis, Blacks & the 2012 Democratic National Convention (Washington, DC: Joint Center for Political and Economic Studies, 2012), www.jointcenter.org/research/blacks-and-the-2012-democratic-national -convention.

16. U.S. Census Bureau, "Table 401. Reported Voting and Registration Among Native and Naturalized Citizens by Race and Hispanic Origin: 2010," Statistical Abstract of the United States: 2012, www.census.gov /compendia/statab/2012/tables/12s0401.pdf.

17. David A. Bositis, Blacks & the 2012 Republican National Convention (Washington, DC: Joint Center for Political and Econominc Studies, 2012), www.jointcenter.org/research/blacks-and-the-2012-republican-national -convention.

18. U.S. Census Bureau, "Table 401. Reported Voting and Registration."

19. Paul Taylor, "The Growing Electoral Clout of Blacks Is Driven by Turn out, Not Demographics," December 26, 2012, Pew Research on Social & Demographic Trends, www.pewsocialtrends.org/files/2013/01/2012_Black _Voter_Project_revised_1-9.pdf.

20. Frank Newport, "Obama Remains Women's Presidential Pick; Romney, Men's," Gallup, August 23, 2012, www.gallup.com/poll/156848 /obama-remains-women-presidential-pick-romney-men.aspx.

21. Taylor, "Growing Electoral Clout of Blacks."

22. Cynthia Gordy, "The War on Black Voters," The Root, December 10, 2011, www.theroot.com/views/war-black-voters.

23. Wolf, "Voting Rights Act."

24. Brennan Center for Justice, "Voting Laws Roundup 2013," May 10, 2013, www.brennancenter.org/analysis/election-2013-voting-laws-roundup.

25. Christopher Uggen, Sarah Shannon, and Jeff Manza, *State-Level Estimates of Felon Disenfranchisement in the United States, 2010* (Washington, DC: The Sentencing Project, 2012), 1, www.sentencingproject.org/doc/publications/fd_State_Level_Estimates_of_Felon_Disen_2010.pdf.

26. Ibid., 1–2.

27. Ibid., 2.

28. Campus Compact, "Service Statistics 2008: Highlights and Trends of Campus Compact's Annual Membership Survey," 2009, www.compact.org/wp-content/uploads/2009/10/2008-statistics1.pdf.

29. Nancy Hooyman and H. Asuman Kiyak, *Social Gerontology: A Multidisciplinary Perspective* (Boston: Pearson/Allyn & Bacon, 2005).

30. Andrew Billingsley and Cleopatra Howard Caldwell, "The Church, the Family, and the School in the African American Community," *Journal of Negro Education* 26, no. 1 (1991): 60.

SCIENCE AND TECHNOLOGY

1. National Action Council for Minorities in Engineering, "African Americans in Engineering," *NACME Research and Policy Brief* 2, no. 4 (2012), www.nacme.org/user/docs/AfricanAmericans12.pdf.

2. National Action Council for Minorities in Engineering, *American Engineers: The Key to Global Competitiveness: NACME 2012 Annual Report* (White Plains, NY: National Action Council for Minorities in Engineering, 2013), www.nacme.org/user/docs/AR2012Final.pdf.

3. U.S. Department of Labor, "The African American Labor Force in the Recovery," February 29, 2012, 6, www.dol.gov/_sec/media/reports/BlackLaborForce/BlackLaborForce.pdf.

4. Karen de Sá, "African-American Science Fair Attracts Record Numbers of Students to Buck the Odds in Silicon Valley," *San Jose Mercury News*, January 27, 2013.

5. College Board, "AP Stem Access Program," n.d., www.collegeboard.org/ap-stem-access-program.html.

6. National Science Foundation, "Table 2-8. Intentions of Freshmen to Major in S&E Fields, by Race/Ethnicity and Sex: 2010," Women, Minorities, and Persons with Disabilities in Science and Engineering, 2013, www.nsf.gov/statistics/wmpd/2013/pdf/tab2-8.pdf.

7. National Action Council for Minorities in Engineering, "African Americans in Engineering."

8. U.S. Census Bureau, "Table 814. Doctorates Conferred by Characteristics of Recipients: 2000 and 2009," *Statistical Abstract of the United States: 2012*, www.census.gov/compendia/statab/2012/tables/12s0814.pdf.

9. National Action Council for Minorities in Engineering, "African Americans in Engineering."

10. National Science Foundation, "Table 2-8. Intentions of Freshmen."

11. U.S. Census Bureau, "Table 814. Doctorates Conferred."

12. National Action Council for Minorities in Engineering, "African Americans in Engineering."

13. National Science Foundation, "Table 5-12. Top 20 Academic Institutions Awarding S&E Bachelor's Degrees, by Race/Ethnicity of Minority Graduates: 2006–10," Women, Minorities, and Persons with Disabilities in Science and Engineering, 2013, www.nsf.gov/statistics/wmpd/2013/pdf/tab5-12.pdf.

14. National Science Foundation, "Table 7-10. Top Baccalaureate Institutions of Black S&E Recipients, 2006–2010," Women, Minorities, and Persons with Disabilities in Science and Engineering, 2013, www.nsf.gov/statistics/wmpd/2013/pdf/tab7-10.pdf.

15. National Action Council for Minorities in Engineering, "African Americans in Engineering."

16. National Science Foundation, "Table 9-6. Employed Scientists and Engineers, by Occupation, Highest Degree Level, and Race/Ethnicity: 2008," Women, Minorities, and Persons with Disabilities in Science and Engineering, 2013, www.nsf.gov/statistics/wmpd/2013/pdf/tab9-6.pdf.

17. National Science Foundation, "Table 9-34. Occupations of Scientists and Engineers Employed by the Federal Government, by Race/Ethnicity: 2006–09," Women, Minorities, and Persons with Disabilities in Science and Engineering, 2013, www.nsf.gov/statistics/wmpd/2013/pdf/tab9-34.pdf.

18. National Science Foundation, "Table 8-3. Location and Type of Postgraduate Activity for U.S. Citizen and Permanent Resident S&E Doctorate Recipients with Definite Postgraduate Plans, by Race/Ethnicity: 2010," Women, Minorities, and Persons with Disabilities in Science and Engineering, 2013, www.nsf.gov/statistics/wmpd/2013/pdf/tab8-3.pdf.

19. Donna K. Ginther, Walter T. Schaffer, Joshua Schnell, et al., "Race, Ethnicity, and NIH Research Awards," Science 333, no. 6045 (2011): 1015–19, doi:10.1126/science.1196783.

20. Ibid.

21. Kathryn Zickuhr and Aaron Smith, Digital Differences (Washington, DC: Pew Internet & American Life Project, 2012), pewinternet.org/Reports/2012/Digital-differences.aspx.

22. Dmitri Williams, Nicole Martins, Mia Consalvo, and James D. Ivory, "The Virtual Census: Representations of Gender, Race, and Age in Video Games," New Media & Society 11, no. 5 (2009): 815–34, doi:10.1177/1461444809105354.

23. Victoria J. Rideout, Ulla G. Foehr, and Donald F. Roberts, Generation M2: Media in the Lives of 8- to 18-Year-Olds (Menlo Park, CA: Henry J. Kaiser Family Foundation, 2010), www.kff.org/entmedia/upload/8010.pdf.

24. Williams et al., "Virtual Census."

25. Ibid.

26. Rideout et al., Generation M2.

27. Latanya Sweeney, "Discrimination in Online Ad Delivery," Queue 11, no. 3 (2013), queue.acm.org/detail.cfm?id=2460278.

28. "Two Atlanta HBCUs Participating in Major Robotics Research," Journal of Blacks in Higher Education, August 22, 2011, www.jbhe.com/2011/08/two-atlanta-hbcus-participating-in-major-robotics-research/.

29. Andrea Foster, "NSF Grant Promotes Robotics at Historically Black Colleges," Wired Campus blog, Chronicle of Higher Education, January 9, 2008, chronicle.com/blogs/wiredcampus/nsf-grant-promotes-robotics-at-historically-black-colleges/3594.

30. NASA, "List of Universities with a Robotics Program," n.d., robotics .nasa.gov/students/robo_u.php.

31. Mike Swift, "Blacks, Latinos and Women Lose Ground at Silicon Valley Tech Companies," *San Jose Mercury News*, February 13, 2010.

BLACK FEMALES

1. See Erikka Yancy, "Confessions of a Hair Weave Addict," *Huffington Post*, April 15, 2013, www.huffingtonpost.com/erikka-yancy/hair-weave -addiction_b_3065875.html.

2. H. Fields Grenee, "What Spending a Half a Trillion Dollars on Hair Care and Weaves Says About Us," MadameNoire, May 11, 2011, madame noire.com/57134/what-spending-a-half-a-trillion-dollars-on-hair-care-and -weaves-says-about-us/.

3. Target Market News, *The Buying Power of Black America*, 17th ed. (Chicago: Target Market News, 2013).

4. Dana Towns, "2012 Taliah Waajid Natural Hair Show Hosted at the Georgia International Convention Center," *West Georgian*, October 23, 2012, thewestgeorgian.com/2012-taliah-waajid-natural-hair-show-hosted -at-the-georgia-international-convention-center/.

5. Michelle Healy, "Natural Hair Is Making Waves Among Black Women," *USA Today*, December 26, 2011, yourlife.usatoday.com/your -look/story/2011-12-21/Natural-hair-is-making-waves-among-black -women/52147456/1.

6. Auden C. McClure, Susanne E. Tanski, John Kingsbury, et al., "Characteristics Associated with Low Self-Esteem Among U.S. Adolescents," *Academic Pediatrics* 10, no. 4 (2010): 238–44.e2, doi:10.1016/j.acap .2010.03.007.

7. John Blake, "Return of the 'Welfare Queen,'" CNN Politics, January 23, 2012, www.cnn.com/2012/01/23/politics/weflare-queen.

8. Office of Family Assistance, "Characteristics and Financial Circumstances of TANF Recipients, Fiscal Year 2010," U.S. Department of Health and Human Services, August 8, 2012, www.acf.hhs.gov/programs/ofa /resource/character/fy2010/fy2010-chap10-ys-final.

9. Joint Economic Committee, "Understanding the Economy: Long-Term Unemployment in the African American Community," U.S. Senate, March 2010, www.jec.senate.gov/public/index.cfm?a=Files.Serve&File_id =f7a324ea-4998-4a96-aeea-0265a3a68aae.

10. Washington Post–Kaiser Family Foundation Poll, October 6– November 2, 2011, www.washingtonpost.com/wp-srv/politics/polls/post kaiserpoll_110211.html.

11. Blake, "Return of the Welfare Queen."

12. Daniel P. Moynihan, *The Negro Family: The Case for National Action* (Washington, DC: Office of Planning Policy and Research, U.S. Department of Labor, 1965), www.dol.gov/oasam/programs/history/webid-meynihan .htm.

13. Office of Civil Rights, "Discipline," U.S. Department of Education, March 2012, www2.ed.gov/about/offices/list/ocr/docs/crdc-2012-data -summary.pdf.

14. Center for Labor Research and Education, "Annual Report: Black Employment and Unemployment in 2011," University of California, Berkeley,

January 17, 2012, laborcenter.berkeley.edu/blackworkers/Black_Employ ment_and_Unemployment_2011.pdf; Center for Labor Research and Education, "Annual Report: Black Employment and Unemployment in 2012," University of California, Berkeley, February 12, 2013, laborcenter.berkeley .edu/blackworkers/Black_Employment_and_Unemployment_2012.pdf.

15. Charles Puzzanchera, Benjamin Adams, and Sarah Hockenberry, *Juvenile Court Statistics 2009* (Pittsburgh, PA: National Center for Juvenile Justice, 2012), 20, staging.ncjj.org/pdf/jcsreports/jcs2009.pdf; Melissa Sickmund, "Juveniles in Corrections," *Juvenile Offenders and Victims National Report*, June 2004, www.ncjrs.gov/pdffiles1/ojjdp/202885.pdf; Office of Juvenile Justice and Delinquency Programs, *Easy Access to the Census of Juveniles in Residential Placement: 1997–2010*, Office of Juvenile Justice and Delinquency Programs, ojjdp.ncjrs.org/ojstatbb/ezacjrp/.

16. Puzzanchera et al., *Juvenile Court Statistics 2009*, 26.

17. Sickmund, "Juveniles in Corrections."

18. Alice Randall, "Black Women and Fat," *New York Times*, May 5, 2012

19. Office of Minority Health, "Obesity and African Americans," U.S. Department of Health and Human Services, September 6, 2012, minority health.hhs.gov/templates/content.aspx?ID=6456.

20. Jeannine S. Schiller, Jacqueline W. Lucas, Brian W. Ward, and Jennifer A. Peregoy, "Table 31. Age-Adjusted Percent Distributions of Body Mass Index Among Persons Aged 18 Years and Over, by Selected Characteristics: United States, 2010," in "Summary Health Statistics for U.S. Adults: National Health Interview Survey, 2010," *Vital and Health Statistics* 10, no. 252 (2012): 106–8, www.cdc.gov/nchs/data/series/sr_10 /sr10_252.pdf.

21. Danice K. Eaton, Laura Kann, Steven Kinchen, et al., "Table 101. Percentage of High School Students Who Were Obese and Who Were Overweight, by Sex, Race/Ethnicity, and Grade—United States, Youth Risk Behavior Survey, 2011," in "Youth Risk Behavior Surveillance—United States," *Morbidity and Mortality Weekly Report* 61, no. 4 (2011): 149, www .cdc.gov/mmwr/pdf/ss/ss6104.pdf.

22. Rachael Rettner, "Hair Concerns Keep Some Women from Gym," LiveScience, December 17, 2012, www.livescience.com/25619-hair-care -african-american-women-exercise.html.

23. Maya Rockeymoore, "Are Black Women Fat Because They Want to Be?," *Huffington Post*, May 8, 2012, www.huffingtonpost.com/dr-maya -rockeymoore/black-women-and-obesity_b_1498145.html.

24. Washington Post–Kaiser Family Foundation Poll, October 6– November 2, 2011.

25. U.S. Census Bureau, "Table 2. Marital Status of the Population 15 Years and Over by Sex, for Black Alone and White Alone, Not Hispanic, 2011," Black Alone Population in the United States: 2011, www.census.gov /population/race/data/ppl-ba11.html.

26. U.S. Census Bureau, "Table 6. Households by Type, for Black Alone and White Alone, Not Hispanic Households: 2011," Black Alone Population in the United States: 2011.

27. Washington Post–Kaiser Family Foundation Poll, October 6– November 2, 2011.

28. U.S. Census Bureau, "Table 4. Nativity and Citizenship Status by Sex, for Black Alone and White Alone, Not Hispanic: 2011," Black Alone Population in the United States: 2011.

29. U.S. Census Bureau, "Table 5. Year of Entry of the Foreign-Born Population by Sex, for Black Alone and White Alone, Not Hispanic: 2011," Black Alone Population in the United States: 2011.

30. U.S. Census Bureau, "Table 1. Population by Sex and Age, for Black Alone and White Alone, Not Hispanic: 2011," Black Alone Population in the United States: 2011.

31. U.S. Census Bureau, "Table 16. Regional Distribution of the Population by Sex, for Black Alone and White Alone, Not Hispanic: 2011," Black Alone Population in the United States: 2011.

32. U.S. Census Bureau, "Table 15. Housing Tenure by Family Type, for Black Alone and White Alone, Not Hispanic Families: 2011," Black Alone Population in the United States: 2011.

33. U.S. Census Bureau, "Table 2. Marital Status."

34. Washington Post–Kaiser Family Foundation Poll, October 6–November 2, 2011.

35. Ibid.

36. Ibid.

37. Ibid.

38. Ibid.

39. Ibid.

40. "Highest % of Women Historically Black Colleges and Universities," CollegeStats.org, n.d., collegestats.org/colleges/historically-black/highest -women.

41. U.S. Census Bureau, "Table 229. Educational Attainment by Race and Hispanic Origin: 1970 to 2010," Statistical Abstract of the United States: 2012, www.census.gov/compendia/statab/2012/tables/12s0229 .pdf.

42. Ibid.

43. David Cooper, Mary Gable, and Algernon Austin, "The Public Sector Jobs Crisis," Economic Policy Institute, May 2, 2012, www.epi.org /publication/bp339-public-sector-jobs-crisis/.

44. U.S. Equal Employment and Opportunity Commission, "2011 Job Patterns for Minorities and Women in Private Industry (EEO-1)," 2012, www1.eeoc.gov/eeoc/statistics/employment/jobpat-eeo1/2011/index .cfm.

45. Sophia Kerby, "The State of Women of Color in the United States," Center for American Progress, July 17, 2012, www.americanprogress.org /wp-content/uploads/issues/2012/07/pdf/women_of_color_brief.pdf.

46. Washington Post–Kaiser Family Foundation Poll, October 6–November 2, 2011.

47. Office of Minority Health, "Chronic Liver Disease and African Americans," U.S. Department of Health and Human Services, August 24, 2012, minorityhealth.hhs.gov/templates/content.aspx?ID=6204.

48. Kenneth D. Kochanek, Jiaquan Xu, Sherry L. Murphy, et al., "Table 17. Age-Adjusted Death Rates for 113 Selected Causes, Enterocolitis Due to Clostridium Difficile, Drug-Induced Causes, Alcohol-Induced Causes, and Injury by Firearms, by Hispanic Origin, Race for Non-Hispanic Population,

and Sex: United States, 2009," in "Deaths: Final Data for 2009," *National Vital Statistics Report* 60, no. 3 (2011): 75–80, www.cdc.gov/nchs/data/nvsr /nvsr60/nvsr60_03.pdf.

49. Schiller et al., "Table 2. Age-Adjusted Percentages of Selected Circulatory Diseases Among Persons Aged 18 Years and Over, by Selected Characteristics: United States, 2010," in "Summary Health Statistics for U.S. Adults: National Health Interview Survey, 2010," 19–21.

50. "Table 71. Cholesterol Among Persons 20 Years of Age and Over, by Selected Characteristics: United States, Selected Years 1988–1994 Through 2007–2010," in *Health, United States, 2011: With Special Feature on Socioeconomic Status and Health* (Hyattsville, MD: National Center for Health Statistics, 2012), 246–49, www.cdc.gov/nchs/data/hus/hus11 .pdf.

51. U.S. Census Bureau, "Table 101. Abortions—Number and Rate by Race: 1990 to 2007," *Statistical Abstract of the United States: 2012*, www .census.gov/compendia/statab/2012/tables/12s0101.pdf.

52. Matthew J. Hickman and Brian A. Reaves, "Local Police Departments, 2003," NCJ 210118, Bureau of Justice Statistics, May 2006, 7, www.bjs.gov /content/pub/pdf/lpd03.pdf.

53. Washington Post–Kaiser Family Foundation Poll, October 6– November 2, 2011.

54. Puzzanchera et al., *Juvenile Court Statistics 2009*, 25.

55. U.S. Sentencing Commission, "Table 7. Age, Race, and Gender of Offenders, Fiscal Year 2011," in *2011 Sourcebook of Federal Sentencing Statistics*, www.ussc.gov/Research_and_Statistics/Annual_Reports_and _Sourcebooks/2011/Table07.pdf.

56. Charles Puzzanchera, Benjamin Adams, and Melissa Sickmund, *Juvenile Court Statistics 2008* (Pittsburgh, PA: National Center for Juvenile Justice, 2011), www.ncjj.org/pdf/jcsreports/jcs2008.pdf

57. E. Ann Carson and William J. Sabol, "Prisoners in 2011," NCJ 239808, Bureau of Justice Statistics, December 2012, 8, www.bjs.gov /content/pub/pdf/p11.pdf.

58. Allen J. Beck and Candace Johnson, "Sexual Victimization Reported by Former State Prisoners, 2008," NCJ 237363, Bureau of Justice Statistics, May 2012, bjs.ojp.usdoj.gov/content/pub/pdf/svrfsp08.pdf.

59. Marc Mauer, *The Changing Racial Dynamics of Women's Incarceration* (Washington, DC: The Sentencing Project, 2013), sentencingproject .org/doc/publications/rd_Changing%20Racial%20Dynamics%202013.pdf.

60. Stephanie Bush-Baskette, *Misguided Justice: The War on Drugs and Black Women* (Bloomington, IN: iUniverse, 2010), 85.

61. Puzzanchera et al., *Juvenile Court Statistics 2009*, 25.

BLACK MALES

1. Ivory A. Toldson, "More Black Men in Jail than College? Wrong," *The Root*, February 28, 2013, www.theroot.com/views/more-black-men -jail-college-wrong.

2. E. Ann Carson and William J. Sabol, "Prisoners in 2011," NJC 239808, Bureau of Justice Statistics, December 2012, 8, www.bjs.gov/content/pub /pdf/p11.pdf.

3. U.S. Census Bureau, "Table 279. College Enrollment by Selected

Characteristics: 1990 to 2009," *Statistical Abstract of the United States: 2012*, www.census.gov/compendia/statab/2012/tables/12s0279.pdf; U.S. Census Bureau, "Table 1. Educational Attainment of the Population 18 Years and Over, by Age, Sex, Race, and Hispanic Origin: 2010," Educational Attainment: 2010—Detailed Tables, www.census.gov/hhes/socdemo /education/data/cps/2010/tables.html.

4. Center for Labor Research and Education, "Annual Report: Black Employment and Unemployment in 2011"; Center for Labor Research and Education, "Annual Report: Black Employment and Unemployment in 2012."

5. Washington Post–Kaiser Family Foundation Poll, October 6– November 2, 2011, www.washingtonpost.com/wp-srv/politics/polls/post kaiserpoll_110211.html.

6. Devah Pager, "The Mark of a Criminal Record," *American Journal of Sociology* 108, no. 5 (2003): 937–75, www.princeton.edu/~pager/pager _ajs.pdf.

7. William Elliott III, "Examining Minority and Poor Youth's College Aspirations and Expectations: The Potential Role of College Savings." Working Paper No. 07-06, Center for Social Development, Washington University, 2007, www.usc.edu/dept/chepa/HRYANG/publications/111.pdf.

8. Traci Danielle Davis, "Field of Dreams: Exploring African American Male Students' Career Aspirations and Their Relationship to School Engagement" (PhD dissertation, University of Miami, 2011), rave.ohiolink .edu/etdc/view?acc_num=miami1304299566.

9. J. Luke Wood and Robert T. Palmer, "Understanding the Personal Goals of Black Male Community College Students: Facilitating Academic Achievement and Psychosocial Development," *Journal of African American Studies* 17, no. 2 (2013): 222–41, doi:10.1007/s12111-013-9248-3, jlukewood .com/wp-content/uploads/2012/06/Luke-and-Rob.pdf.

10. Nicki King, Ella R. Madsen, Marc Braverman, et al., "Career Decision-making: Perspectives of Low-Income Urban Youth," *Spaces for Difference: An Interdisciplinary Journal* 1, no. 1 (2008): 21–41, www.escholarship.org /uc/item/86m528db.

11. U.S. Census Bureau, "Table 4. Nativity and Citizenship Status."

12. U.S. Census Bureau, "Table 5. Year of Entry."

13. U.S. Census Bureau, "Table 1. Population by Sex and Age."

14. U.S. Census Bureau, "Table 16. Regional Distribution."

15. Washington Post–Kaiser Family Foundation Poll, October 16– November 2, 2011.

16. U.S. Census Bureau, "Table 2. Marital Status."

17. U.S. Census Bureau, "Table 6. Households."

18. U.S. Census Bureau, "Table 15. Housing Tenure."

19. Washington Post–Kaiser Family Foundation Poll, October 6– November 2, 2011.

20. Ibid.

21. Ibid.

22. Ibid.

23. Ibid.

24. Ivory A. Toldson, "Debunking Education Myths About Blacks," *The Root*, July 19, 2012, www.theroot.com/views/debunking-education-myths -about-blacks.

25. Shaun R. Harper and Andrew C. Porter, *Attracting Black Male Students to Research Careers in Education: A Report from the Grad Prep Academy Project* (Philadelphia: University of Pennsylvania, Center for the Study of Race and Equity in Education, 2012), www.gse.upenn.edu/equity/sites/gse.upenn.edu.equity/files/publications/Harper%20and%20Porter%20%282012%29_0.pdf.

26. Washington Post–Kaiser Family Foundation Poll, October 6–November 2, 2011.

27. U.S. Equal Employment and Opportunity Commission, "2011 Job Patterns for Minorities and Women in Private Industry (EEO-1)."

28. National Science Foundation, *Women, Minorities and Persons with Disabilities in Science and Engineering: 2013* (Arlington, VA: National Center for Science and Engineering Statistics, 2013), www.nsf.gov/statistics/wmpd/2013/pdf/nsf13304_digest.pdf.

29. Washington Post–Kaiser Family Foundation Poll, October 6–November 2, 2011.

30. Ibid.

31. Ibid.

32. "Table 74. Healthy Weight, Overweight, and Obesity Among Persons 20 Years of Age and Over, by Selected Characteristics: United States, Selected Years 1960–1962 Through 2007–2010," in *Health, United States, 2011,* 257–63.

33. Schiller et al., "Table 31. Age-Adjusted Percent Distributions of Body Mass Index Among Persons Aged 18 Years and Over, by Selected Characteristics: United States, 2010," "Summary Health Statistics for U.S. Adults: National Health Interview Survey, 2010," 106–8.

34. "Table 75. Obesity Among Children and Adolescents 2–19 Years of Age, by Selected Characteristics: United States, Selected Years 1963–1965 Through 2007–2010," *Health, United States, 2011.*

35. Danice K. Eaton, Laura Kann, Steven Kinchen, et al., "Table 101. Percentage of High School Students Who Were Obese and Who Were Overweight, by Sex, Race/Ethnicity, and Grade—United States," in "Youth Risk Behavior Surveillance—United States, 2011," *Morbidity and Mortality Weekly Report* 61, no. 4 (2012), www.cdc.gov/mmwr/pdf/ss/ss6104.pdf."

36. Office of Minority Health, "Chronic Liver Disease and African Americans."

37. Schiller et al., "Table 2. Age-Adjusted Percentages of Selected Circulatory Diseases." Note that statistics refer to the years 2007–10.

38. "Table 71. Cholesterol," *Health, United States, 2011.* Note that statistics refer to the years 2007–10.

39. Matthew J. Hickman and Brian A. Reaves, "Local Police Departments, 2003," NCJ 210118, Bureau of Justice Statistics, May 2006, 7, www.bjs.gov/content/pub/pdf/lpd03.pdf.

40. Charles Puzzanchera, Benjamin Adams, and Sarah Hockenberry, *Juvenile Court Statistics 2009* (Pittsburg, PA: National Center for Juvenile Justice, 2012), 20, staging.ncjj.org/pdf/jcsreports/jcs2009.pdf.

41. Ibid., 25.

42. U.S. Sentencing Commission, "Table 7. Age, Race, and Gender," in *2011 Sourcebook of Federal Sentencing Statistics.*

43. Puzzanchera et al., *Juvenile Court Statistics 2009,* 25.

44. Pew Charitable Trusts, *Collateral Costs: Incarceration's Effect on Economic Mobility* (Washington, DC: Pew Charitable Trusts, 2010), www.pewstates.org/uploadedFiles/PCS_Assets/2010/Collateral_Costs(1).pdf.

45. Ibid.

46. Carson and Sabol, "Prisoners in 2011," 7.

47. Ibid., 8.

48. Allen J. Beck and Candace Johnson, "Sexual Victimization Reported by Former State Prisoners, 2008," NCJ 237363, Bureau of Justice Statistics, May 2012, bjs.ojp.usdoj.gov/content/pub/pdf/svrfsp08.pdf.

ABC network, 35
abolitionism, 115
abortion, 80, 147–48
abuse, 90
Academy of Motion Picture Arts
    and Sciences, 36
accumulated disadvantage.
    See under justice system
    statistics
ACT college readiness exam, 19
actors, 33–35
Advanced Placement (AP)
    exams, 17–18
advertising, 112–13
affordable housing, 91
African Americans. See Black
    Americans
age breakdown, of Black
    Americans, 2
agricultural sciences, 126. See
    also farming
AIDS, 53–54, 76
air pollution, 27–28
alcohol abuse, 52–53
Alexander, Michelle, 59
A&M College, 128
American Bar Association, 69
American Recovery and
    Reinvestment, 23
American Revolution, 93
antipsychotic medications,
    90–91
AP (Advanced Placement)
    exams, 17–18
arrests, 63–65, 79, 148, 157
art, 37–38. See also
    entertainment statistics
assault, sexual. See sexual
    assault
Associated Press Sports
    Editors, 42
associate's degrees, 4, 125
asthma, 28
athletes, 32, 39–40
Attention Deficit Hyperactivity
    Disorder (ADHD), 50
Attucks, Crispus, 93

baby boomers, 85
Baker, Paxton, 40
Ball, M.V., xiii
banking habits, 107–8
bankruptcy, 109

baseball, 39–41
basketball, 32, 39–41
Batson v. Kentucky, 71
behavioral issues, of children, 9
Bennett College, 146
BET network, 35
Beyoncé, 37
Big Data, 164n1
biological sciences, 126
birth control, 48
birthing trends, 47–48
Black Americans
    ancestry of, ix
    as subjects of memes, x, 137
    See also specific headings
blood pressure, 57, 147, 157
boarding schools, 8
body weight, 141–42, 157
Bowie State University, 152
BP oil spill, 22, 30–31
Braun, Carol Moseley, 116
breast cancer, 55
breastfeeding, 47
Broadway theater, 35–36
Brooke, Edward, 116
Brookings Institution, 104
Bruce, Blanche, 116
Bullard, Robert, 22
bullying, 67
Burris, Roland, 116
Bush, George H.W., 117
Bush, George W., 116
business degrees, 4
business ownership, 24–25, 109
Byrd, Steven, 37

cancer:
    breast, 55
    colorectal, 54–55
    and environmental
        conditions, 23
    in females, 147
    intrahepatic bile duct, 147,
        157
    lung, 55
    in males, 157
    prostate, 55
carbon footprint, 23, 25–26
CARD Act, 109
Carver, George Washington,
    123
Catholic church membership, 91
cell phone usage, 123, 131–32

CEOs, 100, 109
charter schools, 10
Cheadle, Don, 32
chemical dependency, 49–53, 80
cholesterol, 147, 157
chronic illness, 53–57
churches, 49, 122
cigarette use, 53, 55
civic participation, 122
civil rights, 70, 115, 120, 164n4
classical music, 38
climate change, 22, 28–29
Clinton, Bill, 116
coal industry, 24, 26–27
cocaine, xv, 52, 79, 148
Cole, Nat King, 32
College Board, 17
college degrees, 3–4, 128
college faculty, 6
college presidents, 7
colleges and universities, 20–21
    for black engineering students,
        126–28
    community, 20
    Historically Black, 21, 45–46,
        145–47
    preparedness for, 19–20
    See also individual institutions
colorectal cancer, 54–55
"color line," ix, xvii
comedy, 38–39
community colleges, 20
computer science, 125
consumption patterns, 26, 114
contraception trends, 48
Cook, Will Marion, 36
Cornell University, 46
Cosby, Bill, 33
court fairness, 71–73
Cowan, William "Mo," 116
crack cocaine, xv, 52, 79, 148
credit card debt, 108
crime, 66–68. See also justice
    system statistics
criminal conviction histories, 151
criminalization, of students, 12–13
criminal justice system. See justice
    system statistics
cultural incompetence, 50

data
    as essential component in racial
        equity, ix

    as reflection of social contexts,
        xv
    See also statistics on Black
        Americans
Davis, Angela Y., 58
death penalty, 77–78
debt, 108–9, 156–57
decision making, xvii–xviii
Deepwater Horizon oil spill, 22,
    30–31
degrees:
    associate's, 4, 125
    business, 4
    college, 3–4, 128
    doctoral, 4, 125, 129–30
    engineering, 126–28
    law, 4
    master's, 4, 129
    medical, 4, 45–46
    professional, 4
Democratic Party, 118, 119
demographics:
    of females, 143
    of males, 153
    overview of, 1–2
dental assistants, 45
depression, 30, 50
Derham, James, 45
Destiny's Child, 37
detention, 74–77
diabetes, 55–56
digital divide, 123
disabilities, 13, 14, 97
discrimination. See racial profiling
disease, 53–57
disenfranchisement, voter, 121–22
disorderly conduct offenses, 73
disparity, ix
divorce, 88
doctoral degrees, 4, 125, 129–30
doctors, 44–47, 49
"Don't Ask, Don't Tell" law, 96
Douglass, Frederick, 45, 115
Drew, Charles, 45
Drexel University, 47, 128
drop-out rates, school, 14–15
drug enforcement, xv–xvi
drugs:
    abuse of, 49–53, 80
    arrests based on, 64, 74, 158
    war on, 79–80, 149
Du Bois, W.E.B.:
    on charity toward Blacks, xviii

Du Bois, W.E.B. (*continued*)
and the "color line," ix, xvii
on criminal justice system, 58
social science data collected by,
xiii–xvi
on stupidity, xiii
Duke University, 47

early childhood education, 7–8
Economic Policy Institute, 99
economic power, xvii
education statistics:
and barriers to education, 59
on degrees, 3–4
on educators, 4–7
on females, 145–46
on higher learning, 20–21
on males, 150, 155–56
on school discipline and push-
out, 12–15
and social factors, xvi
on student performance, 15–20
on students, 7–12
Elders, Joycelyn, 45
electoral politics, 59, 116–22
electricity:
expenditures on, 26
renewable, 23–24
Emancipation Proclamation, 1
Emory University, 46
employment, 100–106
barriers to, 59
during college years, 21
in educational settings, 4–7
and high school dropout rates,
15
of men, 151, 156–57
of women, 146–47
energy industry, 24–25
engineering industry. *See*
STEM (science, technology,
engineering, and math) fields
English teachers, 6
entertainment statistics, 32–39
on film and TV, 32–36
on music and art, 37–38
on theater, 36–37
environmental statistics, 22–31
on black-owned businesses,
24–25
on carbon footprint, 23, 25–26
on climate change and global
warming, 22, 28–29

on coal industry, 24, 26–27
on consumption, 26
on disasters, 29–31
on green jobs, 23–25
on negative environmental
consequences, 27–28
eugenics, 48

Fair Sentencing Act, 79
family, 49, 144, 154
farming, 23, 25
fast food restaurants, 142
Federal Bureau of Prisons, 74
Federal Gun Free School Act, 64
felony disenfranchisement, 121–22
females, 137–49
on "being black," 144–45
body weight of, 141–42
demographics of, 143
difficulties faced by, 140–41
educational experiences of,
145–46
financial standing of, 108, 146–47
free time of, 83
and gender wage gap, 104
hair care habits of, 137–38
health of, 55–57, 147–48
HIV rates in, 54
household and marital status of,
143–44
imprisonment of, 74
and justice system, 140–41,
148–49
in medical school, 21
in military, 96
on public assistance, 138–39
and relationships, 84, 144
as single parents, 142–43
in sports media, 41
in STEM fields, 125
in teaching profession, 4–5
tobacco use by, 53
and war on drugs, 149
50 Cent (rap artist), 37
film, 20, 32–36
financial industry, 101–2
fishing industry, 25, 30
flood damage, 30
Florida A&M University, 127
Florida State University, 46, 127
Floyd v. the City of New York, 59
food deserts, 56–57
football, 32, 39–41

forced sterilization, 48
foreign language teachers, 6
forestry industry, 25
fossil fuel extraction, 24
foster care, 90–91
fracking, 28
Frasier, Robin, 40
Frazier, Njema, 123
Freeman, Morgan, 33
Front Row Productions, 37

gangs, street, 67
Garrison, William Lloyd, 45
GATE (Gifted and Talented
     Education) programs, 17
gay marriage, 92, 144
gender identity. See
     transgendered people
gender wage gap, 104
Generation Y, 85
Georgia Institute of Technology,
     128
Georgia State University, 126, 128
Gifted and Talented Education
     (GATE) programs, 17
global warming, 28–29
Goldman Sachs, 102
governors, 117
Graduate Record Examination
     (GRE), 155
graffiti, 73
grants, science, 130
GRE (Graduate Record
     Examination), 155
greenhouse gas emissions, 25–26
green jobs, 23–25
Gulf Coast, 22
guns, 64, 66, 67, 81–82
Gustafson, Kaaryn, 138–39

HAART (Highly Active
     Antiretroviral Therapy), 54
hair care habits, of Black women,
     137–38
Hall, Juanita, 36
Hampton University, 46, 128
Harry, Beth, 9
Hart, Kevin, 39
Harvard University, 131
hate crimes, 69
HBCUs. See Historically Black
     Colleges and Universities
health aides, 45

health care access, 47
health insurance, 28
health statistics, 43–57
     on contraception, 48
     on disease and chronic illness,
          53–57
     on females, 55–57, 147–48
     on health care access, 47
     infant mortality rate, 48–49
     life expectancy, 49
     on males, 55–57, 157
     on medical professionals, 44–47
     on mental health and chemical
          dependency, 49–53
     on pregnancy and birthing
          trends, 47–48
     on respiratory disorders, 23,
          27–28
     on veterans, 97–98
heart disease, 57, 147
heating costs, 26
"heat islands," 29
higher learning, 20–21
Highly Active Antiretroviral
     Therapy (HAART), 54
hip-hop music, xvii, 37. See also
     rap music
Historically Black Colleges and
     Universities (HBCUs), 21, 45–
     46, 145–46
HIV/AIDS, 53–54, 76
hockey, 40–41
home health aides, 45
homelessness, 98, 107
home ownership, 109–10
homeschooling, 10
homicide. See murder
housing:
     affordable, 91
     barriers to, 59
     lead poisoning in, 28
     residential segregation, xvii
     spending on, 109
Howard University, 45, 46, 127
Hughes, Jan, 5
hunting industry, 25
Hurricane Katrina, 22, 29–31
Hurricane Rita, 22

IBD (intrahepatic bile duct) cancer,
     147, 157
identity
     racial, 2

identity (*continued*)
  sexual, 92, 96, 144, 154
  transgendered (*see*
    transgendered people)
  See also lifestyle statistics
identity theft, 67, 68
illness, chronic, 53–57. *See also*
  health statistics
immigration, illegal, 80–81
incarceration, 74–77, 148–49, 154,
  158–59
income, 104–6, 110–11
Indiana University, 46
Individual Retirement Accounts
  (IRAs), 107
infant mortality rate, 29, 48–49
Internet usage trends, 130
intimate partner violence, 66
intrahepatic bile duct (IBD) cancer,
  147, 157
investments, financial, 107
Iraq War, 96, 98
IRAs (Individual Retirement
  Accounts), 107
Isaacs, Cheryl Boone, 36

Jackson, Michael, 38
Jackson, Samuel L., 33, 34
jail. *See* incarceration
Jay-Z, 37
jazz music, 38
Jemison, Mae, 123
Jim Crow laws, xiii, 59
JLWOP. *See* Juvenile Life Without
  Parole
job satisfaction, 6
Johnson, Earvin "Magic," 40
Johnson, Lyndon B., 117
Johnson, Robert, 99
Joint Center for Political and
  Economic Studies, 118
Jones, Alia, 37
Jordan, June, 83
Jordan, Michael, 40
judges, in U.S. courts, 70
jury selection, 71–73
justice system statistics, 58–82
  on accumulated disadvantage,
    77–78
  on arrests, 63–65
  on black judges in U.S. courts, 70
  on black lawyers, 69–70
  on crime and safety, 66–68

  on females, 140–41, 148–49
  on incarceration and detention,
    74–77, 148–50, 154–55
  on jury selection and court
    fairness, 71–73
  on law enforcement, 60–62,
    65–66
  on males, 158–59
  on sentencing, 73–74
  and September 11th, 69
  on the war on drugs, 79–80
juvenile justice systems, 58, 64–65,
  74, 76–78, 148
Juvenile Life Without Parole
  (JLWOP), 76–77

Keogh Plans, 107
Keys, Alicia, 37
King, Rodney, 72
knowledge, xvi
Kyoto Protocol, 25

law degrees, 4
law enforcement, 60–62, 65–66,
  148, 157
Lawrence, Martin, 34
law school, 21
lawyers, 69–70
lead poisoning, 28
LGBT individuals, 54, 90, 92, 144–
  45, 154
licensed practical nurses (LPNs), 45
licensed vocational nurses (LVNs),
  45
life expectancy, 49
lifestyle statistics, 83–92
  on daily activities and priorities,
    83–88
  on household and marital status,
    88–91
  on marriage equality, 92
  on religious practices, 91
  on sexual identity, 92
Ligon v. City of New York, 59
LIHEAP (Low Income Home Energy
  Assistance Program), 26
liquor stores, 56–57
liver disease, 55
López, Ian Haney, ix
Louisiana State University, 128
Low Income Home Energy
  Assistance Program (LIHEAP),
  26

LPNs (licensed practical nurses), 45
lung cancer, 55
LVNs (licensed vocational nurses), 45

Major League Baseball (MLB), 39–41
Major League Soccer (MLS), 39–41
Malcolm X, 3
males, 150–59
  on "being black," 154–55
  demographics of, 153
  education of, 150, 155–56
  employment opportunities for, 151
  financial outcomes for, 155–57
  free time of, 83
  and gender wage gap, 104
  health of, 55–57, 157
  household and marital status of, 153
  imprisonment of, 74
  and justice system, 158–59
  professional aspirations of, 152
  and relationships, 84, 154
  in sports media, 41
  in STEM fields, 125, 156
  in teaching profession, 5
  tobacco use by, 53
  transmission of HIV amongst, 53–54
manslaughter, 63, 65, 66
Marable, Manning, x
marijuana use, 79–80
marital status statistics, 88–91, 143–44, 153
marriage equality, 92, 144
Marshall, Thurgood, 117
Martin, Trayvon, 81, 82
master's degrees, 4, 129
math. See STEM (science, technology, engineering, and math) fields
math teachers, 6
media
  engagement of Black Americans by, 112–13
  sports, 41–42
  time spent using various, 85
  See also entertainment statistics
Medical College of Wisconsin, 47
medical degrees, 4, 45–46
medical professionals, 44–47

medical schools, 20–21, 45–46
medications, 51, 90–91
Meharry Medical College, 46
Memphis Minnie, 43
men. See males
mental health, 49–53, 97–98
men who have sex with men (MSM), 54
military service, 93–98
misdiagnoses, of mental health conditions, 50
mixed heritage, 2
Morehouse School of Medicine, 46, 128, 132
Morgan State University, 128
Moynihan, Daniel Patrick, 139–40
MSM (men who have sex with men), 54
murder, 63, 66, 73, 76
Murphy, Eddie, 33
Murray, Albert, xvi
music, 37–38
Muslim communities, 92

NAEP (National Assessment of Educational Progress), 16–17
NAIS (National Association of Independent School) schools, 8
narratives, of Black Americans, x
NASA, 132
National Assessment of Educational Progress (NAEP), 16–17
National Association of Independent School (NAIS) schools, 8
National Basketball Association (NBA), 39–41
National Football League (NFL), 39–42
National Guard, 94
National Hockey League (NHL), 40
National Institutes of Health, 130
National School Lunch Program, 11
The Nat King Cole Show, 32
natural disasters, 29–30
Nelly, 37
New York Police Department (NYPD), 59
New York Stock Exchange, 101
Niagara Movement, 43
nicotine use, 53, 55

No Child Left Behind Act, 10
non-profit organizations, xvii–xviii, 101
North Carolina A&T State University, 127, 128
nursing profession, 45
NYPD (New York Police Department), 59

Oakwood University, 46
Obama, Barack:
  as commander in chief, 93
  on Deepwater Horizon incident, 30
  election of, 116, 119
  judges appointed by, 70
  powerful imagery with election of, x
  support for gay marriage by, 92
Obama, Michelle, 152
obesity, 56, 141–42, 157
Ohio State University, 46
Operation Enduring Freedom, 96
Operation Iraqi Freedom, 96
Operation New Dawn, 96
The Oprah Winfrey Show, 33
overdiagnosis, of mental health conditions, 50
oyster farms, 30, 172n45
ozone pollution, 27

parole, 75
Paterson, David, 117
Patrick, Deval, 117
Peck, David Jones, 45
penal systems, 58
Perry, Tyler, 33
The Philadelphia Negro (W.E.B. Du Bois), xiv, xviii
phlebotomists, 45
physical appearance, ix
physical education teachers, 6
physical therapists, 45
Pinchback, Pinckney, 117
Pitts, Steven, 104
police. See law enforcement
police brutality, xv
police harassment, 65
political parties, 118–19
politics, 115–22
  civic participation, 122
  electoral, 59, 116–22

Pollard, Frederick Douglass "Fritz," 40
pollution, 27–28
pornography, 80
post-traumatic stress disorder (PTSD), 97
poverty, 106–14
  after Hurricane Katrina, 30
  of black students, 7
  high-poverty schools, 11–12
  and public assistance, 139–40
  of veterans, 98
  visibility of, xvii
Powell, Colin, 116
Prairie View A&M University, 128
pregnancy statistics, 47–48
preschool, 7–8
prescription medications, 51, 90–91
Prince (singer), 37
prison. See incarceration
private schools:
  attendance at, 8
  teachers in, 5
probation, 75
professional aspirations, 152
professional degrees, 4
property offenses (criminal justice), 75
prostate cancer, 55
Protestant church membership, 91
PTSD (post-traumatic stress disorder), 97
public assistance, 138–39
public order offenses (criminal justice), 73, 75
public schools, 5, 8, 10
purchasing habits, 114
Purple Rain (music album), 37

race, as social construction, ix
racial equity, ix
racial identity, 2
racial profiling:
  by juries, 71
  by law enforcement, 62
  in voting, 120
  in workplace, 103
racism, 145
radio, 33
Radio One, 33
Randolph, A. Philip, 99
rape. See sexual assault

rap music, 37, 38. *See also* hip-hop
R&B music, xvii, 37
reading habits, 39
Reagan, Ronald, 139
Recession of 2007-2010, 23, 111–12
Reconstruction, 59, 164n4
registered nurses (RNs), 45
relationships, romantic, 84, 144, 154
religious practices, 91. *See also* churches
renal disease, 55
renewable electricity, 23–24
Republican Party, 118
respiratory disorders, 23, 27–28
retirement plans, 107
Revels, Hiram, 116
Rice, Condoleezza, 116
RNs (registered nurses), 45
robberies, 63, 65, 68–69, 73
Robeson, Paul, 32
robotics, 132
Rockeymoore, Maya, 142
romantic relationships, 84, 144, 154
Rutgers University, 46

safety, 67–68
San Antonio Independent School District v. Rodriguez, 3
SAT performance, 18–19, 94
Scheindlin, Shira, 59
school discipline, 12–15
school lunch programs, 11
science grants, 130
science industry. *See* STEM (science, technology, engineering, and math) fields
science teachers, 6
Scott, Tim, 116
Screen Actors Guild, 35
second-class data, xv
segregation:
    and black students, 7, 9
    early statistical work on, xiv
    and lifestyles of Black Americans, 83, 88
    residential, xvii
self-employment, 100
sentencing (justice system), 73–74
Sentencing Project, 121

September 11th terrorist attacks, 69
sexism, 145
sexual abuse, 90
sexual assault:
    in prisons, 74, 148, 159
    public opinion on, 69
    rates of, 66, 73
    school-based zero tolerance policies on, 64
sexual identity, 92, 96, 144, 154
sexually transmitted diseases, 44, 53
Shelby County v. Holder, 120
shoes, purchasing of, 114
shopping habits, 114
single-parent households, 89, 142–43
slavery, 58, 164n4
Smith, James McCune, 45
Smith, Will, 33, 34
soccer, 39–41
social sciences, 125–26
Soul Train, 33
Southern University, 128
"The Spawn of Slavery" (W.E.B. Du Bois), 58
special education, 6, 9–10
Spelman College, 46, 127, 132, 146
sports, 32, 39–42
standardized testing:
    ACT college readiness exam, 19
    Graduate Record Examination, 155
    pedagogical debates regarding, 3
    and punitive educational practices, 13
    SAT performance, 18–19, 94
stand-up comedy, 38–39
Stand Your Ground (SYG) laws, 81
state legislatures, 117–18
statistics on Black Americans
    bias of, xviii
    historical use of, xiii–xiv
    See also specific types, e.g.: education statistics
status offenses (criminal justice), 75
STEM (science, technology, engineering, and math) fields, 123–33
    females in, 125

STEM (science, technology, engineering, and math) fields (*continued*)
  gaming and technological innovation in, 123, 131–33
  males in, 125, 156
  representation of Black Americans in, 102, 124–30
stereotypes, 20
sterilization, forced, 48
stop-and-frisk practices, 58
students, 7–12, 15–20. *See also* education statistics
substance abuse, 49–53
substance abuse treatment, 91
suicide trends, 51
SYG (Stand Your Ground) laws, 81
syphilis, 44

TANF (Temporary Assistance for Needy Families), 139
teachers, 4–7
technical education courses, 6
technical violations (criminal justice), 75
technology, data collection, xv
technology industry. *See* STEM (science, technology, engineering, and math) fields
teen pregnancy rates, 47–48
television, 32–36
Temporary Assistance for Needy Families (TANF), 139
terrorism, 68, 69
testing, school. *See* standardized testing
text messaging, 130
theater, 36–37
Thomas, Clarence, 117
Thriller (music album), 38
tobacco use, 53, 55
Toldson, Ivory, 150
Tony Awards, 37
transgendered people:
  employment of, 102, 103, 106
  HIV rates in, 54
  incarceration of, 76
  police harassment of, 65–66
transportation jobs, 23, 25
Tuskegee Airmen, 93–94
Tuskegee syphilis experiment, 43–44
TV shows, 32–36

UC Berkeley Center for Labor Research and Education, 104
unemployment statistics, 97, 99, 102–3, 139, 151
union membership, 100–101
universities. *See* colleges and universities
University of Florida, 127
University of Illinois, 46
University of Maryland, 46, 126, 128
University of Miami, 46
University of Phoenix, 6, 21, 127
University of South Carolina, 46
University of South Florida, 46, 126
University of Texas, 46
U.S. Air Force, 94, 96
U.S. Army, 95, 96
U.S. Bureau of Labor Statistics, 23, 103
U.S. Congress, 116
U.S. Department of Defense, 93
U.S. Department of Education, 14
U.S. Department of Justice, 120
U.S. House of Representatives, 115
U.S. Marine Corps, 95, 96
U.S. Military Academy, 94–95
U.S. Navy, 95, 96
U.S. Office of Minority Health, 50
U.S. Senate, 115
U.S. Sentencing Commission guidelines, 73, 158
U.S. Stock Exchange, 99
U.S. Supreme Court, 3, 71, 117, 120
Usher, 37

VA (Veterans Administration) hospitals, 98
veterans, 75, 96–97
victimization, 66–68, 76–77. *See also* sexual assault
video games, 123, 131–33
violence, 66–68
vocational education, 6
volunteering, 122
voter ID laws, 120
voting, 59, 116–22
Voting Rights Act, 115, 120

Waajid, Taliah, 137
Wake Forest University, 141

warehousing sector, 25
war on drugs, 79–80, 149
Washington, Denzel, 34
Washington, Kerry, 32
Weber, Max, xiii
weight. *See* body weight
Wilder, Douglas, 117
Williams, Daniel Hale, 45
Winfrey, Oprah, 33, 99
women. *See* females

Women's National Basketball
    Association (WNBA), 39–41
writers, film and television, 35

Xavier University, 46, 127

Young, Charles, 93

zero-tolerance school policies, 64
Zimmerman, George, 81

PUBLISHING IN THE PUBLIC INTEREST

Thank you for reading this book published by The New Press. The New Press is a nonprofit, public interest publisher. New Press books and authors play a crucial role in sparking conversations about the key political and social issues of our day.

We hope you enjoyed this book and that you will stay in touch with The New Press. Here are a few ways to stay up to date with our books, events, and the issues we cover:

- Sign up at www.thenewpress.com/subscribe to receive updates on New Press authors and issues and to be notified about local events
- Like us on Facebook: www.facebook.com/newpress books
- Follow us on Twitter: www.twitter.com/thenewpress

Please consider buying New Press books for yourself; for friends and family; or to donate to schools, libraries, community centers, prison libraries, and other organizations involved with the issues our authors write about.

The New Press is a 501(c)(3) nonprofit organization. You can also support our work with a tax-deductible gift by visiting www.thenewpress.com/donate.